Modern Cultural Theorists

Theorists

Jacques Lacan

CW00553486

Modern Cultural Theorists

Jacques Lacan

Madan Sarup

Homerton College, Cambridge

HARVESTER
WHEATSHEAF

New York   London   Toronto   Sydney   Tokyo   Singapore

First published 1992 by
Harvester Wheatsheaf,
Campus 400, Maylands Avenue
Hemel Hempstead
Hertfordshire, HP2 7EZ
A division of
Simon & Schuster International Group

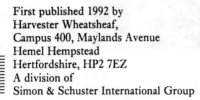

Typeset in 10 on 12 point Ehrhardt
by Inforum, Rowlands Castle, Hants

Printed and bound in Great Britain by
Biddles Ltd, Guildford and King's Lynn

British Library Cataloguing in Publication Data

A catalogue record for this book is available from
the British Library

ISBN 0–7450–0637–X (hbk)
ISBN 0–7450–0638–8 (pbk)

---

1   2   3   4   5   96   95   94   93   92

Contents

Acknowledgements

In this book I will show how Lacan's psychoanalytical theory, his discourse, has deeply affected how people think of themselves, about philosophy, about language, about desire, sexuality and about film and literature. I am indebted to Peter Dews, who first introduced me to the thought of Jacques Lacan. Since then I have studied on an informal basis with the Centre for Freudian Analysis and Research and I am most grateful to Bice Benvenuto, Bernard Burgoyne, Richard Klein and Darian Leader, founder members of this Lacanian centre, for their rigorous teaching. I am, of course, wholly responsible for the opinions and views expressed in this book. I would also like to thank Paul Maltby, Felizardo Nakano and Claire Pajaczkowska for discussing these ideas with me. My life has been enriched by the emotional support and intellectual stimulus given to me by many friends, particularly Ariella Altzman, Maud Blair, Eileen Jebb, Desa Phillipi, Tasneem Raja and Gudrun Schwinge.

Preface

Who was Jacques Lacan? What did he do? Why is he so famous? Lacan made psychoanalysis into the dominant intellectual discipline in France. From 1953 on, he held weekly or bi-weekly lectures in Paris, which he called seminars. Lacan used to speak to an audience of approximately 800 people squeezed into a room meant for 650. Over the years, many writers and intellectuals attended his seminars; among them were Althusser, Barthes, Derrida, Foucault, Jakobson, Kristeva, Leiris, Mannoni, Merleau-Ponty, Ricoeur, Sollers and others. These public seminars were given for twenty-six years. Their original purpose was to teach psychoanalysts how to read Freud closely. Their second aim was that of developing and extending psychoanalytical theory.

Lacan's favourite interlocutors were not academic psychologists but luminaries, as he called them, of the past: Aristotle, Hegel, Kant, Socrates, Spinoza, Shakespeare and Sophocles. His close friends included surrealist poets, film stars and the great structuralists, Benveniste, Jakobson and Lévi-Strauss. Many major figures in European intellectual life have been influenced by Lacan in important ways, and for a considerable number of people, inspired by his work, the study of feminism, film and literature have become exciting enterprises.

Fully to understand Lacan's thought and his enormous cultural influence we must have a look at a wide range of discourses: Saussurean semiology, Jakobsonian rhetorical analysis; Freud's Oedipal schema; Benveniste's linguistics; Lévi-Strauss's idea of women as exchange; Hegel's concept of desire . . . Lacan said that, from the age of twenty onwards, he did nothing other than explore philosophers on the subject of love. It is therefore unsurprising that many of these pages are about the pain, 'lack', the loss of love, and the force of desire.

Jacques Lacan 1901–1981
Chronology

1901   Jacques Lacan born in Paris, the eldest son of
        prosperous, bourgeois parents. After attending a
        well-known Jesuit school – he was raised a Catholic
        but did not practise Catholicism – he studies
        medicine and then psychiatry.

1927   Begins his clinical training and then works in
        several psychiatric hospitals in Paris.

1932   Receives his doctorate in psychiatry with a thesis on
        the relationship of paranoia to personality structure.
        This attracts considerable interest in surrealist
        circles. His interests in paranoia, language,
        phantasy and symptoms, the main concerns of the
        surrealists, bring him close to them. The main idea
        in the first period of Lacan's work, 1932–48, is the
        domination of the human being by the image.

1933   Publishes articles in *Minotaure*. Starts attending
        Kojève's lectures on Hegel.

1934   Enters analysis with Rudolph Loewenstein and
        becomes an active member of the Société
        Psychanalytique de Paris (SPP).

1936	Reads a major paper to the International Psychoanalytic Association (IPA) on the mirror-stage theory which remains unpublished (the version included in *Ecrits* dates from 1949).
1938	Accepted as training analyst by the International Psychoanalytic Association.
1939–45	Second World War. The SPP is decimated and the society effectively ceases to exist. Lacan works in a military hospital.
1948–60	In the second period of Lacan's work the function of the image is subordinated and the dominant field of knowledge in his thinking is linguistics.
1951	The SPP's Training Commission begins to raise the issue of Lacan's use of 'short sessions' in his analyses. By 1951 Lacan is writing about the Imaginary, Symbolic and the Real.
1952	The SPP, the Paris society, moves ahead on its plan to start a separate training institute. Lacan takes a strong exception to Nacht's conception of psychoanalysis as a discipline within neurobiology.
1953	There is a split in the SPP over the question of lay analysis. (Should only medical doctors be allowed to become psychoanalysts?) Lacan resigns his membership of the SPP and joins the Société Française de Psychanalyse (SFP).
	Holds his first public seminar (on Freud's papers on technique). These seminars continue for twenty-six years.
	Delivers the important paper 'The function of language in psychoanalysis'. Often called the 'Rome report', this is the founding statement of the view that psychoanalysis is a theory of the speaking subject. Psychoanalysis is now increasingly seen as a linguistic science in close touch with structural anthropology and mathematics.
1955	Attacks the work of ego-psychologists (Hartmann, Kris, Loewenstein and others).

1960–80   In the third period of Lacan's work the key idea is that of the three 'orders', the Imaginary, Symbolic and the Real.

1963   Expelled, finally, from the International Psychoanalytic Association, because of his unorthodox practice and teaching methods.

1964   In response to the hostility of the International Psychoanalytic Association Lacan founds his own school, L'Ecole Freudienne de Paris (EFP). His audience begins to change; there are fewer psychiatrists and more philosophers, anthropologists, linguists, mathematicians and literary critics. Gives seminar on *The Four Fundamental Concepts of Psychoanalysis*.

1966   Publishes his first book: *Ecrits*. The project of publishing Lacan's twenty-five annual seminars is undertaken by his son-in-law and director of his school, Jacques-Alain Miller. There is increasing interest in his work in France and abroad.

1967   Introduction of the highly controversial *la passe* which marks the transition from analysand to analyst. Lacan sees the decision to become an analyst as analogous to the act of becoming a poet.

1968   Student uprising in Paris, the 'May events'. The publication of the first issue of the official journal of the Freudian School, *Scilicet*.

1974   The Department of Psychoanalysis at Vincennes, which opened after the 'May events' of 1968, is reorganised and renamed Le Champ Freudien with Lacan as scientific director and Miller, his son-in-law, as president. There is a stress on the mathematical formalisation of psychoanalytic theory.

1977   Publication in English of *Ecrits – A Selection*.

1980   Lacan unilaterally announces the dissolution of the Ecole Freudienne de Paris. The foundation of La Cause freudienne.

1981   Lacan dies in Paris at the age of eighty.

Historical and cultural context: The emergence of French psychoanalytic culture

When Freud went to the United States in 1909 he was amazed at the welcome given to him by Clark University; compared with those in Europe, he found the professors astoundingly unprejudiced and open. But only five years after his visit, Freud noted that something was going wrong in America. Americans were accepting psychoanalysis *too* easily, and Freud took this as a sign that they were misunderstanding it, watering it down and sweetening it to their taste. He felt that his ideas about sexuality and the unconscious were being diluted.

Freud believed that too easy an acceptance meant that psychoanalysis was being denatured, and he also believed the converse: resistance to psychoanalysis suggested that it was being taken seriously. By 1914 it was already clear that it was in France that resistance to psychoanalysis was the greatest. French philosophers and scientists found it unacceptable; they rejected psychoanalysis as a German inspiration. Indeed, there was no psychoanalytic society in France till 1926, and for nearly quarter of a century it remained small, its members stigmatised by medical peers.[1] And then there was the Second World War. Many members of the psychoanalytic society were killed, and its activities ceased.

In the post-war years existentialism was extremely popular. Part of its popular appeal was that it provided a way to think through the issues of choice and individual responsibility that had been raised by the war years. As a theory of the self, existentialism did not go very far towards breaking away from the Cartesian heritage. Its psychology tended to portray the individual as a rational, conscious actor who could understand the basis of his or her action. It remained firmly rooted in a philosophy of individual autonomy and rational choice. It could be said that the social changes reflected in the work of existentialists, new novelists and new filmmakers are those that, by isolating and psychologising the experience of the individual, paved the way for the emergence of a psychoanalytic culture.

In the course of the 1960s the French attitude towards psychoanalysis swung from denigration and resistance to infatuation. And in the last twenty years psychoanalysis has emerged as an amazing social phenomenon. Public interest in psychoanalysis has climbed to new heights. Psychoanalytic discourse has invaded French life and language, it is changing the ways people think about politics and their personal relationships, discuss books and films, and address their children. Psychoanalysis has colonised vast areas of culture. Books, magazines, newspapers, radio and television are communicating psychoanalytic ideas to millions of people. These ideas include: that there is an unconscious, that people are not the autonomous thinkers and actors they often believe themselves to be, and that every action has a meaning (one that is often so threatening that we work hard not to let it surface). The social diffusion of psychoanalysis now extends deep into intellectual and popular culture.

How did all this happen? In 1963 the Marxist philosopher Louis Althusser invited Jacques Lacan to bring his seminar to the Ecole Normale Supérieure. After its move from the Saint Anne Hospital to the Ecole Normale, Lacan's seminar became a meeting place for the most prominent figures in Parisian intellectual circles, among them critics Roland Barthes, Julia Kristeva and Phillipe Sollers, philosophers Michel Foucault and Jacques Derrida, and anthropologist Claude Lévi-Strauss. (After the 1966 publication of Lacan's *Ecrits*, as many as a thousand people tried to get into his seminars!) It certainly seems to be the case that during this period bridges between Lacan and the left were strengthened by Lacanian connections with Marxist circles at the Ecole Normale.

Traditionally, Marxists have reproached psychoanalysts for stressing the individual instead of seeing things in terms of the economic, political and historical context. In the 1960s with de-Stalinisation and the new policy of peaceful coexistence, there was a shift towards reconciliation and dialogue. Louis Althusser, a professor of philosophy and a Communist Party member, began to argue that Freud and Marx have a lot in common. Just as Marx discovered a new object of knowledge (the mode of production) and a new way of knowing, Freud discovered the unconscious as an object of science. Freud, too, defined a new science, a new way of knowing about man and society.

This interpretation of psychoanalysis relies heavily on Lacan's reading of Freud, and Althusser expressed his view in a famous 1964 article, 'Freud and Lacan'.[2] The importance of this short article is that it extended interest in Lacan's work beyond the circle of Althusser's own students. Althusser explains that both Marx and Freud, in constructing their new sciences, had to fashion them out of the materials of the past, that is from scientific concepts that were constituted to serve entirely different ends from their own. Thus, Freud and Marx were both weighed down by the cultural baggage of their time. Freud 'thought' his discovery in concepts borrowed from the biology, mechanics and psychology of the day. Marx 'thought' his discovery using Hegelian notions of the subject. Althusser is trying to rethink Marxism without any reference to Hegel's absolute subject, and he sees a kindred spirit in Lacan, who is trying to rethink psychoanalysis without reference to a unified conception of self or ego.

In the 1968 events the students wanted to run all institutions as participatory democracies where self-expression would be given free rein. Attempts at self-expression in structures of democratic self-management led to preoccupation with the self. During the May events many people believed that a liberated politics could emerge only from liberated interpersonal relationships.

There was an explosion of interest in psychoanalysis after 1968, and in the years following the May events, French psychoanalysis came to be reconciled with two ideological currents, existentialism and Marxism, with which it had formerly had hostile relations. The form taken by the post-1968 psychoanalytical culture was powerfully influenced by the events of 1968. Everywhere, students insisted on the continuity of politics with the world of everyday personal relationships. Many activists of the troubled late 1960s began to search for personal solutions when a political solution seemed to have failed.[3] There was an outburst of interest in transformations of the psyche. Psychoanalysts came on to the public stage where they started using a new language. And, of course, the language that we use to talk about a problem is inseparable from the way in which we think about it. In the post-1968 years in France, a psychoanalytic language that referred the visible back to the invisible, the manifest back to the latent, the public back to the private, became the standard discourse. Perhaps the discourse of psychoanalysis offers a new framework for thinking; in the personal sphere it offers itself as a way of addressing new insecurities. Psychoanalytic ideas about the individual are now welcome because people seem to find them relevant to their experience.

It could be argued that involvement with the new psychoanalytic culture was a way of continuing contact with the personal and political issues which May 1968 brought to the surface. Thinking through the events required a theory which could integrate politics and the person. Lacanian psychoanalysis helped people to think about questions of desire, sexuality and self-expression.[4]

French psychoanalytic culture is now deeply involved in social and political issues. While in America ego-psychology promised that self-improvement was possible without calling society into question, in France psychoanalysis became deeply involved in radical social criticism. Since 1968, French Marxism, feminism, antipsychiatry and psychoanalysis have become so tied up with one another that they resemble a complex knot. All these disciplines and approaches have been mediated by the thought of Jacques Lacan. A plan of the book follows:

Chapter 1, on Freudian theory, provides an outline of some of Freud's main ideas: an introduction to his models of the mind, the relationship between unconscious wishes and repression, the Oedipus complex and the threat of castration. There is an emphasis on the study of dreams, slips, jokes and the mechanisms involved. There is then a focus on psychoanalysis as a practice which includes a discussion about symptoms and transference. The second part of the chapter consists of a sketch of Lacan's main interests; how Lacan returns to Freud's early work which is concerned with language, the unconscious and sexuality. There are also sections on his distinctive style, on what Lacan is against, and the different ways in which his theory has been interpreted.

Lacan's thought is profoundly marked by his encounter with surrealism. And so in Chapter 2 Lacan is placed in the contexts of the aims and interests (the unconscious, sexuality, language) of the movement. I refer to the work of Dali, Magritte and others, and give a brief exposition of Lacan's early writings.

Chapter 3 deals with Lacan's wide-ranging interests in philosophy. There are sections on the influence of Spinoza, Hegel, Heidegger, and reflections on some of the similarities in the thought of Lacan and Sartre. The chapter concludes with a discussion of Lacan's theory of the four discourses. It is suggested that Lacan, in later years, objected to the totalising ambitions of philosophy and there is a discussion about why this was the case.

Chapter 4, on the functions of language, begins with the argument that the biological is always interpreted through language. Saussure's linguistic theory and Lacan's emendation of it is explained. Lacan's concept of the Symbolic is then linked with the structuralism of Lévi-Strauss. Another influence on Lacan was Roman Jakobson and so this leads to a section on metaphor and metonymy. After a discussion on human subjectivity, I outline one Heideggerian strand in Lacan's thinking about language: 'empty' and 'full' speech. Finally, there is a consideration of the analyst–patient situation and the importance of listening.

In Chapter 5, having provided a cultural context, I outline the development of Lacan's theory chronologically. Beginning with his early work on feminine paranoia and its criminal manifestations, I go on to explain the mirror phase, the distinction between need, demand and desire, and other Lacanian concepts. After examining the reasons why he is against ego-psychology, I present his arguments for the variable length of the analytic session. I then outline Lacan's conception of the unconscious and his views on interpretation.

Chapter 6 is a discussion of the key themes contained in Lacan's *Ecrits*. It includes explanation of the three orders, the Imaginary, Symbolic and the Real, the distinction between empty and full speech, and the role of the analyst. Other topics discussed include Lacan's revision of Saussurean linguistics (with a focus on metaphor and metonymy), the significance of the phallus, the relationship between truth and the unconscious, between desire and *jouissance*.

Chapter 7 includes a further discussion of the theory of the three orders, the Imaginary, the Symbolic and the Real. There is a consideration of the relationship between image, identity and identification. The shift of focus in Lacan's thought from image to language is noted, and his view of psychosis studied. Lacan's fascination with models and mathematical statements is then examined and the chapter ends with some criticisms of his thought.

Chapter 8 considers some important issues in sexuality, love and feminism. It begins with Lacan's interpretation of the Oedipus and castration complexes. There is then a discussion of his views on feminine sexuality and romantic love, which he sees as a phantasy of oneness. The last section deals with the complex interrelationship between psychoanalysis and feminism, and the provocative ideas of three French feminists – Cixous, Irigaray and Kristeva – are discussed.

In Chapter 9 there is a discussion of the idea: in what ways are films like dreams? This leads to a consideration of the dream-work and the role of condensation and displacement. The pleasure in looking is commented upon and the construction of the film-viewer is explained. Finally, there are some reflections on voyeurism and fetishism in the cinema.

It is argued in Chapter 10 that Lacanian psychoanalysis has greatly contributed to the revitalisation of literary theory. I focus on two case studies first, I present Freud's view of Hamlet, and then I summarise Lacan's comments on the play. This leads us to a consideration of the play as a tragedy of desire, to the topics of the compulsion to repeat and the death drive. The second case study consists of Lacan's analysis of a famous story by Edgar Allan Poe, 'The Purloined Letter'. It is suggested that the story is an allegory, partly, about the repetition compulsion. It may also be a parable about psychoanalysis.

CHAPTER ONE | *The Freudian terrain*

Introduction

This chapter provides a brief account of some of the main ideas of Freud's theory. I will discuss the different ways Freud considered the human mind, the concept of repression, the Oedipus complex; dreams, slips, jokes; and psychoanalysis as a practice. This account is inevitably selective (I do not deal with the first phase when Freud was working with patients suffering from hysteria, nor with the last phase when Freud was speculating about society and human culture).[1] At the end of the chapter I will focus on Lacan's main interests and the way he has refashioned Freudian theory.

It has been said that Sigmund Freud contributed to something much wider than merely the growth of a scientific discipline. He has contributed to the whole cultural milieu of the twentieth century in that he has given us a way of seeing things. He fashioned a new image of what it is to be human. Freud, by the power of his writings and by the breadth and audacity of his speculations, revolutionised the thought, the lives and the imagination of an age.[2]

Sigmund Freud (1856–1939) considered the human mind from three points of view: the 'dynamic', the 'economic' and the 'topographical'. These are not mutually exclusive interpretations but emphasise different aspects of the whole. All three are evidence of Freud's attempt to derive the mind from the body.[3]

The dynamic point of view stresses the interplay of forces within the mind, arising from tensions that develop when instinctual drives meet the necessities of external reality. What is necessarily given at the start are the needs of the body itself: these are inseparably connected to feelings of pleasure and pain.

From the 'economic' point of view pleasure results from a decrease in the degree to which the body is disturbed by any stimulus.

1

Unpleasure results from an increase in disturbance. In the interaction of the body with the external environment a part of the mind Freud calls the 'ego' evolves to mediate the actions of the body so as to achieve optimal satisfaction of its needs. The ego is particularly concerned with self-preservation. This implies that there has to be control of the basic instincts if there is to be adjustment to reality. Under the economic model this is viewed as a struggle between the 'reality principle' and the 'pleasure principle' in which the body has to learn to postpone pleasure and accept a degree of unpleasure in order to comply with social demands.

The third point of view is the 'topographical', of which there are two versions. The psychic apparatus is here conceived of in a spatial metaphor as divided into separate subsystems. In the first of the two versions Freud sees the mind as having a threefold division, conscious, preconscious and unconscious. He equates consciousness with the perception system, the sensing and ordering of the external world; the preconscious covers those elements of experience which can be called into consciousness at will; the unconscious is made up of all that has been kept out of the pre-conscious–conscious system. From observations Freud posited that the unconscious system contained basic instincts and drives which he thought were primarily sexual – he called the energy behind these drives the 'libido'. Gradually, as Freud extended the range of phenomena subjected to his scrutiny, this topographical model began to appear simplistic.[4]

The second version of the topographical schema was introduced by Freud in 1923 when he came to view the mind as having three distinct agencies: the id, a term applied retrospectively to the instinctual drives that spring from the constitutional needs of the body; the ego as having developed out of the id to be an agency which regulates and opposes the drives; and the superego, as representative of parental and social influences upon the drives. The superego acts as a conscience constantly castigating the ego for failing to control the id. The ego is seen to be the vital arbiter between the conflicting demands of the id, the external world, and the superego.

> The ego's relation to the id might be compared with that of a rider to his horse. The horse supplies the locomotive energy, while the rider has the privilege of deciding on the goal and of guiding the powerful

animal's movement. But only too often there arises between the ego and the id the not precisely ideal situation of the rider being obliged to guide the horse along the path by which it itself wants to go.[5]

During the last phase of Freud's thinking, which coincides with the last twenty years of his life, it was the opposition of ego and id that was in the forefront of his attention. Freud described the change in his thinking as a shift in interest from the repressed to the repressing forces in the mind. Freud found that though the ego, as the repressing agency was called, was in large part conscious, in so far as it was responsible for repression it operated unconsciously.

With this model of mind Freud saw psychoanalysis as having a quite specific task. He expressed the view that psychoanalysis was an instrument to enable the ego to achieve a progressive conquest of the id:

> Its intention is . . . to strengthen the ego, to make it more independent of the superego, to widen its field of perception and enlarge its organization so that it can appropriate fresh portions of the id. Where it was, there ego shall be. It is the work of culture – not unlike draining the Zuider Zee.[6]

For Freud, psychoanalytical investigation was rather like archaeology. Just as an archaeologist investigates the buried remains of a city, the analyst investigates 'buried' childhood. He wrote: 'There is, in fact, no better analogy for repression, by which something in the mind is at once made inaccessible and preserved, than burial of the sort to which Pompeii fell a victim and from which it could emerge once more through the work of spades. '[7]

The id wants its wishes satisfied whether or not they are compatible with external demands. The ego feels itself threatened by the pressure of the unacceptable wishes. Memories of these experiences, that is images and ideas associated with them, become charged with unpleasurable feeling, and are thus barred from consciousness. This is the operation known as repression.

Every human being has to undergo this repression of what Freud named the 'pleasure principle' by the 'reality principle'. (We are all repressed to some degree but for some of us the repression may become excessive and make us ill.) Repression serves to keep guilt-laden wishes out of conscious experience. The symptoms, dreams and slips of the tongue that occur in everyday life represent the 'return of the repressed', a mechanism that marks both the emergence of the forbidden wish and the resistance to it. Unconscious wishes strive continually to break through against the counterforce exerted by the ego. The censorship of the ego can, however, be subverted; the drives or wishes can get through in disguise, as the so-called 'compromise formations' of the return of the repressed.

The Oedipus complex

Freud maintained that infantile sexuality emerged 'spontaneously from internal causes'. Sexuality is undifferentiated in terms of both its object and aim; Freud called this condition the 'polymorphously perverse' state. From its unstructured state the child's libido develops through specific phases in which the sexual instinct is attached to, and finds release through, the various 'erotogenic zones'. Freud suggested that human sexual development follows a course through quite specific phases: the oral stage, the anal stage, the phallic stage and the latency period. Freud regarded the discovery of the 'polymorphously perverse' nature of infant sexuality and the 'erotogenic zone' conception of development as two of the most fundamental ideas of psychoanalysis.

Freud argued, in short, that sexual identity is not merely anatomically determined, but psychically constructed. Until this is achieved the infant's sexuality is 'polymorphous'; it is at the mercy of the component instincts, functioning independently and varying in their aim, their object and their source.

The match of biological sex with the sexual role determined by society is achieved, not given. For Freud this matching is accomplished through the combined workings of the Oedipus complex and the castration complex. Freud sees the child's relationship with its parents as critical for the achievement of its proper sexual identity. Love of the mother is dominant in the early formative years. Later, the perception of the father as rival becomes insistent for the boy-child to the point where he is drawn into phantasies of the killing of this rival and of possessing the mother. This is the Oedipus complex.[8]

The early dyadic or two-term relationship between infant and mother now opens up into a triangle consisting of child and both parents; and for the child, the parent of the same sex will come to figure as a rival in its affections for the parent of the opposite sex.

What persuades the boy-child to abandon his incestuous desire for the mother is the father's threat of castration. The father is experienced as the source of all authority. The threat need not necessarily be spoken; but the boy, in perceiving that the girl is herself 'castrated', begins to imagine this as a punishment which might be visited upon himself. The boy thus abandons his love for the mother and moves towards identification with the father, with the understanding that he too can in time occupy such a position of power.

The trajectory for the girl-child is not so straightforward. In her case the complexes work in reverse, and the castration complex ushers in the Oedipus complex. She interprets the absence of a penis as a failure in provision on the part of the mother. Under the influence of this disappointment she turns away in hostility from her mother, but in the unconscious the wish for a penis is not abandoned; it is replaced by the wish to bear the father a child. Hence the girl becomes the rival of the mother for the father's love. Freud saw the fading of the Oedipus complex in the girl-child as a more uncertain process, because the identification with the father's law, facilitated by the anticipation of power, is not so secure.

I want to emphasise the centrality of the Oedipus complex because it is the nucleus of desire, repression and sexual identity. It is the point at which we are produced and constituted as subjects. The Oedipus complex represents for Freud the beginnings of morality, conscience, law and all forms of authority. The father's real or imagined prohibition of incest is symbolic of all the higher authority to be later encountered; and in introjecting this patriarchal law the child begins to form what Freud calls the 'superego', the punitive voice of conscience within it. Maturity and growth are conceived by Freud in terms of the successful resolution of the Oedipus complex. The struggle to overcome the complex, however, is never quite resolved, and one of its residues is a life-long ambivalence towards the keeping and breaking of taboos and laws.

Dreams, slips and jokes

Dreams, slips of the tongue, jokes and symptoms all provided material for Freud's model of the mind. It was on this seemingly trivial foundation – that the unconscious could be studied through the messages it sent out – that Freud went on to colonise other ostensibly unrelated fields: religion, anthropology, art criticism, literary studies.

Freud said that dreams are the 'royal road' to the unconscious.[9] Dreams have a meaning and can be interpreted: for Freud they are essentially symbolic fulfilments of unconscious wishes. They are cast in symbolic forms because if this material were expressed directly then it might be shocking and disturbing enough to wake us up, and so the unconscious conceals, distorts its meanings, so that our dreams become symbolic texts which need to be deciphered.

Dreams, then, arise from an unconscious impulse seeking fulfilment, a desire not fulfilled in waking life. Dreams usually contain material, both from recent experience (the day's residues) and from distant memories involving infantile sexual wishes. However, the censorship, the force of repression, will not allow these powerfully charged memories to reach representation in their original form. This is why a dream is a disguised fulfilment of a repressed wish. Evading censorship by a disguise, the dream is a compromise between the demands of impulse and the intensity of the repressing force.[10]

The dream is not just the 'expression' or 'reproduction' of the unconscious: between the unconscious and the dream a process of 'production' or transformation intervenes. The dream itself is the product of an intensive transformation of these materials, known as the 'dream-work'. The dream-work transforms the 'latent' content of the dream, the forbidden dream-thoughts, into the 'manifest' dream-stories – what the dreamer remembers.

The operations of the dream-work take four forms: condensation, displacement, considerations of representability, and secondary revision.

Condensation is the process in which there is a superimposition of elements; composite figures and structures are formed so that as little as possible is left out. A figure can be produced, for example, by uniting the actual features of two or more people into a single dream-image. It is condensation that prevents there being any neat one to one correspondence between the elements of the manifest content and those of the latent content.

The second activity of the dream-work is displacement. The elements in the manifest dream replace elements in the latent dream-thoughts via a chain of associations for the purpose of disguise. This results in the intensity of an idea becoming detached from it and passing to other ideas, which in themselves are of little value. Both condensation and displacement can produce visual and auditory images for abstract thoughts, thus contributing to the actual process of representation in dreams.

Considerations of representability, the way the dream-thoughts achieve representation in the dream via images, is the third activity of the dream-work. Representation is rather like a rebus (a picture-puzzle), a series of ideograms or pictographs. Freud writes that there are dreams in which the most complicated intellectual operations take place, statements are contradicted or confirmed, ridiculed or compared, just as they are in waking thought. Even the most abstract thoughts are transposed with great ingenuity into imagery by the dream work. For example, dreams reproduce logical connection by simultaneity in time. Here they are acting like a painter of the School of Athens or Parnassus who represents in one group all the philosophers or all the poets. It is true that they were never in fact assembled in a single hall or on a single mountain-top; but they certainly form a group in the conceptual sense.

The analyst is not the first interpreter of the dream: in narrating a dream the dreamer already acts as his or her own biased interpreter. One stage of the dream-work, known as 'secondary revision', consists in the reorganisation of the dream so as to present it in the form of a relatively consistent and comprehensible narrative. Secondary revision systematises the dream, fills in its gaps and smooths over its contradictions, reorders its chaotic elements into a more coherent fable. Secondary revision is at work when the dream is presented in the form of a verbal account. The conscious mind prefers to put the irrational dream-sequence into recognisable and familiar logical order, involving a further distortion of the 'distortion' already achieved by the other mechanisms discussed above.[11]

Dreams provide our main, but not our only, access to the unconscious. There are also what Freud calls 'parapraxes', unaccountable slips of the tongue, failures of memory, misreadings which can be traced to unconscious wishes and intentions. So important did Freud think these apparently casual accidents that in 1901 he wrote a whole book on the subject, *The Psychopathology of Everyday Life*. In 1905 Freud published a work on the subject of jokes or of wit. Although appearing some time after *The Interpretation of Dreams* and *The Psychopathology of Everyday Life*, the book can be seen as being directly related to them, and as being a product of the same period and concerns. As with his earlier work on dreams and slips, Freud spent some time classifying jokes and then explaining how each type – word plays, puns, jests, innocent jokes, tendentious ones involving obscenity or hostility – could be rendered intelligible in terms of the release in psychic energy they produced. Just as the mechanism of dreams served as a means whereby dammed-up psychic energy could be released harmlessly, so jokes fulfilled a similar function. The mechanism of repression can be outwitted in the process of joking, and the suppressed desire can find partial fulfilment, thereby producing a measure of satisfaction.

Psychoanalysis as a practice

There is a parallel between dreams and symptoms. It was Freud's mature view that the symptom is the expression of a wish, a repressed wish. As with dreams, Freud went on to connect the repressed wish that the symptom expresses with sexuality. Every symptom is the expression of a sexual wish. The symptom expresses not only a repressed wish (or set of wishes) but also the forces of repression. This phenomenon is called compromise formation; the symptom must make concessions to the forces of repression, otherwise it too would be repressed. A symptom, then, is the expression and the satisfaction of a desire. We have to consider not only what the symptom achieves but also what it avoids. If it is a poor or substitute form of satisfaction for the impulse, it is vastly preferable to denying or renouncing the impulse altogether. For, if the impulse is denied, anxiety ensues.

Sometimes we have internal conflicts which result in what we call neurosis. Neuroses may be obsessional (having to touch every lamp-post in the street), hysterical (developing a paralysed arm for no good organic reason), or phobic (being unreasonably afraid of open spaces or certain animals). Behind these neuroses, psychoanalysts discern unresolved conflicts whose roots run back to the individual's early development. The aim of psychoanalysis is to uncover the hidden causes of the neurosis in order to relieve the patient of his or her conflicts, so dissolving the distressing symptoms.

Much more difficult to cope with, however, is the condition of psychosis, in which the ego, unable to repress the unconscious desire, actually comes under its sway. If this happens, the link between the ego and the external world is ruptured, and the unconscious begins to build up an alternative, delusional reality. The psychotic, in other words, has lost contact with reality at key points, as in paranoia and schizophrenia. 'Paranoia' refers to a more or less systematised state of delusion, under which Freud includes not only delusions of persecution but delusional jealousy and delusions of grandeur. Schizophrenia involves a detachment from reality and a turning in on the self, with an excessive but loosely systematised production of phantasies.[12]

Psychoanalysis is not only a theory of the human mind, but a practice for curing those who are considered mentally ill or disturbed. An important aspect of the cure in Freudian theory are two processes called transference and counter-transference. *Transference* was for Freud the displacement of feelings from one idea to another; it is a mode of investing persons and objects with positive and negative qualities, according to our early memories of significant experience of familial figures.

In the course of the treatment the patient, or analysand, may begin unconsciously to 'transfer' on to the analyst the psychic conflicts from which he or she suffers. This poses a problem for the analyst, since such repetition or ritual re-enactment of the original conflict is one of the patient's unconscious ways of avoiding having to come to terms with it. We repeat, sometimes compulsively, what we cannot properly remember.

The mechanism of transferring past experience on to the figure of the analyst is set in motion just when the repressed wish is in danger of emerging.[13] The nearer the analyst gets to the repressed complex which induced the illness the more the patient's behaviour becomes pure repetition and divorced from present reality. S/he is in the grip of the 'repetition compulsion', the uncontrolled return of the repression. It is partly because of transference, and the insights and interventions which it permits the analyst, that the patient's problems are gradually redefined in terms of the analytic situation itself.

Freud saw counter-transference as the analyst's uncontrolled response to the patient's transference. It has been defined as 'the whole of the analyst's unconscious reactions to the individual analysand – especially to the analyst's own transference'.[14] Some analysts have suggested that there is transference and countertransference on the side of the analyst and the analysand.

This concludes my exposition of Freud's chief ideas, but I will continually be referring to his theories and relating them to Lacan's work in the text. (I do not believe in the view that holds that one should study Freud first and Lacan much later.) I think Lacan should be studied, dialectically, with a constant reference to Freud.

Lacan's main themes

Having given an account of the principal ideas of Freud, I now want to signal some of the ways Lacan has developed the Freudian heritage. Lacan's work is a strikingly original attempt to 'rewrite' Freudianism in ways relevant to all those concerned with the question of the human subject, its place in society, and above all its relationship to language. One of the things Lacan has done is to reinterpret Freud in the light of structuralist and post-structuralist theories of discourse.

Lacan emphasises the importance of an intense and personal reexamination of Freud's original texts. He has emended our understanding of Freud's work and, some would say, his reading of Freud has created a new version of psychoanalysis. Lacan's psychoanalytical ideas have made possible new theorisations of the individual and society, and new forms of social criticism.

Lacan, taking from Freud his desire to establish a system of knowledge, has made use of (and criticised) ethology, psychology, philosophy, linguistics, logic and mathematics. He has put psychoanalysis in touch with other disciplines, with new areas of thought.

He has, for example, revised Freudian theory by the use of Saussure's structural linguistics, a discipline not available to Freud. Lacan has made people aware of language in the theory and practice of psychoanalysis.

Lacan has made a radical critique of the psychoanalytic institution itself. There is considerable controversy over Lacan's unorthodox ideas. He sees psychoanalysis more as a calling than as a career. He personifies a conception of analysis not as a quasi-medical technique focused on 'cure' but as a scientific discipline and a process of individual research and self-discovery. (If a cure comes at all in psychoanalysis it comes as a kind of bonus or secondary gain.) For Lacan, psychoanalysis is not a system of cure, it is not a method of explaining or guaranteeing knowledge, but is a series of techniques for listening to and questioning desire.

One interesting point is that the *reception* given to Lacan's theory has varied from country to country; each set of circumstances has emphasised different aspects of his work. In France, and in Latin countries in general, the influence of Lacan has been mainly clinical and closely linked with psychoanalytic practice. In Anglo-Saxon countries the clinical aspect has, to a large extent, been absent and the influence of Lacan has been crucial in the areas of feminism, film and literature.

We should also bear in mind that there are many *interpretations* of Lacan's work. For example, in France, there are differences between the older and younger 'generations'. On the one hand there is the approach of the old school, or first generation, of Lacanians (Octave and Maud Mannoni, Serge Leclaire, Moustafa Safouan and others) who emphasise clinical problems and the crucial role of language in the psychoanalytical process – an approach largely based on Lacan's writings in the 1950s, the era of high structuralism. On the other hand, the younger generation, led by Jacques-Alain Miller, have emphasised the formalisation of Lacanian psychoanalysis into mathematical statements ('mathemes'), and have pointed out the differences between the different stages of his teaching.

While Freud's work is haunted by biology, Lacan's work, on the other hand, has a strong anti-biological tendency. Lacan wants to focus on what is distinctively human in the human mind, on the cultural rather than the 'natural' determining forces, and on anthropology and sociology rather than on biology.

In Anglo-Saxon countries the dominant interpretation of Freudian thought is that the unconscious is close to the basic instincts or the biological needs of human beings. This viewpoint is derived from Freud's later works. Lacan's 'return to Freud' is essentially a return to the spirit of the *earlier* works, the three books which show Freud's fascination with language and the unconscious: *The Interpretation of Dreams, The Psychopathology of Everyday Life*, and *Jokes and Their Relation to the Unconscious*.[15] In Lacan's work there is also an emphasis on language, but it is not the usual notion of language which involves the understanding and consciousness of a subject. Inspired by the linguistic theories of Ferdinand de Saussure and Roman Jakobson (whose ideas were not available to Freud), Lacan's view of language is different: it is not only man who speaks, but that in man and through man *it* speaks.

By reinterpreting Freudianism in terms of language, Lacan permits us to explore the relations between the unconscious and human society. He makes us realise that the unconscious is not a private region 'inside' us, but is an effect of our relations with one another. The unconscious exists 'between' us, as our relationships do. The unconscious surrounds us and weaves itself – rather like language – through us. Indeed, Lacan regards the unconscious as structured like a language. For Lacan the unconscious is a particular *effect* of language, but this language, for Lacan as for the structuralists, is never something entirely within our individual control.

In England it was assumed for a long time that Lacan was a structuralist. This impression was fostered by influential studies like Anika Lemaire's *Jacques Lacan*.[16] She discusses Lacan only in linguistic terms and prioritises the influence of Ferdinand de Saussure, Roman Jakobson and Lévi-Strauss. Lemaire takes the systematicity of Lacan's work for granted and reads it in purely synchronic terms. Structuralist references dominate everything; Lacan's debts to Hegel and Kojève, Heidegger, Sartre and others simply disappear.

There are, then, many problems in trying to understand Lacan's life-work. Was he a poet or a mathematician? Was he, basically, a surrealist or a structuralist? I think it is wrong to polarise his work in a dichotomous, 'either/or' way. Perhaps it is better to think of his work as having different periods or phases. There are numerous differences between the many periods of his work and it is difficult to define his concepts because they are always changing.

It will be argued that Lacan integrates feeling and reason, that he is both poet and mathematician, surrealist and structuralist. I want to stress that Lacan's early philosophical roots are in phenomenology and that he was particularly influenced by Kojève's reading of Hegel. Later, in the early 1950s, Lacan drew heavily on linguistics and structuralism.

Those commentators who focus largely on the structuralist aspects tend to stress Lacan's antagonism to humanistic philosophy and psychology, disciplines that treat man as an actor who wills his action. In contrast, Lacan sees man as a submitting object of processes that transcend him. Structuralist theories emphasise the possibility of discovering universal laws about man and society. Lacan's affirmation of the centrality of language to thought and his emphasis on logical and mathematical formalisation is meant to lay the groundwork for a unification of knowledge.

Though Lacan often spoke of the primacy of language he always believed that there was more to experience than language. He never accepted the pure priority of language. Lacan was always concerned with the interface of experience and structure.

Lacan stresses the role of language *and* the role of desire. For Lacan, once the child has the capacity for language there is a qualitative change in his or her psychical structure – s/he becomes a subject. We are speaking subjects. However, in language, we can never completely express what we want. There is always a gap between what we say and what we mean. Language is linked with desire. Desire is a fundamental lack, a hole in being. The desire of the subject is in perpetual movement but it can never find fulfilment. Lacan, in short, wants to convert our feeling of powerlessness to an understanding of logical impossibility.

But even if you find some of these reasons for studying Lacan convincing there is still the problem of reading. Lacan's style is difficult. It has been called incomprehensible, esoteric, and obscure. His style belongs to a French tradition that can be traced back to poets like Mallarmé. Indeed, Catherine Clément has written of Lacan not only as a founder of a new psychoanalytic theory but as she experienced him, a shaman, a sorcerer possessed by a poetic inspiration.[17]

One characteristic of Lacan's style is his use of jokes and puns.

As Freud taught us, jokes are an expression of the unconscious; puns contain many nuances of meaning. Lacan uses puns to demonstrate how the analyst works: to interpret is to play on words.

Early in his career, Lacan wrote poems and articles in the surrealist *Minotaure*. In this journal appeared the work of Breton, Eluard, Dali, Masson, Picasso and many others. He saw a great deal of the surrealists. As everyone knows, the surrealists were heavily influenced by Freud's work. They loved language and playing with words. They liked the Freudian idea that when you use the wrong word, when you say a word other than the one you meant to say, it is not really you who are speaking. You are spoken.

In trying to understand a new theory it is often helpful to know what the theorist is *against*. Lacan is fundamentally antagonistic to the Anglo-Saxon philosophical tradition. Within this tradition the British, in particular, emphasise the virtues of 'common-sense'. It is assumed that common-sense is, in some way, real. It is taken for granted that we can act rationally on the basis of common-sense. In the field of psychoanalysis the British tend to stress the ability of the analyst. Such beliefs are contested by the Lacanian school, who see these ideas as ideological.

These ideological views are expressed most clearly in the work of the ego-psychologists. Ego-psychology, a powerful movement, began in Vienna in the 1920s and 1930s. Heinz Hartmann, Ernst Kris and Rudolph Loewenstein, the most famous members, were supported by Anna Freud in London. Looking at mental conflict, they held that there was a conflict-free zone in the ego. In their, view, patients came to the analyst because they had a weak ego, and had to model their ego on the strong one of the analyst. The aim of analysis is to enable patients to love and to work. When the ego-psychologists emigrated to the United States it became particularly noticeable that they stressed *adaptation* to group norms. There was pressure to conform; for example, the ego-psychologists stressed genital sex as being the only 'wholesome' form and implied that other forms of sexual activity were deviant. Ego-psychology fitted in with the dominant sociology of the time, the consensual structural functionalism of Talcott Parsons. One of Lacan's achievements is that he has made us aware that psychoanalysis should not be used for the purpose of social adjustment, it should not be an apparatus for the regulation of the human subject and its adaptation to 'reality'.

Lacan stresses the fact that psychoanalysis is about human sexuality and the unconscious. For psychoanalysts sexuality can never be equated with genitality, nor is it the simple expression of a biological drive. It is always psychosexuality, a system of conscious and unconscious human phantasies involving activities that produce pleasure beyond the satisfaction of any physiological need. The psychosexual drive arises from various sources, seeks satisfaction in many different ways, and makes use of many diverse objects for its aim of achieving pleasure. Some analysts, like Ernest Jones, described the acquisition of sexual identity in terms of *ego* development. Lacan is strongly against this; in his view, the unconscious never ceases to challenge our apparent identity as subjects.

In contrast to the ego-psychologists, Lacan stresses the unconscious. He insists that the unconscious is governed by its own laws. Its images do not follow each other as in the sequential logic of consciousness but are condensed into each other or are displaced on to something else. Because it is *unconscious*, direct access to it is impossible, but, nevertheless, its manifestations are apparent most notably in dreams, everyday slips of the tongue, jokes, in neurotic and psychotic behaviour, and in *symptoms*. It needs to be emphasised that all psychoanalytic practice is based on the ability to hear something other than what the patient says, on the capacity to hear, within the conscious message enunciated by the speaker, the patterns produced by the unconscious.

Lacan is antagonistic to all those who assume that the human subject (the individual) exists from the beginning. For Lacan neither sexuality nor the unconscious are pre-given facts; they are *constructions*. The human subject is constructed in and through language. Language does not arise from within the individual; it is always out there in the world outside. In short, the human animal is born into language and it is within the terms of language that the human subject is constructed.

Lacan's thought disrupts and challenges many assumptions about knowledge and subjectivity common to the social sciences and humanities as well as in everyday life. Lacan's fusion of language-like processes with Freud's notion of sexuality and the unconscious are very useful to thinkers in a wide variety of disciplines in which questions of subjectivity, desire, reading and interpretation are usually ignored. His interest in psychoanalysis as a science of interpretation gives him an appeal far beyond the psychoanalytic community itself.

Writers in many domains are now making extensive use of Lacan's concepts and considerable developments are taking place in feminist thought, literary studies and film criticism through the use of Lacanian theory. Indeed, I want to argue that Lacanian thought has stimulated important intellectual advances throughout cultural studies. What is identity and how are subjects constituted? What is the relationship between the political and the personal? What are the functions of language in everyday life? What is the nature of desire? These are all questions about which Lacan has something interesting to say.

CHAPTER TWO | *The legacy of surrealism*

Introduction: The aims and aspirations of the movement

I begin this chapter by explaining why the surrealists were so fascinated by Freud, and outline the ways in which they explored the workings of the unconscious through the use of various techniques. After suggesting some of Lacan's connections and convergences with the surrealists, I consider the influence of Caillois on Lacan. In conclusion I describe the case of Aimée, an early patient of Lacan's who was also a *cause célèbre* for the surrealists.

Lacan's discourse is deeply marked by his encounter with surrealism. Lacan's work, a storehouse of images, allusions and references to surrealism, cannot be fully understood without a knowledge of the aims and aspirations of the movement. As Bice Benvenuto has remarked, surrealism's overturning of the place of conscious reason, its questioning of the reality of the object, its cultivation of the absurd, and its emphasis on the omnipotence of desire, seem to have provided Lacan with many of his basic attitudes.[1]

The surrealist movement had great intellectual breadth and verve and it is difficult for us now fully to understand its original aura of excitement and revolt. Surrealism was a highly politicised, inflammatory movement which had a radical concept of freedom.[2] Its aim was nothing less than the liberation, in art and in life, of the resources of the unconscious mind. The surrealists' spiritual ancestors were de Sade, Baudelaire, Rimbaud and Lautréamont. Deeply influenced by the lessons of Marx and Freud, surrealists, like André Breton, Paul Eluard, Louis Aragon and others, saw the new revolution occurring simultaneously on two fronts: the one political and external, the other exploring the deepest recesses of the human mind and unfolding its truths in the work of art.

Why were the surrealists so interested in Freud? And why were these artists so interested in the exploration of the relationship between the conscious and the unconscious?

The surrealists believed that the value of a work of art lay in the effort of the artist to encompass the whole psychophysical field of which the conscious mind represented only one small part. They thought of human experiences in the form of a pyramid, the narrow peak of which is the limited range of the conscious state, and the broad base the full, subterranean strata of the unconscious.[3] André Breton, the theoretical leader of the movement, believed that the surrealists' search for an extra-empirical reality was within the traditions of Western thought, and he consistently demanded that the barriers which ignore the worlds of the primitive, the child and the mad person be broken down.

Surrealism inherited from Dada a hostility towards conventional definitions of art. For Breton, surrealism was not merely an artistic style; it was closer to being a transcendental world-view.[4] Surrealism attempted to go beyond and above all forms of realism and to attain the realm of pure, unmediated thought and perception. This interest in the transcendental lies at the heart of the surrealists' subsequent enthusiasm for Hegel, who was seen as a potential ally in transcending the contradictions of bourgeois order.[5] The surrealists hoped for nothing less than the fusing of all the sources of human creativity – the dream, the unconscious, the conscious, the irrational – into a heightened reality that might alter the very shape of the world as well as men's and women's understanding of that world.

Freud published an essay in 1907 on Jensen's novel *Gradiva*.[6] In subjecting the novel to the psychoanalytic method, Freud showed the economy of the unconscious, its relationship to conscious action, and the role played by dream in this nexus. This essay provided many of the themes of the surrealists: the mechanism of repression, the dynamism of the repressed, the myth of love and the primacy of desire. One of Freud's conclusions was that both scientist and artist arrive ultimately at the same understanding of the unconscious; one proceeds through conscious observation of abnormal mental processes in others, the other directs his or her attention to his or her own unconscious and gives it artistic expression. The surrealists were quick to seize on Freud's conclusion that science and art confirm rather than contradict one another in their explication of the unconscious. They found in Freud's essay an explicit justification for their own attempt to determine the tortuous relationship between artistic expression and the unconscious.

The surrealists were concerned with the replacing of the image derived from nature by that drawn from an *interior* model. The work of art was to exist not as an aesthetic end, but only as a means to the exploration and expression of an inner psychic reality. Surrealist work of the 1920s and 1930s relied, whether implicitly or explicitly, on the discoveries of Freud. The surrealists, preoccupied with the sources of creativity, probed the working of the unconscious through many means. These included automatism, collage, dream interpretation, exploration of myth and the use of the paranoiac-critical method.

Automatism, the practice of automatic writing, was one of the first techniques the surrealists used. This process became for them a form of self-administered psychoanalysis. Automatic writing consisted of writing down as rapidly as possible, without revision or control by the conscious, everything that has passed through the mind when the writer had been able to detach her- or himself sufficiently from the world outside. The possibility of applying the techniques of automatic writing to painting was envisaged at this time. They also studied hypnosis and mediumship and made transcripts of what trance subjects said. Experiments of this kind produced a sort of intoxicated exhilaration. Writing, painting and sculpture became aspects of one single activity: that of calling empirical 'reality' into question.

The surrealists often attempted to fuse the polarities of dream and reality, the unconscious and the conscious in a single image. They did this through the technique called collage (the sticking together of disparate elements to make a picture). Surrealists depended on the devices of condensation, displacement and juxtaposition, to create a visual world analogous to but not reflecting any known perceptible reality. Max Ernst, for example, used old engravings and photo-mechanical reproductions as a means of violating conventional ideas about the rational structure of that same world. His figurative paintings, stripped of logical connections, remind one of the processes of the dream-work.

Although automatism and collage were the first 'Freudian' techniques used by the surrealists, Freud's major contribution to surrealism lay in his explication of the role of language in dream and dream interpretation. The formal structure of the dream – the condensation that results in a density of imagery, displacement of the senses of time and space and the importance of figurative language – is reconstituted in the works of the movement. The surrealists argued for a view of the relationship between dream and waking in which both states are perceived as fluid, their contents ceaselessly intermingled. They foresaw the ultimate achievement of dream study as the integration of the two states, in appearance so contradictory, of dream and reality into one sort of absolute reality which they called surreality.

Like Freud, the surrealists were fascinated by mythological themes such as Oedipus, Narcissus and others. In the area of surrealist painting, where there exists no single and identifiable surrealist 'style' and where the value of the work is determined almost exclusively on the basis of its content, myth becomes one way of organising and synthesising surrealist beliefs within a recognisable set of symbols.[7] From their reading of Freud the surrealists realised that automatism, dream and myth all shared common characteristics: condensation, a displacement of the sense of time and space, a similar symbolism. Freud had viewed dreams as the residues of daily activity; myth as the collective heritage of centuries. For him the two modes of unconscious thought shared a symbolism that derived from their common origin in childhood, whether individual or cultural.[8]

Another form of Freudian experimentation was the intentional simulation of states of mental abnormality. The most flamboyant and provocative exploitation of this technique was by Salvador Dali. Dali became fascinated by Millet's 'Angelus' and was quick to recognise that the work's universal appeal could not be fully explained by its overt content, two peasants bowing their heads as the Angelus peels from a distant tower. His earlier reading of Freud led Dali to an examination of the latent sexual content of a work which he saw as 'the most erotic picture ever painted, a masterpiece of disguised sexual repression'.[9] When a visitor to the Louvre drove a hole through the canvas Dali became even more convinced of the work's disquieting quality. It was Jacques Lacan, a frequent contributor to *Minotaure* with articles on the relationship between paranoia and artistic creativity, who interviewed the vandal. Lacan's interest in such 'deviants' should not surprise us. He worked for a year in a clinic attached to the Préfecture de Police, and his main task was to prepare psychiatric reports on criminals and vagrants.

Unable satisfactorily to explain the enigmatic aspects of 'The Angelus', Dali set about examining the painting in the light of the paranoiac-critical method which he had developed earlier. It was during the 1930s that Dali developed his 'paranoiac-critical' method, a process by which he deliberately induced psychotic hallucinatory states in himself for exploitation in his art and life. We know that this practice caught the attention of Lacan, who subsequently visited Dali, whereupon Dali further developed his theory.[10]

Freud had used the psychoanalytical device of free association to trace the symbolic meaning of dream imagery to its source in the unconscious. Dali applied the same method to pictorial imagery, and particularly to that imagery which arises as a result of the visual hallucinations which Dali had exploited since childhood. By using the external world as the source and stimulus for the delusion and by rendering the hallucinatory results with the clarity and precision of Dutch seventeenth-century still-life, Dali hoped to destroy all belief in the idea of a stable external reality without recourse to abstraction, which would violate the essentially figurative structure of mental images.

Lacan's connection with the surrealists

One of the main characteristics of surrealist work is the juxtaposition of images and objects far removed from one another. Breton borrowed Lautréamont's idea of beauty: 'Beautiful as the unexpected meeting, on a dissection table, of a sewing machine and an umbrella.' Breton's analysis of his dreams contributed to the imagery of the poetry. The experience of what the surrealists called 'convulsive beauty' (of something that shakes the subject's self-possession, bringing exultation through a kind of shock), is rather like Freud's notion of the *uncanny*, where shock, mixed with the sudden appearance of fate, engulfs the subject.

All this implies a definite break with a purely instrumental or representational view of language. For surrealist poets like Aragon, Breton and Eluard, language is not a nomenclature or a transparent medium. Meaning is seen as being produced through the juxtaposition of images and the clash of associations rather than as deriving from some ideal correspondence between sign and referent.

One surrealist painter, René Magritte, quite consciously began to explore a theory of meaning, in the late 1920s, that was surprisingly close to contemporary linguistic theory. Many of his paintings are an investigation of the relationship between the process of depiction and the object depicted. His painting, 'Use of Speech', which depicts a smoking pipe and is inscribed with the words *'Ceci n'est pas une pipe'* (This is not a pipe), is a familiar one. This painting is, in part, a comment on the non-correspondence between the visual image and the object it represents.[11] An image of a pipe is not a pipe. In other words, the relationship between signifier, signified and referent is shown to be arbitrary.

I am mentioning all this because it will help us to understand not only Lacan's views on language but his own particular use of it. Lacan's style, with its puns and word games, is part of a highly self-conscious intellectual tradition. Just as Marcel Duchamp's 'ready-mades' challenged conventional assumptions about the nature of the art object, word play can be seen as a challenge to the notion that language is transparent. Many of Lacan's contemporaries such as Duchamp, Leiris, Queneau, were masters of glossological games.

There are many references to surrealism in Lacan's *Ecrits*.[12] The frequency with which Lacan alludes to surrealism is all the more striking in that it is not a major reference for the post-war avant-garde. (Neither Barthes, Sollers nor Kristeva has anything positive to say about it.) Of the forty or so French literary authors included in the name index, more than half belonged to the surrealist group at one time or another, or were claimed by the surrealists as their forebears.

Lacan has said that he felt a great personal connection with surrealist painting. In short, surrealism provides Lacan with a constant stock of allusions and illustrations, as when Magritte's window paintings are used in the 1962 seminar to illustrate the structure of phantasy (the idea that a phantasy is like a picture fitted into the opening of a window).[13]

There is also an indirect reference to surrealism in Lacan's comments on Hans Holbein's painting 'The Ambassadors' (1533), which is in the National Gallery, London. This work, one of the surrealists' favourite classical paintings, depicts two splendidly dressed men. In the foreground there is a strange, vaguely phallic object and, if one stands at a certain angle, one can see a skull appear, a continual reminder of the presence of death. This painting is a perfect example of the use of anamorphosis (a distorted image which will look normal if viewed from a certain angle or in a curved mirror) in painting.[14] Lacan writes that 'Holbein makes visible for us something that is simply the subject nihilated', and suggests that Dali belongs to the same tradition as Holbein, and it is true that anamorphosis is an important feature of Dali's paintings.[15]

Besides being on close terms with Dali, the young Lacan associated with the group surrounding Breton. While Lacan was publishing clinical articles on neurology in medical journals he was also contributing to surrealist reviews; it was, in fact, in surrealist circles that his doctoral thesis on paranoia received its most enthusiastic welcome.

It is an irony that psychoanalysis met with considerable and lasting resistance in French medical circles and that it was in the literary milieu that it found its first favourable reception. Some writers tried to absorb psychoanalysis into an established literary discourse by arguing that it could be fitted into a theory of literary introspection. For the surrealists, psychoanalysis had a very different function: it was a means with which to attack bourgeois values. They believed that the primary function of psychiatry was one of social repression. They agreed with the psychoanalytical view that the distinction between the normal and abnormal is not self-evident.

The first issue of the surrealist journal *Minotaure* contains work by Dali and Lacan. It has been said that there are definite parallels between their thinking at this time (Dali met Lacan in 1933). Certain of Dali's double or multiple images might be illustrations of Lacan's views on the mirror phase, and the narcissistic construction and function of the ego.[16] (I will explain these ideas presently.)

The ideas of Caillois

Many important articles were published in *Minotaure*. We know that Lacan was greatly influenced by Roger Caillois, a sociologist and avant-garde writer, who published two long essays in the above journal, the first on the praying mantis, the second on the phenomenon of mimicry. He wrote about how some animals, such as the praying mantis, stick insects and others, camouflage themselves. At that time it was generally held that this mimeticism was good for the creature and for the species. Caillois denies this; he argues that mimeticism is not good and he gives several arguments to illustrate why it is not successful. He writes about how these creatures subject themselves to the structure of an image, and how the structure to which they have to conform does not actually foster their survival. Indeed, it has a catastrophic effect on them.

The female mantis's sexual practices – in certain species, its consumption of its mate after or even during copulation – and its voracity made it the perfect symbol of the phallic mother, fascinating, petrifying, castrating. It is not surprising that the image of the praying mantis is found everywhere in the surrealist work of the period.[17]

In his subsequent exploration of mimicry Caillois writes that the mantis comes stunningly to resemble a machine when, even decapitated, it can continue to function and thus to mime life:

> In the absence of all centres of representation and of voluntary action, it can walk, regain its balance, have coitus, lay eggs, build a cocoon, and, what is most astonishing, in the face of danger can fall into a fake cadaverous immobility. I am expressing in this indirect manner what language can scarcely picture, or reason assimilate, namely death.[18]

Most scientific explanations for animal mimicry relate it to adaptive behaviour. It is usually argued that the insect takes on the coloration, the shape, the patterning of its environment in order to fool either its predator or its prey. Caillois shows that the adaption hypothesis founders on two counts. First, the fusion of the insect with its environment can and often does work against survival, as when the animal is mistakenly eaten by its own kind or cannot be perceived by members of its species for purposes of mating. Second, this phenomenon, which functions exclusively in the realm of the visual, is largely irrelevant to predators' hunting habits, which are a matter of smell and motion. In Caillois's view, mimicry is a function of the visual experience of the insect itself.

Tying mimicry to the animal's own perception of space, Caillois hypothesises that the phenomenon is in fact a kind of insectoid psychosis. He argues that the life of any organism depends on the possibility of its maintaining its own distinctness, a boundary within which it is contained, the terms of what we could call its self-possession. Mimicry is the loss of this possession, because the animal that merges with its setting becomes dispossessed, de-realised, as though yielding to a temptation exercised on it by the vast outsideness of space itself, a temptation to fusion. In case all this seems far-fetched, Callois reminds his readers of primitive sympathetic magic in which an illness is conceived of as a posses-sion of the patient by some external force, one that dispossesses the victim of his or her own person, one that can be combated by drawing it off from the patient through the mimicry performed by a shaman in a rite of repossession.

Caillois's essay on mimicry had a great influence within the psychoanalytic circles developing in Paris in the 1930s.[19] Lacan expressed his debt to Caillois, particularly in his working out of the concept of the mirror phase.[20] This phase refers to the moment when the child assumes an imaginary unity with its body image, in the way that some animals alienate their true nature, in mimetically hiding in their surroundings. It is the child's first en-counter with its image in a mirror which results in a fictional self-projection that influences subsequent identity formation.

Lacan's theory of subjectivity – in his early work – is partly derived from Caillois. Caillois's main thesis is that the organism is constructed by forces and structures beyond the control of the subject. Influenced by Caillois's ideas about how some insects are captured by the image, Lacan argues that the human being, like the praying mantis, is captivated by the image. At the time Lacan was interested in narcissistic identification and he drew on Caillois's work to argue that we are dominated by a structure of images and that this has a toxic, poisonous effect on the human subject.

The case of Aimée

An important moment in the history of surrealism is the convergence of the concern for language and the interest in psychoanalysis and psychiatry. The surrealists argued that the pathological is not meaningless and that it is a mode of expression which has its own validity. It is possible that Lacan's famous slogan 'the unconscious is structured like a language' may owe much to the surrealists' attention to the linguistic expression of psychic phenomena. It has been suggested that some surrealist texts prefigure aspects of Lacanian theory. Indeed, it could be argued that the surrealists were the first to realise that psychoanalysis is essentially a question of language. They fully understood why the method introduced by Freud and Breuer was given the name 'the talking cure' by Anna O., one of Breuer's patients.[21] Besides language, the surrealists were interested in certain aspects of femininity. 'Woman-as-victim' is a common theme in surrealist art.

Lacan's first articles were published between 1926 and 1933 while he was training as a psychiatrist. During this time he studied many patients suffering from delusions and became interested in their disorders of language. His research convinced him that no psychical phenomenon could arise completely independently of the subject's personality.

The major work of this period was his doctoral thesis: 'Paranoid psychosis and its relation to the personality' (1932), which included a study of a female psychotic whom he called Aimée.[22] While not a psychoanalyst, Lacan used some analytical concepts in his account of his patient at a time when Freud was not well known in France. Lacan's thesis was one of the first attempts in France to interpret a psychosis in terms of the total history of the patient.

Aimée was a thirty-eight-year-old railway clerk who inexplicably attacked one of the best-known actresses in Paris, wounding her with a knife as she entered the theatre one evening. Aimée consistently maintained that the actress, and others, had been spreading slander about her. She had never met her alleged persecutors. Aimée had literary ambitions, but her novels and poems had been repeatedly rejected by one publisher after another.

It was the unusual nature of her writings which first led Lacan to take an interest in her case. In his view, Aimée attacked an ideal image of a woman who enjoys social freedom and power, the very type of woman she hoped to become by pursuing a literary career. The dominating woman she envied, and who became her persecutor, was initially embodied by her sister and then by a close woman friend to whom Aimée once admitted: 'I feel that I am masculine.' Aimée's condition, then, was rooted in a problem of identification, in a confusion of self and other. She wished to be a rich, influential novelist, and attacked the incarnation of her ambition: an actress who represented her ego-ideal.

In Lacan's view Aimée was clearly suffering from delusions of being persecuted. A remarkable feature of Aimée's delusions was that when she was found guilty before the law and imprisoned, the delusions disappeared. The wish behind her delusions was one of unconscious self-punishment, probably in order to deal with her guilt feelings. Her psychosis was 'self-punishment paranoia'. This was one of Freud's concepts and referred to those who are criminals from a sense of guilt.[23] Freud described how certain criminal acts give relief to subjects who suffer from oppressive feelings of guilt before the crime. He also wrote how children can quite often be naughty on purpose to provoke punishment, and then are quiet and settled after the punishment.

Lacan's observations led him to the conclusion that Aimée's assault on the actress was in fact a means of punishing herself by attacking her ideal. Lacan's comments rely heavily on Freud's argument that paranoia is in part a defence against homosexuality, a process of disavowal (a refusal to acknowledge) which gives rise to the delusion of persecution and to the identification of the loved one with the persecutor. In this case, and another which Lacan discusses concerning the Papin sisters, self and other merge all too easily and gender becomes uncertain.

Aimée was not only a patient of Lacan's, but was also a *cause célèbre* for the surrealists. Lacan's thesis included a selection of Aimée's copious writings, which were produced at the height of her psychosis and which virtually stopped when it abated. The literary qualities of Aimée's work were much appreciated and discussed by members of the surrealist movement of which Lacan was a part. I will discuss the Aimée case again, in more detail, in a later chapter.

CHAPTER THREE | *The uses of philosophy*

Introduction

One of Lacan's achievements is that he has linked psychoanalysis with philosophy, linguistics and literature, and has, at the same time, stressed its status as a science. Let us begin by looking at some of the interconnections between Lacan and philosophy.

Freud disliked the speculations of philosophy but this did not prevent him from advancing his own speculative hypotheses. They are, however, subject to subsequent modifications and revisions. Freud's empiricism implies a high degree of conceptualisation. He believed that advances in knowledge are impossible without the constant renewal and enrichment of the work of conceptualisation. This is what Lacan has tried to do in his own work.

Like Freud before him, Lacan objects strongly to the totalising ambitions of philosophy, its tendency to see itself as the primary form of explanation, and to its claims to being able to tell the whole truth. But whereas Freud chooses to identify his work with the slow, halting march of science, Lacan opposes philosophical totalisation on the ground that it is simply not possible to tell the whole truth. The words that might allow one to do so are simply not there.

Among psychoanalysts, Lacan's interest in philosophy and his willingness to enter into theoretical controversy are the exception to the rule. He is constantly referring, for example, to St Augustine, Descartes, Hegel, Kierkegaard, Malebranche, La Rochefoucauld, Spinoza and many others. Philosophy provides Lacan with an arsenal of references and allusions which can be used to make illustrative or pedagogic points.

Lacan's career spans fifty years of French intellectual life, and it is only to be expected that it should reflect many of the cultural shifts that have occurred over that period. There are many references to different philosophical movements, and finally (after 1953) to a linguistically based structuralism. In this chapter I want to delineate the concerns of some philosophers who have influenced Lacan's work. I will focus on those aspects of Spinoza, Hegel, Sartre and Heidegger which help explain Lacan's thinking.

The influence of Spinoza

When we read Lacan's work we become aware of certain underlying assumptions about the nature of life, and the objects that we love. These assumptions owe a great deal to his study of Spinoza's *Ethics*.[1] The first thing to understand about Spinoza is that he was a determinist and believed that all things which come to pass, come to pass according to the eternal order and fixed laws of nature. He thought that all our actions are determined by our past experience, our physical and mental constitution, and by the state of the laws of nature. Second, we should note that he was a relativist. He held that nothing is good or bad in itself, but is so only in relation to someone. Since the same thing may at different times affect the same person differently, the goodness or badness of such a thing cannot be considered as an inherent property of it, but only as a property which comes into existence depending upon what relation it has to a human being at a specific historical moment.

Given, therefore, the two facts that all events are determined by natural laws so that human subjects are not free, and also that things are not good or bad in themselves, then in what does the good life for human beings consist? For Spinoza, such a life consists in the possession of a certain attitude towards the world. This attitude is in part emotional and in part rational. The rational part of it consists in the recognition of the truth that all events are determined, the emotional part in an acceptance of this fact.

Spinoza maintains that the idea that human beings have free will is false, an illusion engendered by not knowing what the causes of our actions are. On the other hand, he says, there is such a thing as human servitude or bondage. Human bondage consists in being induced to act by some causes rather than others. There are some causes – passive emotions such as fear, anger and hatred – which are generated in us by the frustrating influence of the parts of the world that are outside us. But as well as these, he believes, we have active emotions, those generated by an understanding of our circumstances in the world, a knowledge of what is really going on. The more our activities are caused by active emotions and the less by passive ones, the less we are in bondage, the more we are ourselves.

Spinoza believed that if there was confusion in the mind there was pain in the body. In passion, we are being acted upon (passivity). Clear ideas create the possibility of acting, the opposite of passion (activity). His view is that by the exercise of the intellect in gaining an understanding, we can make the passive emotions fade away so that their place comes to be occupied by the active emotions.

Spinoza's philosophy offers guidance to people which, if followed, will enable them to avoid fear, anxiety and unhappiness. These arise only when we become slaves to our emotions; a person who does not take the broad view is a person 'in human bondage'. In short, people can liberate themselves by understanding that the course of nature is predestined and also by understanding that 'nothing is good or bad in itself', but that it only becomes good or bad depending upon how it affects us.

To put it in another way, Spinoza is arguing that human beings will be happy when they come to understand that there are limits to human power; by understanding that everything which happens must happen necessarily, people will no longer dissipate their energy in struggling against these events. By looking at every event as part of a larger system ('in the context of eternity', to use his phrase), one will no longer be upset and frightened by the events that occur in life.

Spinoza is important because he stresses the idea that discovering what the hidden sources of your feelings and actions are will in some way be liberating, even though it does not literally increase your freedom. It frees you from the frustration induced by being at the mercy of forces you do not understand. This thought is, of course, central to the ideas of Freud and Lacan.

Drawing on Spinoza, Lacan suggests that we should analyse and develop clear ideas, and that patients (analysands) should learn to act (but this, of course, is different from 'acting out'). Though we cannot avoid being subjects we *can* have some understanding of the processes involved. Lacan thinks that at the end of analysis there is a conclusion; people can come to a conclusion about their desire. Rather than be victims of their passion, analysands can act.

It seems to me that Lacan has been influenced by Spinoza's determinism, his relativism and his view of the importance of understanding 'the passions'. The precise interconnections between their thought will become apparent as I explain Lacan's constantly evolving and dialectical 'system' in succeeding chapters.

Hegel's master–slave story

Lacan belonged to the same generation as Sartre and Lévi-Strauss, a generation which was antagonistic to the academic philosophy of the 1920s and 1930s. It was a generation that reacted bitterly against the domination of neo-Kantianism and the Cartesian tradition. This was a tradition that excluded Hegel from serious consideration.

It was not the academic philosophers who imported Hegel and Heidegger into France but more marginal figures, many of them immigrants like Kojève, whose lectures on Hegel were to have an immense impact. Alexandre Kojève gave a series of lectures, between 1933 and 1939, which were regularly attended by intellectuals such as Aron, Bataille, Breton, Klossowski, Merleau-Ponty, Queneau and Lacan. Many elements of the 'left Hegelianism' and Marxist humanism of the post-war decades can be traced back to these lectures. Kojève's lectures describe a violent world-view and focus upon moments of rupture and struggle rather than synthesis. For Kojève it is Hegel's *Phenomenology of Spirit* which is the key text and, within that text, it is the master–slave dialectic which is foregrounded to the exclusion of almost everything else. The central moment in the emergence of individuality revolves around Desire in so far as it implies a dialectic between self and other.

As Lacan was greatly influenced by Kojève's lectures on Hegel's *Phenomenology of Spirit* I will now give a brief summary of Kojève's exposition of the nature of human desire, the struggle for recognition, and the parable of the master–slave relation.[2]

Man is self-consciousness. He is conscious of himself, conscious of his human reality and dignity; and it is in this that he is essentially different from animals. Man becomes conscious of himself when, for the first time, he says 'I'.[3]

The man who contemplates is 'absorbed' by what he contemplates; the knowing subject loses himself in the object that is known. The man who is 'absorbed' by the object that he is contemplating can be 'brought back to himself' only by a Desire; by the desire to eat, for example. It is in and by – or better still as – 'his' Desire that man is formed and is revealed, to himself and to others, as an I . . .

In contrast to the knowledge that keeps man in a passive quietude, Desire disquiets him and moves him to action. Born of Desire, action tends to satisfy it, and can do so only by the 'negation', the destruction, or at least the transformation, of the desired object: to satisfy hunger, for example, the food must be destroyed or, in any case, transformed. Thus, all action 'is negation'.

But negating action is not purely destructive, for if action destroys an objective reality, for the sake of satisfying the Desire from which it is born, it creates in its place, in and by that very destruction, a subjective reality. The being that eats, for example, creates and preserves its only reality into its own reality by the 'assimilation', the 'internalisation' of a 'foreign', 'external' reality. Generally speaking, the I of Desire is an emptiness that receives a real positive content only by negating action that satisfies Desire in destroying, transforming and 'assimilating' the desired non-I.

Human Desire must be directed towards another Desire. Thus, in the relationship between man and woman, for example, Desire is human only if one desires, not the body, but the Desire of the other; if he wants 'to possess' or 'to assimilate' the Desire taken as Desire – that is to say, if he wants to be 'desired' or 'loved' or, rather, 'recognised' in his human value, in his reality as a human individual.

To desire the Desire of another is in the final analysis to desire that the value that I am or that I 'represent' be the value desired by the other: I want him to 'recognize' my value as his value. In other words all human Desire is, finally, a function of the Desire for 'recognition'.[4] It is only by being 'recognised' by another, by many others, or – in the extreme – by all others, that a human being is really human, for himself as well as for others.

The human being can be formed only if at least two of these Desires confront one another. Each of the two beings endowed with such a Desire is ready to go all the way in pursuit of its satisfaction; that is, is ready to risk its life . . . in order to be 'recognised' by the other, to impose itself on the other as the supreme value; accordingly, their meeting can only be a fight to the death.

Human reality is created, is constituted, only in the fight for recognition and by the risk of life that it implies. Man is human only to the extent that he wants to impose himself on another man, to be recognised by him . . . If one of the adversaries remains alive but kills the other, he can no longer be recognised by the other; the man who has been defeated and killed does not recognise the victory of the conqueror. Therefore, it does the man of the fight no good to kill his adversary. He must overcome him 'dialectically'. That is, he must leave him life and consciousness, and destroy only his autonomy. In other words, he must enslave him.

By refusing to risk his life in a fight for pure prestige, the Slave does not rise above the level of animals. Hence he considers himself as such, and as such is he considered by the Master. But the Slave, for his part, recognises the Master in his human dignity and reality, and the Slave behaves accordingly.

The Master is not the only one to consider himself Master. The Slave, also, considers him as such. Hence, he is recognised in his human reality and dignity. But this recognition is one-sided, for he does not recognise in turn the Slave's reality and dignity. Hence, he is recognised by someone whom he does not recognise. And this is what is tragic in his situation. The Master has fought and risked his life for a recognition without value for him. For he can be satisfied only by recognition from one whom he recognises as worthy of recognising him. The Master's attitude is an existential impasse.

The Master is fixed in his Mastery. He cannot go beyond himself, change, progress. As for the Slave, there is nothing fixed in him. He wants to transcend himself by negation of his given state. He has a positive ideal to attain, the ideal of autonomy, of Being-for-itself. The Master forces the Slave to work. In becoming Master of nature by work, then, the Slave frees himself from his own nature. The future and history hence belong not to the warlike Master, who either dies or preserves himself indefinitely in identity to himself, but to the working Slave.

The Master, who does not work, produces nothing stable outside of himself. He merely destroys the products of the Slave's work. Work is repressed Desire, it forms and educates. The Slave can work for the Master only by repressing his own desires. Hence, he transcends himself by working – or, perhaps better, he educates himself.

Man achieves his true autonomy, his authentic freedom, only after passing through Slavery, after surmounting fear of death by work performed in the service of another. Without work that transforms the real objective world, man cannot really transform himself.

The Master can never detach himself from the world in which he lives, and if the world perishes, he perishes with it. Only the Slave can transcend the given world and not perish. Only the Slave can transform the world that forms him and fixes him in Slavery and create a world that he has formed in which he will be free. And the Slave achieves this only through forced work carried out in the Master's service. To be sure, this work by itself does not free him. But in transforming the world by this work, the Slave transforms himself, too, and thus creates the new objective conditions that permit him to take up once more the liberating fight for recognition that he refused in the beginning for fear of death. And thus, in the long run, all slavish work realises not the Master's will but the will – at first unconscious – of the Slave who, finally, succeeds where the Master, necessarily, fails.

Lacan is deeply indebted to Hegelian thought. Indeed, one critic has written that it is not an overstatement to say that the entire first phase of Lacan's work as a psychoanalyst from 1936 to 1953 is dominated by the elaboration of this Hegelian account of the dilemmas of self-consciousness and their resolution.[5] I think Lacan draws on Hegel's work in the following ways. Hegel's analysis of the power situation of the master and slave and their co-dependence has greatly influenced Lacan who, as we shall see, often refers to and makes use of the master–slave dialectic. Second, I would argue that Hegel's parable about how the master and the slave strive for recognition of desire forms an essential part of Lacan's thought. It is said that Lacan combined Freud's concept of libido with Hegel's concept of recognition to produce his particular concept of desire. For Lacan there is no simple relation between desire and an object that will satisfy it; in fact, he shows how desire is linked in a complicated fashion to the desire of the Other.[6]

On Sartre and Heidegger

Despite Lacan's criticisms of the absolute autonomy of the self
assumed by existentialism, he recognises in Sartre a fellow
Hegelian. When Lacan wishes to discuss problems of alternation
and ambivalence he often turns towards the analysis of the dialectic of self and other, of seeing and being seen, of humiliation and
domination to be found in Sartre's *Being and Nothingness.*
   Let me briefly outline some of the *similarities* between the discourses of Lacan and Sartre. Lacan described *Being and Nothingness* as essential reading for psychoanalysts because of the acuity of
its presentation of the other and of the gaze.[7] Sartre believed that
the gaze is not located just at the level of the eyes. The eyes may
well not appear; they may be masked. The gaze is not necessarily
the face of our fellow being; it could just as easily be the window
behind which we assume he is lying in wait for us. It is an X, the
object when faced with which the subject becomes object.
   Lacan also has important things to say about this topic. The
eyes, as one of the modes of access for libido to explore the world,
become the instrument of the 'scopic drive'. A drive, we must
remember, is not just pleasure-seeking, but is caught up in a
signifying system. This signifying process comes to affect all looking. The eye is not merely an organ of perception, but also an
organ of pleasure. There is, of course, a difference between the eye
and the look. The subject can, in a way, be seized by the object of
its look. As Lacan points out, 'it is, rather, it that grasps me'.[8]
   Lacan recommends Sartre's phenomenology as essential reading
because it can contribute to our understanding of inter-
subjectivity. The latter's phenomenology of 'being in love' is
judged 'irrefutable'. Sartre believes that the self remains irre-
mediably opposed to the Other. Drawing on Hegel's parable, of
the master–slave relation, Sartre reinterprets the struggle for recognition and argues that the attempt by each self to reduce the
other to an object is impossible. What happens is this: to the other
person, who looks at me from the outside, I seem an object, a
thing; my subjectivity with its inner freedom escapes his gaze.
Hence his tendency is always to convert me into the object he sees.
The gaze of the Other penetrates to the depths of my existence,
freezes and congeals it. It is this, according to Sartre, that turns

love into perpetual conflict. The lover wishes to possess the beloved, but the freedom of the beloved cannot be possessed; hence
the lover tends to reduce the beloved to an object for the sake of
possessing it. Love is menaced always by a perpetual oscillation,
between sadism and masochism. In sadism I reduce the other to a
mere lump, to be beaten and manipulated as I choose, while in
masochism I offer myself as an object, but in an attempt to entrap
the other and undermine his freedom.[9]

One of the most important concepts in Lacan's thought is desire. This is, of course, one term in the need–demand–desire triad.
I shall briefly attempt to explain the meaning of these terms. Like
his mentor, Hegel, Lacan begins from the experience of physical
need. We all realise that the child is for a long time dependent upon
others for the satisfaction of its basic wants. Need can be defined in
basically biological terms. Lacan argues that a crucial transformation takes place when the child's plea for satisfaction begins to be
expressed in language, since the request for satisfaction is now
accompanied by a plea for recognition as the subject of the need to
be satisfied. This is what Lacan calls *demand*. It is out of this
process that there emerges what Lacan terms desire. *Desire* is that
which goes beyond demand and conveys the subject's wish for
totality. It can never be fulfilled.

I mention this because there are close connections between Lacan's and Sartre's concept of desire. Lacan's term *désir* comes from
Hegel, through Kojève, and phenomenology. Sartre speaks of man
being torn between a 'desire to be' and a 'desire to have'. For both
Sartre and Lacan desire is defined in terms of a 'lack of being'.

Some parallels can also be found between Lacan's 'mirror phase'
and Sartre's early work. In both cases the ego is viewed as an
illusory representation, as a source and focus of alienation. Optical
metaphors are used by both authors. Lacan introduced the mirror
phase in 1936. With the mirror phase Lacan began to work with a
concept of the human subject who does not have his own unity in
himself, but with a subject who finds his unity only in the other,
through the image in the mirror. This gives us the matrix of a
fundamental dependency on the other, a relationship defined not
in terms of language but in terms of image. In philosophical terms
Lacan's mirror phase takes its inspiration from Kojève's Hegel,
whereas Sartre's pure phenomenology owes its primary inspiration
to Husserl. I should add, in parentheses, that though Lacan was

influenced by Sartrean existentialism he was also critical of it. He could not accept its bleak pessimism, its faith in self-consciousness, the search for liberty within a situation of enslavement, and its denial of the efficacy of action.[10]

Another similarity between Lacan and Sartre is their interest in Heidegger. Lacan makes considerable reference to Heidegger's thought, and specifically to the 'existentialist' Heidegger of *Being and Time*. It was with the publication of this book, his first major work, in 1927, that Heidegger reworked Husserl's original method and gave phenomenology an existentialist orientation. Instead of asking what does it mean to *know*, he asks what does it mean to *be*? Later, in the 1930s, Heidegger's thinking underwent its famous 'turn' from a phenomenology of human existence, based on a concrete description of man's moods and projects as a being-in-the-world, to a phenomenology of language which stressed the priority of the word of Being over the human subject. In this later work Heidegger argues that language functions poetically as 'a house of Being' where genuine thinking is fostered. In his view we do not represent language to ourselves; language presents itself to us and speaks through us.

According to Heidegger I am not some free-floating disembodied *cogito*, but inherit a world that is not of my making, a world into which I have been thrown. I remain free to choose how I will reappropriate the meanings of this world for myself in order to project them into an open horizon of futural possibilities. Heidegger argues that Man is not a fixed object among objects, a self-identical entity; he is a being who is perpetually reaching beyond himself towards the world, towards horizons of meaning beyond his present given condition. The essence of human being is temporality, for we can only understand ourselves in the present by referring to the temporal horizons of our existence, that is by recollecting our past and projecting our future.

In Heidegger's view, human thought can never elevate itself from its immersion in the past into a position of panoramic survey. He believes that our attempt to grasp our own rootedness in the past is driven by the urgency of a need to establish an authentic relation to our still-to-be-realised possibilities of being. Heidegger's stress on the temporal dimension of the *future* is shared by Lacan. In this view the actions of the subject cannot be seen as causally determined by his or her past; what is important is the *interpretation*. For Lacan, it is the way in which we understand our past which determines how it determines us.[11] But this understanding is itself intimately related to our orientation towards the future.

Heidegger in *Being and Time* considers temporality as 'being towards', an anticipatory mode of being.[12] In Lacan's theorisation of the mirror phase there is also a temporal as well as a visual dimension. In the mirror phase the illusory or alienating nature of the ego's identifications involve an anticipatory, futural dimension.

The centre of Heidegger's concern is the meaning of Being. This quest leads him to language where Being manifests itself. Language speaks Being as thinking. Thinking in Heidegger, especially in the later works, reveals that language speaks Being. And Being, as such, dwells in language. Heidegger and Lacan have the following similarities: they both reject the traditional view that language is an instrument for the extension of man's will. They would agree with the statement, 'Man acts as though he were the shaper and master of language, while in fact language remains the master of man.'[13] Both suggest, in their different ways, that we are locked in a prison house of language. Neither Heidegger nor Lacan is interested in mere explanation; both are far more interested in elucidation and illumination. They want not to inform but to evoke.

I think Lacan's reading of Heidegger had a considerable impact on his thinking about language. Let me give an example. Lacan's notion of empty and full speech owes something to Heidegger's *Gerede* (idle talk) and *Rede* (discourse). While *Gerede* is associated with gossiping and chatter, *Rede* is to do with the disclosure of truth and Being.[14] Lacan believes that empty speech is alienated, inauthentic speech; full speech means ceasing to speak of oneself as an object. These concepts will be discussed fully in the next chapter on language.

The theory of the four discourses

It is important to remember that while Barthes, Derrida, Foucault and Lévi-Strauss were university teachers Lacan was a practising psychoanalyst, known for his emphasis on 'the return to Freud'. At the beginning of the 1950s Lacan took this 'return to Freud' as a slogan with which to attack ego-psychology. I have already made a few brief remarks about Lacan's antagonism to ego-psychology and how he considered it as non-Freudian and even anti-Freudian. As a critique of ego-psychology runs through all of Lacan's post-war work, we should be clear about what ego-psychology is.

Though it is often thought of as American, its origins are actually European. Its founders are Heinz Hartmann, Ernest Kris and Rudolph Loewenstein, and their work is based largely on Freud's second topology of id, ego and superego. For Hartmann and his associates, the three agencies, id, ego and superego, can be defined in terms of their functions: id functions are centred upon basic needs and a striving for instinctual gratification, ego functions centre upon adaptation to external reality and the superego functions focus upon moral demands.

Freud vacillated between two quite different views of the ego which can be called the realist and the narcissistic. The 'realist' view is that the ego is an agency which intervenes in the conflict between the sexual wishes, which originate in the id, and the demands of reality. The ego acts like a filter in both directions, from the id to reality and from reality to the id. As already mentioned, Freud likens the ego to the rider of a horse; the horse signifies the energies of the id, energies which must be correctly harnessed if the rider is to keep his/her seat. Reality is represented by the path or destination the rider must entice and control the horse to follow.

In this view, the ego protects the norms of social reality by modifying the 'unreasonable', impossible demands of the id, on the one hand; while on the other, the ego protects the id by shielding it from excessively strong stimuli coming from reality – from harsh judgements, the absence of desired objects. It should be noted that in the above, realist model, two terms are given and unquestioned, the id being a function of biology, and reality an unalterable, ahistorical system, 'civilisation'.

It is claimed by ego-psychologists that the ego contains within it elements which mature and develop into a 'conflict-free ego sphere' which transcends conflicts and which is regarded as autonomous. Ego-psychologists focus on the way the ego neutralises instinctual drives and the strength of the id, harnesses them and uses them to further the work of adaptation. According to ego-psychologists the aim of analysis is to strengthen the ego. The analysis is seen as a process whereby the patient, the analysand, comes to identify with the strong ego of the analyst.

Where ego-psychology refers to the realist view, Lacan relies on Freud's second or narcissistic account of the ego. The narcissistic ego is fluid and mobile, consisting of a series of identifications, internalisations of images/perceptions. In contrast with the ego psychologists Lacan believes that 'the core of our being does not coincide with the ego'. Drawing on Freud's paper 'On narcissism', Lacan argues that the ego is not organised by the reality system, precisely because all its structures are characterised by the effect of misrecognition.[15] In Lacan's view the ego cannot judge reality, or mediate between reality and desire because it is always marked by error, misrecognition or lack.

Lacan often refers to the 'perverse genius' of La Rochefoucauld and asserts that the Nietzsche of *On the Genealogy of Morals* and La Rochefoucauld were the precursors of Freud. Rochefoucauld is the great theorist of *amour-propre* (self-love), or what we may now call 'narcissism'. He believed that self-love was the mainspring behind all human behaviour and that it concealed itself behind countless masks and disguises. For Lacan the notion of *amour-propre* represents a glimpse into the narcissistic structure of the ego.[16] He establishes an opposition between La Rochefoucauld and Descartes. Lacan's new view of the subject challenges the European philosophical tradition, often personified for Lacan by Descartes. Descartes's proposition 'I think, therefore I am' implies the importance of thought, of the conscious. The Cartesian subject is identified with the ego. Lacan wants to emphasise the unconscious, which he never sees as 'primitive', 'dark' or 'negative'. Lacan is always on good terms with the unconscious; he therefore reverses Descartes's maxim and says: 'I think where I am not, therefore I am where I do not think'.[17]

Lacan is antagonistic to those forms of thinking based on 'the centre' and 'the fixed point'. He declares that the Copernican Revolution failed to dislodge the prestige of the centre: it shifted from man and the earth to the sun, but it is still the idea of the centre that controls discourse. Kepler was more radical than Copernicus in his thinking because of his notion of the ellipsis, which had no centre. This point is important because Lacan's critique of the individual ego is based on his objection to the notion of centring, of making the centre the point of view from which to assess and evaluate human being.

It was argued by Lacan that in the classical philosophers one always finds (in one place or another) a fixed point, which gives the mind repose and makes truth into a stable relationship: with the known object, with the knowing subject, with Reason or with History. He believed that you can never tell the whole truth because in order to say everything, you would need more time, more words: 'I always speak the truth. Not the whole truth, because there's no way, to say it all. Saying it all is literally impossible: words fail.'[18] Lacan saw truth as a relationship between a subject and the unconscious. But where the unconscious is involved, nothing is guaranteed. No certainty remains.

I will conclude this chapter by returning to the theme with which I began: Lacan's objection to the totalising ambitions of philosophy and to its pretentions to be able to tell the whole truth. In 1969 Lacan gave a seminar on the four fundamental structures of discourse. A discourse is a mode of human relatedness mediated by speech, and the human subject is a subject of speech. The subject – transitory, evanescent, always elsewhere – emerges when it is inserted into the signifying system of the symbolic order as soon as it begins actively to speak. The subject is an effect of the signifiers that represent it, sliding from one to another along the signifying chain. I speak without knowing it. I speak with my body, and this without knowing it. I always say more than I know.

Now, the four modes of discourse are those of the master, the university, the hysteric and the psychoanalyst. These four modes rarely exist in pure form. In the concrete they are often a blend of several modes; in their schematised form they serve the purposes of analysis and exposition only.

This is Lacan's most overtly political seminar; we must remember that the students had only recently participated in the struggles of May 1968. Lacan's objections to totalisation are expressed in the critique of the 'discourse of the master'. Very simply, the discourse of the master originates in the attempt to attain the moment of absolute knowledge described by Hegel in *The Phenomenology of Mind*. For Lacan such knowledge can only be illusory in that it implies an unattainable unity, that is to say, a knowledge which brings together truth and the knowing self in a unity. In Lacanian terms, unity – or the illusion of it – belongs within the realm of the imaginary and of the narcissistic functions of the ego. There is, in other words, a clear link between the illusion of mastery and absolute knowledge or power, and the illusory identity of the ego.

I said above that the discourse of the master was related to the illusory moment of absolute knowledge. In later years Lacan made the discourse of the master synonymous with the discourse of philosophy. The philosopher, like the master, seeks a totality of illusory knowledge.

At the other extreme, the hysteric constantly re-enacts the Socratic role of asking questions, demanding knowledge from the master. Incidentally, it is at the insistent urging of the hysteric that science 'takes off'; after all, was it not female hysterics who stimulated Freud into discovering psychoanalysis itself?[19] Master and hysteric thus coexist in a state of symbiosis, with the hysteric demanding knowledge and the master striving to attain absolute knowledge in response.

The discourse of the university is that of the master reinforced by mystification and obscurantism. It, too, is concerned with mastery in the sense that one might speak of mastering a discipline, but at every stage it is forced to confess to the inadequacy of its acquired knowledge, thereby reproducing the non-mastery of its students.

Psychoanalytic discourse subverts the discourses of both the master and the university by insisting that *the whole truth can never be spoken, that totality is an imaginary, illusory notion*. At the same time it allows the hysteric to speak, thus stimulating the drive towards knowledge, but also undercutting the hysteric's illusion that the master knows all. Lacan insists that these four discourses exist within a system of permutations – the theory seems to be a universal system of classification – and that they require one another's existence. The hysteric and the analyst need one another, and the university requires a master to justify its teachings.

I find the discourses of the master and the psychoanalyst particularly interesting because one is the reverse of the other. In the discourse of the master a certain mastery or control is manifest. Medical discourse would be one example. (But note that the word master connotes 'slave' at one time and 'disciple' at another.) The discourse of the master involves the exercise of power and an expanding body of knowledge. In contrast, the task of psychoanalytic discourse is to follow the flow of the signifying chain, not for its own sake, but in order to discern the course of desire in its quest for *objet-petit-à* (the object which unchains desire). What characterises the discourse of the analyst is the primacy of the subject in futile quest for the irretrievable object that causes its desire.

Towards the end of his life, Lacan became increasingly concerned with mathematical formalism and, by about 1972, he seems to have become alienated from philosophy. He began to think of philosophy as no more than a variation of the discourse of the master. Why was this?

One explanation for this is that metaphysics (a central part of metaphysics is ontology. This studies Being), by reason of its abstraction, partakes of the same generality and disregard of the unique subjectivity as the discourse of the master. Second, philosophy, by reason of its pretension to articulate truth, aspires to an analogous power.

Some thinkers, like Heidegger for example, believe that the proper object of philosophy is Being. For Lacan, what is primordial in specifically human experience is not being but language and speech. He insists that there is no pre-discursive reality. Every reality is founded in and defined by a discourse. Men, women and children are only signifiers; being is a function of speech.

It could be argued that Lacan's ultimate rejection of philosophy is a direct consequence of his thesis about the primacy of language over (metaphysical) Being. It is because of this primacy that the next chapter is devoted to language, what Lacan calls the Symbolic. I agree with the suggestion that the irreducible difference between the philosophic and the psychoanalytic must be respected.[20] If one allows that philosophy's concern is with being, one must also recognise that the concern of psychoanalysis is with lack-of-being.

CHAPTER
FOUR | *The functions of language*

Introduction

In the first three preparatory chapters, on Freudian psychoanalysis, surrealism and philosophy, I have often alluded to
language. In this chapter I want to focus on Lacan's constantly
changing (and complex) view of language, and show how he draws
on the work of Saussure, Jakobson, Lévi-Strauss and Heidegger.
Some of the topics I will discuss include: Lacan's emendation of
Saussure's theory, the importance of metaphor and metonymy, the
relationship between language and human subjectivity, and the
meaning of 'full' and 'empty' speech.

In his attempt to define a new way of studying human
phenomena Lacan was deeply influenced by the methods of
phenomenology. This is a method of philosophical enquiry elaborated by Edmund Husserl and, more recently, by Jean-Paul Sartre
and Maurice Merleau-Ponty. The phenomenological method concentrates on the subjects' own account of themselves. They are not
seen as objects of investigation, but instead as sources of meaning.
The facts of desire are as real to the subject as the facts of nature
viewed by positive science.

I want to begin by saying something about the relationship
between biology and language, on how the biological is always interpreted through language. Among Lacan's contemporaries both
Sartre and Merleau-Ponty were concerned to refute the biologism
and scientism of Freud's work, and both turned to the same sources
as Lacan in order to support their critiques: the thought of Hegel
and Heidegger. In Lacan's (phenomenological) view biological facts
exist in psychoanalysis but only in so far as they are mediated
through language and speech. Biological facts do not exist apart
from the meaning that is given to them during the history of the

44

subject. Here is an example: imagine that you were born a hunchback. You may consider that a calamity and be in despair. On the other hand, like Shakespeare's Richard III, it may help you to hide your ambition, or it may help you to obtain the love of women who are touched by your handicap. (We know that in certain feminine positions the handicap of the other is a condition for desire.) So you may possibly put your hunchback to use in many and various ways.[1] The same thing is true with all biological data. To put this in another way: biological 'facts' become signifiers.

Language, even for the non-speaking infant, is already there in the world before he is born. He is born into a world of language. It is often said that the conversation between his parents before he is born may be the most important discourse concerning him the (unborn) child will ever have.

Lacan believed that the human being in particular is born premature; that is to say, he is dependent for a long time on the environment and on other beings to grow – for an especially long time if you compare him with animal species. A baby cries. From the beginning the satisfaction of biological urgencies necessitates the calling of the other. In that sense the biological urge is already modified because it is clear that what has begun to be more important than the satisfaction of thirst is that *the other respond to the call.* What is more important than the satisfaction of material, biological needs is the desire for recognition and love.

In Chapter 2, I mentioned the fact that in the 1930s Lacan was much influenced by the work of Roger Caillois. By using examples from stick insects and the praying mantis, Caillois suggested that these creatures were seized by the image. Drawing on his work, Lacan argued that the human being (later, he was to use the phrase 'the speaking being') is captivated by the image or imago. There is a constituting image which determines what will be perceived. Our seeing is determined by images. It is not that we see but that we are seen by the imaging structure. Rather like these insects, we are seized by the image and this has a toxic effect. The human subject is alienated and is in bondage to the image.

This is an interesting argument because later, in his second period (1948–1960) Lacan was to argue that *language* has this effect. Human subjects are caught, grasped, by the signifier. It is not the image but the word that has a toxic effect. The speaking being is poisoned by language.

Traditionally, language has been conceived as an instrument for communication, mastered by subjects fully conscious of what they are doing when they speak. In contrast, the Lacanian view of language centres round *the lack of mastery* of the speaking subject (slips of the tongue, and so forth). In this view of language, the subject is formed in a process which turns the small animal into a human child. The subject is seen as constituted by language and it appropriates the world through language. In a Freudian perspective, says Lacan, man is nothing but the subject caught in, and tortured by, language.[2]

Lacan's emendation of Saussure

Lacan is against the idea that communication is a transferral of concepts from one mind to another, an exchange of tokens which already have their meaning clearly stamped upon them. He rejects the view of language as a representation of pre-given objects. Lacan believes that the contractual nature of language requires that, in order for two subjects to name the same object, they must recognise each other as recognising the same object, thereby transcending the struggle for possession. Speech, argues Lacan, is always an inter-subjective *pact*.[3] Lacan stresses that speech is not simply a conveyor of information, but establishes a relation between speaker and hearer. In accordance with the dialectic of recognition the very being of the subject is dependent upon its recognition by other subjects.

Lacan has always been concerned with language and speech; Saussurean linguistics, on the other hand, did not become part of his theory until the 1950s. He believes that the essential property of language is the involvement of an interlocutor – one who takes part in a dialogue. Before it comes to signify something, language signifies for *someone* even though the interlocutor may be imaginary. It implies, then, a signifying intention on the part of the subject. Intentionality can be expressed in one of two modes. Either it is expressed but not understood by the subject (in which case it has to be interpreted), or it is masked by the mechanisms of negation and disavowal.

It was in about 1948, a few years after the Second World War, that Lacan began to focus his attention on the use of Saussurean linguistics in psychoanalysis. In 1953 Lacan gave a paper in Rome ('the Rome Discourse'), 'The function and field of speech and language', which is the founding statement of psychoanalysis as a theory of the speaking subject.[4] It is in this paper that Saussure first emerges as a major influence in Lacan's thinking and where he contends that the human subject is determined by language.

Lacan was indebted to Ferdinand de Saussure's concept of the sign. Saussure argued that there is the signifier, which is an acoustic image, and the signified, which is a concept. In the sign, a signifier and a signified collide and are bonded. Their relationship is an arbitrary one, but once this bonding has taken place the sign becomes a fixity. In Saussure the components of the sign are thought of as symmetrical and *interdependent*. Lacan questions the symmetry and equilibrium between signifier and signified in Saussure. What Lacan does is to reverse Saussure's algorithm and make it S/s (Signifier over signified).[5] The bar separating the two symbols stresses the cleavage between them. Note that the signified is below the signifier; in Lacan's account the signified does 'slip beneath' the signifier and successfully resists our attempts to locate and delimit it.

For Saussure, words are signs, combinations of signifiers and signified. For Lacan, however, signifiers are contrasted with signs. While signs refer to absent objects (for example, Man Friday's footprint in the sand indicates his presence on the island), signifiers do not refer to objects but to the chain of language. They do refer, but to other signifiers. When the signified seems finally to be within reach, it dissolves into yet more signifiers. Lacan often uses the metaphor of 'the signifying chain'; the chain is what limits the speaker's freedom. Yet the chain is mobile; any one of its links can provide a point of attachment to other chains. The signifying chain of speech comprises the 'rings of a necklace that is a ring in another necklace made of rings'. In Lacan's view the characteristic sensations of 'being a person' or 'having a personality' come from the self-perpetuating imperative that propels the signifying chain.

Lacan, then, has emended Saussure in several ways. While Saussure emphasised the co-presence of signifier and signified, Lacan always gives primacy (priority or precedence) to the signifier. He stresses the point that the signifier has an active, colonising power over the signified. It 'anticipates' the signified. He says that sentence openings like 'I shall never . . .', 'All the same it is . . .', 'And yet there may be . . .', are already creating meaning before the arrival of the key terms. Retroaction, too, may be seen at work in sentences, in that they achieve their final 'effect of sense' only when their last word has been given.

The single most important idea which Lacan adopts from structuralism is that of the 'arbitrary' relation between signifier and signified. This arbitrariness entails that there can be no natural, automatic or self-evident transition from signifier to signified, from language to meaning, or from human behaviour to its psychological significance. The bar between signifier and signified is described by Lacan as a barrier resisting 'signification'.

Shortly after 'the Rome Discourse', a rapid and remarkable shift began to take place (about 1953) in Lacan's teaching. The theory of the Imaginary, which had been the central concern in the first phase of Lacan's work, was displaced – or rather, enriched – by the Symbolic. This shift was undoubtedly the result of a growing awareness of structuralist thought, and was marked by a break in the phenomenological vocabulary of his earlier work.

Lacan mapped his concept of the Symbolic on to Freud's concept of the Oedipal process (see Chapter 1). Access to the Symbolic order is achieved by crossing the frontier, out of the Imaginary, the dyadic world of mother and child, into recognition of the Father's Name and his Law. That is out of a body-based, maternal relationship into one created by social exchange, culture and taboos. These are the concerns of Lévi-Strauss.

An important feature of Lacan's theory is its incorporation of some of the ideas of Lévi-Strauss. The leading structuralist of the time, Lévi-Strauss argued that a society should be seen as an ensemble of symbolic systems, in the first rank of which would be language, marriage-rules, economic relations, art, science and religion. Lacan accepts almost without qualification the Lévi-Straussian account of the rules of matrimonial exchange as the foundation of human society.

Lévi-Strauss argues that the family structure manifests a transcendence of all natural order by the establishment of Culture. It alone allows each and every one to know who he or she is. In total promiscuity no one could in fact be called father, son or sister and no one would be able to situate her- or himself or recognise others by the particular place they occupied. Now, the prohibition of incest is duplicated in the sacrifice of sexual relations with the mother or the sister. It is also duplicated by the law of exchange, the obligation to take a wife from another family in order that the relationships of alliance may be established.[6]

In short, the basic thesis of Lévi-Strauss is that marriage is governed by a preferential order of kinship which, like language, is imperative for the group, but unconscious in its structures. Rules governing alliance regulate the exchange of women and there is a prohibition of incest. The Law which governs this whole structure is identical with the law of language. It is on the basis of this argument that Lacan elaborates his theory of the Symbolic, the dimension of culture into which the child must be introduced through the acquisition of language and through the renunciation of incestuous desires for union with its mother.

As far as language is concerned it should be remembered that, though he draws on some of Lévi-Strauss's ideas, Lacan criticises the claims of structuralism to produce an objective decoding of linguistic messages. For Lacan, meaning cannot be objectified; rather, it is characterised by a fundamental elusiveness and unpredictability: since no signifier follows automatically from that which precedes it, in the very gap between signifiers something of the subject is revealed.

The primacy of metaphor

Lacan believes that language is, in essence, metaphorical. This view derives from Roman Jakobson, who argued that metaphor and metonymy are two poles, or two processes in language which are at work everywhere in language.

First of all, it is essential to be clear about the meaning of metaphor and metonymy. Broadly speaking, metaphor is based on a proposed similarity or analogy between the literal subject and its metaphorical substitute, whereas metonymy is based on a proposed contiguous (or sequential) association between the literal subject and its 'adjacent' replacement. Both metaphor and metonymy can be subdivided into other figures. A simile, for example, is a type of metaphor – in both cases there is a felt resemblance. A simile is explicit, while a metaphor simply asserts without explanation. A metaphor has an elliptical concentration which is lacking in the simile.[7]

It is usual to consider synecdoche as a variant of metonymy. A synecdoche is usually defined as the part for the whole, or the whole for the part. A textbook example of metonymy is 'Bordeaux'. It is, first of all, the name of a town; then it began to denote the wine produced there – the product instead of the place of production. This is a type of meaning shift based on contiguity. Words are constantly changing their meanings in this way. Figurative meanings become literal, and there is a growth of new figurative meanings.

As I said in Chapter 1, Freud believed that two processes were important in the formation of dreams, jokes, slips of the tongue or pen, and symptoms in general: condensation and displacement. Freud first came to recognise the mechanism of condensation in the simple fact that the dream itself is much shorter and much more compressed than its verbal representation. In his view, condensation, the 'nodal point' of the dream, always allows multiple interpretations. Displacement is a form of distortion in which censorship displaces the centre of the dream on to objects or words of minor importance.

I mention this because Lacan has sought to correlate Freud's concepts, condensation and displacement, with Roman Jakobson's analysis of the two poles of language. Jakobson argued that metaphor and metonymy are two poles, which are at work in language. It is important to remember that they are not entities. They are categories of distinction, not bags to put things in. Neither describes an isolable thing; they describe a relation.

Jakobson sees metaphor and metonymy as the characteristic modes of binarily opposed polarities which between them underpin the twofold process of selection and combination. An utterance or message is a combination of constituent parts selected from the repository of all possible constituent parts. Messages are constructed by a combination of a 'horizontal' movement, which combines words together, and a 'vertical' movement which selects the particular words from the available inventory of the language. The selective process manifests itself in similarity (one word or concept being 'like' another) and its mode is metaphoric. The combinative process manifests itself in contiguity (one word being placed next to another) and its mode is metonymic. In short, selection (the relation of similarity) and combination (the relation of contiguity) – the metaphoric and metonymic ways – are considered by Jakobson to be the two most fundamental linguistic operations.

Of course, both metaphor and metonymy can be subdivided into other figures (simile is a type of metaphor; synecdoche is a type of metonymy) but the distinction between the two modes is fundamental: it is how language works. Second, as Jakobson reminds us, any metonymy is slightly metaphorical and any metaphor has a metonymic tint.

The distinction has great relevance in aesthetics. It enabled Jakobson, for instance, to contrast cubism (which is metonymic: the object becomes a series of synecdoches where each fragment stands for the whole) with surrealism (which is metaphoric), or to separate the metaphoric romantics and symbolists from the metonymic realists (Anna Karenina is described by Tolstoy through metonymic details, her handbag, her clothes, and so on). Widening his analysis, Jakobson concludes that the two processes appear in all symbolic organisations, for instance in the dream-work: for him displacement is metonymic, but condensation is synecdoche, and identification or symbolism is metaphoric.

Lacan simplifies this by contrasting metaphoric condensation with metonymic displacement. He suggests that these two modes of symbolic representation provide a model for the understanding of psychic functions: the concept of metaphor illuminates the notion of 'symptom' (the replacing of one signifier by an associated one), that of metonymy sheds light on the origin of desire (through the combinative connection of signifier to signifier and the sense this implies of the infinite extension of such a process into uncharted areas). To recapitulate: Lacan assimilates the two processes of the Freudian unconscious, condensation and displacement, to the linguistic axes of metaphor and metonymy. For Lacan unconscious meaning 'insists' in the signifying chain by means of metaphor and metonymy; in his view the symptom is a metaphor and desire is a metonymy.

Lacan also refers to 'horizontal' and 'vertical' aspects of language. This distinction derives from Jakobson's alignment of metonymy with the horizontal dimension of language (the line of Western writing, the syntagmatic) and metaphor with the vertical dimension (the paradigmatic stack of possible selections for any point along the line). These points are important, as I said earlier, in literary studies because Jakobson linked metaphor to poetry, particularly to romantic and symbolist poetry, and metonymy to the realist novel. Lacan, too, links metaphor to poetry and makes an allusion to metonymy's tie to realism. There is, however, no doubt that Lacan's preference is for metaphor.[8]

Language, Lacan writes, can be used metaphorically 'to signify *something quite other* than what it says'.[9] In other words, the metaphoric aspect of language allows it to point the word to something beyond its literal meaning and referent. A metaphor always means more than it says: 'Behind what discourse says, there is what it means (wants to say), and behind what it wants to say there is another meaning and this process will never be exhausted.'

For Lacan, then, all uses of the word are metaphoric. As an example he gives the French word *main*, which signifies 'hand', to show the numerous ways in which the word is used. I looked up the word in an English dictionary and found: at first hand, change hands, come to hand, from hand to hand, get one's hand in, hand in glove, hands off, hands up, have a free hand, have a hand in, lay hands on, lend a hand, offhand, off one's hands and so forth. The point Lacan is making is this: an entire cultural and economic scene is evoked by the variety of uses of a term which is supposed merely to designate a part of the body.

Lacan has also commented on self-conscious uses of metaphor in literature. He refers to the phrase '*soleil de mon coeur*' (sun of my heart). Implied in this phrase is

> the fact that the sun warms me, the fact that it makes me live, and also that it is the centre of my gravitation as well as its producing this half of shade of which Valéry speaks and which is also that which blinds and which gives it all this false evidence and tricking brightness.

It could be said that Lacanian psychoanalysis is akin to poetry in which the interplay of metaphors is a major means of encountering unspeakable truth. In poetry, as in psychoanalysis, language is pushed to its limits, and becomes a struggle with the inexpressible.

But what is the significance of metaphor? Metaphor is a systematic form of classifying and imputing value. Lacan followed closely his friend Jakobson's definition of this trope: it is the trope of selection and substitution. Metaphor implies choice. The ability to choose depends on the ability to sort into categories, and therefore to be able to say, 'this, not that'. In other words, any substitution of one thing for another is the preferring of that thing to the other. Choice implies value judgement.

Language and human subjectivity

I have often referred to one of Lacan's key ideas: the human subject is constituted through language. The subject is the subject of speech and subject to language. Three points that Lacan makes about the symbolic order (language) and the determination of human subjectivity follow.

One: Lacan takes the mirror stage as the model of the ego function itself, the category which enables the subject to operate as 'I'. He supports his argument from linguistics, which designates the pronoun as a 'shifter'. The 'I' with which we speak stands for our identity as subjects in language, but it is the least stable entity in language, since its meaning is purely a function of the moment of utterance. The 'I' can shift and change places because it only ever refers to whoever happens to be using it at the time.

Two: besides the instability in the pronoun, there is equally loss, and difficulty in the word. Language can operate only by designating an object in its *absence*. Lacan argues that symbolisation turns on the object as *absence*. We know, from Freud, that a child hallucinates the object it desires and that in one of its games it often throws a cotton reel out of its cot in order to symbolise the absence and presence of the mother (the 'fort-da' game).[10] Symbolisation begins when the child gets its first sense that something could be missing.

Three: subjects in language persist in their belief that somewhere there is a point of certainty, of knowledge and of truth. But for Lacan this is a phantasy. He argues that the meaning of each linguistic unit can be established only by reference to another. In short, there can be no final guarantee or securing of language.

But if each signification refers to another signification, and that signification refers to another one, in an endless chain, how do we decide what words mean? The Lacanian term *point de capiton* (literally, an upholstery stud) refers to a point of convergence. Just as an upholstery stud or button is the centre for the converging lines or creases on the surface of a taut fabric, so the linguistic *point de capiton* provides a vantage point from which everything that happens in a given discourse can be situated both retroactively and prospectively. The subject attaches significance to certain signifiers; these signifiers, like upholstery buttons, pin down the floating mass of signification. Lacan stresses the fact that we do not understand a sentence until we know we have reached the end; its meaning remains in suspense until the closure. A *point de capiton*, then, is the 'anchoring point' by which the signifier stops the otherwise endless movement of signification. Its diachronic function is to put a halt to the otherwise endless process whereby signifier refers to signifier.

From empty to full speech

One of the interesting features of Lacan's view of language is that *the use of Saussure and Jakobson coexists alongside a Heideggerian exploitation of the poetics of language*. Heidegger took it for granted that there was no Archimedean point of leverage 'outside' language and that it was impossible to step outside language, the 'house of being'. Lacan shares this view. From this perspective, the fact that we are obliged to use language in order to talk about language proves that we cannot escape it in order to arrive at some 'higher' level. There is no metalanguage.

There is, then, a Heideggerian strand in Lacan's thinking about language. He makes a fascinating distinction between full and empty speech; these terms correspond to Heidegger's *Rede* (speech, discourse) and *Gerede* (idle talk) respectively. Heidegger makes an important distinction between authentic and inauthentic forms of existential discourse. The authentic form he calls 'Saying'. This he identifies with our ability to remain responsible for our speech by remaining silent so as to *listen* and thus genuinely respond to the voice of Being. The inauthentic form he calls idle talk, which he goes on to define as opinionated chatter unmindful of human Being. Discourse with the other can easily degenerate into idle talk. This occurs whenever the speaker ceases to respond individually to the address of the other and is content merely to correspond to the anonymous chatter of 'public opinion'. Capitulating to the unthinking sway of the 'They', my speech ceases to be authentically my own.

In idle talk words become strategies for escaping from ourselves; we cease to communicate decisively on the basis of our own lived experience. Our existence is no longer lived by us. And so we fill up the hollow gaps within us by chattering away according to the rules of fashionable gossip. To put this in another way: idle talk operates as a form of closure which suspends any authentic interpretation of our being. Anonymous clichés and catchwords prevent us from using language thoughtfully, and by skimming over the surface of things we contrive to suppress the fundamental question of our rootedness in Being.

I turn now to Lacan's view of 'empty' and 'full' speech. Within the analytical encounter language is not the vehicle for individual expression. For Lacan the subject is trapped in the labyrinthine system of a structure in which signifier refers to signifier. In the analytic session the subject does not speak; s/he is spoken by language, trapped in stereotypical, pathological, discourse. It is, therefore, related to the category of empty speech. Within empty speech the subject is dispossessed, alienated and inauthentic. Empty speech belongs to the register of the Imaginary, and it is an obstacle to positive transference in that it blocks the possibility of full speech. In this process, the transition from empty to full speech, the subject gradually abandons the imaginary autonomy of the ego, in order to accept its true location in the domain of inter-subjectivity. To attain full speech means to cease to speak of oneself as an object. If language and speech are the medium of psychoanalysis, the liberation of full speech is its objective.

Consider the analyst–analysand situation. Unlike many analysts Lacan does not believe in empathy and empathic responsiveness. He stresses that analysis is approached from the point of view of language and speech. (In other words, Lacan substituted references to the sciences of language for the biological references of Freud.) The main aim of an analyst is to elicit talk: say what you like, free associate. Psychoanalysts ask patients to talk about what they do not know. They assume that whatever patients say means something else. The analyst is there to say that what you believe you are saying by chance, is, as a matter of fact, perfectly determined, has a reason, has a cause. Nothing happens without a reason; there is a reason for everything.

Lacan suggests that new ways of understanding can be found by *listening* to subjects without preconceptions. The way that subjects give accounts of themselves, with all their hesitations and omissions, ambiguities and denials, their imaginary formations such as dreams, delusions and phobias, and their moments of incoherence, are phenomena which reveal the mental life of the individual.

There are analysands who chatter compulsively in order *not* to have to say something else. We should always ask ourselves: what is it that people are not saying behind their verbal screens? Although s/he is addressed by the patient's words, the analyst realises that s/he is only taking the place of, or listening, to what Lacan called the patient's Other, that is, to a discourse beyond the involvement of two people. The analyst, according to Lacan, will not miss the truth in what the patient is saying if s/he listens to the patient's Other. Lacan writes: 'The subject . . . begins the analysis by talking about himself without talking to you, or by talking to you without talking about himself. When he can talk to you about himself, the analysis is over.'

One of Lacan's famous statements (typically enigmatic) is that 'the subject receives his message from the other in an inverted form'. The example he gives is the sentence 'you are my husband', which is an attempt to involve the other, to elicit the answer 'I am your wife' and so to get my message back from you in a linguistically inverted form. The meaning of 'you are my master' is 'I am your slave'; in other words, the subject is implicated in an inverted mode of communication.

Now, this form of communication necessarily opens up the possibility of deceit: speech is a gift of faith, but its other side is a feint ('a sham attack intended to deceive'), a lie. The subject's statement implies the possibility of a feint, but that in itself implies the possibility of discovering the truth in an inverted form. You may have heard the famous joke recounted by Freud which illustrates this: 'If you say you're going to Cracow, you want me to believe you're going to Lemburg. But I know you're going to Cracow. So why are you lying to me?'[11]

In one sort of talk (Lacan called it *fides*) meaning is fully apprehended and discourse is an attempt to communicate it, to make the other accept it and endorse it; in lying meaning becomes uncertain, because the other may be deceiving me – but that in itself implies the possibility of discovering the truth in an inverted form. The possibility that you may be lying assures me that you are a subject in your own right.

Conclusion

To conclude this chapter, I will summarise some of the main stages in Lacan's conceptualisation of the symbolic order. In the first period (1932–48) Lacan asserts that the field of psychoanalysis is the field of meaning. He holds the Hegelian phenomenological idea that the word is a death, a murder of a thing. That is to say, as soon as the reality is symbolised, caught in a symbolic network, the thing itself is more present in a word, in its concept, than in its immediate physical reality. In this period the analysis gives meaning, retroactively, to what was in the beginning a meaningless trace. So the final moment of the analysis is reached when the subject is able to narrate to the Other his or her own history in its continuity; when his or her desire is integrated, recognised in 'full speech'.

In the second period (1948–60) Lacan's emphasis shifts from the word, speech, to language as a synchronic structure. He had a 'structuralist' conception of language as a differential system of elements. I have found some of the facts about language that Lacan stressed in the 1950s extremely insightful. He has made me aware, for example, that all speech has an effect, and that there is always a difference between what a speaker means and what the speaker's words mean. Moreover, signifiers produce signification (meaning) and that meaning is often constructed retroactively.

In the early 1960s there was a massive shift towards structuralism in intellectual life, and the question arose: if there is a move from act to structure, what is the role of the human subject? And so Lacan tried to correlate the structure of language with the structure of the subject. He argued that a lack or want-to-be is produced by language. The 'abolished' subject is caught in a signifying chain and is confronted with alienation. We lose our being in language. When we are confronted with the lack of being speech is inadequate, there are moments of silence, of resistance. There is always something that language cannot grasp.

During this second period, in which the symbolic order is conceived as having a mortifying effect on the subject as imposing on him a traumatic loss – and the name of this loss, of this lack, is of course symbolic castration – the final moment of analysis is reached when the subject is ready to accept this fundamental loss.

In the third period (1960–80) the main emphasis of Lacan's teaching is on the Real, that which is excluded from the Symbolic. (I will be discussing this concept in Chapter 7.) The symbolic order has a traumatic element at its very heart, and phantasy is conceived as a construction allowing the subject to come to terms with this traumatic kernel.

Lacan declared, in 1977, that he had come to the conclusion that psychoanalysis was not a science. In his view psychoanalysis was closest to rhetoric. This is, of course, consistent with his long preoccupation with the workings of language. Thus analysis seeks to persuade analysands to recognise things that they know already and to act on their desire.

CHAPTER
FIVE

The development of the
theory

Having provided an introduction to Lacan by examining his
wide-ranging interests in Freudian psychoanalysis, surrealism,
philosophy and language, I now want to outline the development
of his thought. I will give an exposition of Lacan's main ideas
chronologically and will refer to: the early papers that are concerned with feminine paranoia (1926–33); the important work on
the mirror phase (1936); the significant distinctions between
need, demand and desire (1946); his polemic against ego-
psychology and the development of his own techniques (1953–
64); his controversial beliefs about the unconscious and on
interpretation (1953) and, finally, his views on the ethics of
psychoanalysis (1959).

The sheer variety of material that Lacan chooses to discuss is
extraordinary, and so the following trajectory of his work may be
helpful. In the first period, 1936–53, he stressed the idea that the
way we relate to others is often determined by an image. There
are images that 'capture' us. I deal with these concerns in the
section on the mirror phase which is a stage that occurs in the
Imaginary register. The Imaginary is related by opposition to the
Symbolic, hence Lacan's interest in language. It is in the second
period, 1948–60, that Lacan is mainly concerned with language.
But as language is always dialogical, always dependent on the
listener just as much as the speaker – even more so in psychoanalysis – there is a gradual development of an interest in an
ethics of social relations.

First works (1926–33)

Feminine paranoia and its criminal manifestations

In his early work Lacan seems to have been fascinated by mad women and their violent acts. He was so captivated by the 'inspired', paranoiac writing that some of them produced that he incorporated in his own work aspects of the paranoid style. As early as 1931 Lacan presented his observations on a woman who had gone insane. A thirty-four-year-old schoolteacher, Marcelle, produced inspired writings like those of a prophet or a mad person. But what is the difference between them? It is said that the prophet stands on the edge of intelligibility, at the place where his or her linguistic innovations can still be understood by the group. The mad person, in contrast, is too far out, isolated and out of reach. What the mad person writes is often superb but it makes no sense; its meaning cannot be communicated.[1]

A few years later, in 1933, Lacan wrote about the notorious crime of the Papin sisters. What Lacan discovered in his studies of women, and never repudiated thereafter, was the danger of too much closeness, the misfortune of one person's identification with another. Christine and Léa Papin were hard-working maids in the town of Le Mans. They were inseparable from one another. Even on their days off they never went out. One stormy night lightning caused a power failure. When their employers, a woman and her daughter, returned from an evening out, they reprimanded the servants. Usually the two sisters did not respond to their employers' anger. But this time events took a different turn.

Each of the sisters grabbed a victim. They tore their victims' eyes from their sockets and, with their victims on the ground, they crushed their victims' faces, stamped on their bodies, slashed the thighs and buttocks of the two dead women and poured the blood of one over the sex organs of the other. When it was over they carefully washed all the knives, hammers and kitchen tools in the sink. They then washed themselves and went to bed as usual.

When Christine was imprisoned she was separated from Léa. A few months later Christine began to suffer from hallucinations and she attempted to tear her eyes out. Confined in a straitjacket, she refused to eat, engaged in acts of self-punishment and began to rave madly.

The crime left such an indelible mark on the French imagination that Jean Genet used it many years later as the inspiration for his play, *The Maids*. (I described the play to illustrate the master–slave relationship in Chapter 3, note 6.) It is clear that the two sisters had grown up in a climate of extreme emotional deprivation. Their 'acting out' had transgressed the boundary between the imaginary and the real.

Lacan discussed this crime in a long article in *Minotaure*. He suggests that separation was the cause of the delirium, just as the close relationship between the sisters was the cause of the crime. These two sisters found their pleasure together; they found in murder a sacred form of ecstasy. 'I am certain,' said Christine, 'that in another life I was supposed to be my sister's husband.' Actually, she was her sister's husband in this life as well. When another female couple appeared in a hostile guise, the Papin sisters exploded. The root cause of their 'twin insanity' was the 'difficulty of being two', the impossibility of distinguishing themselves from one another, to the point that the other ceased to exist. From these circumstances came loss of identity and madness.

The case of Aimée again

I must recapitulate here the story I told in Chapter 2 about a knife attack on a famous actress. One night a famous actress arrived at a theatre in Paris where she was performing. From among the crowd came a well-dressed woman. She took a knife from her handbag and attempted to stab the actress. The unknown assailant was arrested and hospitalised. This woman became the subject of Lacan's thesis in medicine: Aimée.

Just as Christine and Léa were inseparable, so was Aimée. Over the course of her life she was 'inseparable' not from a single woman but from a succession of different figures: first, her mother, then a fallen aristocrat and after that her own sister. Aimée had an amorous hatred towards her sister, her alter ego. Finally, she left home in the grip of a phantasy: she felt that certain courtesans and actresses were plotting against her and she resolved to do something about it. Lacan writes that each of these female persecutors was in fact merely a new image of the sister whom the patient had taken as her ideal. In other words, they were mere prisoners of Aimée's narcissism.

I want to stress that Aimée's inspired writings greatly impressed Lacan and his surrealist friends. Here is a typical passage: 'I am going to be received as a bridegroom. I shall go to see my fiancée. She will be lost in thought. She will have children in her eyes. I will marry her. She would be too sad, no one would listen to her songs.'[2]

What these stories, concerning the Papin sisters and Aimée, have in common is crime: the transgression of the social norm, the sudden dramatic act committed by an unknown person whose action stupefies society at large. According to Catherine Clément the similarity that links Christine, Léa and Aimée is their status as *women*:

> Just as women alone can experience ecstasy without knowing what its nature is, so these women were able to act out their conflicts once and for all, releasing all their tensions and deciding their fate . . . For acting out, however dangerous it may be, is also therapeutic, monstrously so. A conflict that becomes a deed, a fact, ceases to exist.'[3]

What Lacan discovered in the crimes committed by the Papin sisters and Aimée was the so-called 'mirror phase'. Beyond the twin disturbances of Christine and Léa and the series of masks whereby Aimée identified herself with her various doubles in order to destroy them, Lacan glimpsed the crucial importance of an essential phase in the constitution of the human personality: the moment when one becomes oneself because one is no longer the same as one's mother.

The mirror phase (1936)

In contrast to the Anglo-Saxon tradition which stresses the Lockean assumption of common-sense rationality, the Lacanian view stresses that debility – not ability – is at the heart of human beings. To explain this, let us begin with Freud. At the beginning of his career, in the 1880s, Freud was interested in hypnotism and practised it with his patients. He noticed a strange fact about people who carried out, in a post-hypnotic condition, instructions given them during hypnosis. Asked why they did these (sometimes bizarre) actions, the subjects would always give excuses, invent 'reasons', or provide rationalisations. For example, it was suggested to a patient in hypnosis that after he woke up he should put both his thumbs in his mouth. He did so, and excused his action by saying that his tongue had been giving him pain since the previous day when he had bitten it.

In so far as the unconscious answers to language, language acquires remarkable powers. This is most evident in the stage exploitation of hypnosis when the hypnotist induces the victim to eat a lemon by describing it as a sweet and juicy apple. A hypnotist can implant a connection that will cause the victim, even after 'waking', to bark like a dog whenever somebody whistles.

Freud remarked that in cases in which the true causation evades conscious perception one does not hesitate to attempt to make another connection, which one believes, although it is false. He concluded that when the real connections between the two events are not available, people fill in the 'gaps'. There seems to be a compulsion for the ego, under the influence of the pleasure principle, to make *false connections*.[4] The (conscious) ego is associated with distortion and gloss ('to extenuate, to give a favourable explanation, to explain away').

It was awareness of this problem that led Lacan to formulate the theory of the mirror phase. Taking up this element of Freud's work – incidentally, Freud was not happy with the method of hypnotism and soon gave it up for 'free association' – Lacan argues that the ego is structured by compulsive false connections. The central function of the ego is to misunderstand. He called this misrecognition (*méconnaissance*). But we must begin at the beginning . . .

Lacan has developed a sophisticated theory of human subjectivity which is based on the mirror phase. Lacan borrowed the notion of a mirror from the French psychologist Henri Wallon, but reinterpreted it in psychoanalytic terms. The idea of the mirror stage (I prefer the term phase because it is less rigid) came up through a comparison of apes and humans; they each react differently to their mirror image. The ape can pick out something that moves as it moves, but once it has mastered the idea it gets bored with it. The infant, on the other hand, sees the relation between the movements of the image and those of its own body.

The mirror phase is supposed to occur (usually between the ages of six months and eighteen months) when the child has not fully mastered its own body. The mirror phase is a period at which, despite its imperfect control over its own bodily activities, the child is first able to imagine itself as a coherent and self-governing entity. What happens is this: the child finds itself in front of a mirror. It stops, laughs at its reflection, and turns around towards whoever is holding it. It looks at its mother or its father, and then looks again at itself. For this necessary stage to occur, the child must have been separated from its mother's body (weaned) and must be able to turn around and see someone else *as* someone else. That is, it must be able to sense its discrete separation from an Other, and must begin to assume the burden of an identity which is separate, discrete.

Why does the child turn round to look at the Other? The Other warrants the existence of the child, certifies the difference between self and other. This is the action upon which all subjectivity is based, the moment in which the human individual is born. The mirror phase is crucial because it entails consequences that range from the most secure normality to the most psychotic disintegration of the personality.

In a key passage Lacan writes:

> The mirror stage is a drama whose inner dynamic moves rapidly from *insufficiency* to *anticipation* – and which, for the subject caught in the snares of spatial identification, fashions the series of fantasies that runs from an image of a *fragmented body* to what we may call the *orthopedic vision of its totality* – and to the armour, donned at last, of an alienating identity, whose rigid structure will shape all the subject's future mental development.[5]

Note that the mirror phase is a drama played out between an insufficiency and an anticipation. Insufficiency: this means that the human child's resources at birth are insufficient for its needs. Lacan believes that the child is born unfinished. Consequently, it can neither walk nor talk. 'Specific prematurity' is the term for this. The child is in many ways premature, unable to stand up; it is dependent, unco-ordinated, chaotic. Anticipation: this refers to the fact that the child anticipates in front of the mirror its own shape as an adult. Now, in order to be a subject, in order to be oneself, a structure is required. But this structure is rigid; it encloses and alienates. Lacan believes that the normal subject is alienated, s/he is the prisoner of his or her identity, whereby s/he is a member of a group, the offspring of his or her parents, the bearer of a family name as well as a first name that identifies him or her as an individual.

In the Lacan passage quoted above note also that the subject moves from 'a fragmented body' to an 'orthopedic vision of its totality'. This reference is an allusion to Melanie Klein's thesis that at this stage the child is a fragmented body full of horrible murderous phantasies.[6] The term 'orthopedic' means 'that which helps the child to stand up straight'. Orthopedic devices such as crutches are corrective instruments. There is a suggestion that the identity of the subject is something added, something that helps you to stand up straight within yourself.

However, in obtaining its identity the child, in fact, only manages to achieve identification. The two things are radically different. The subject will never be truly 'himself' or 'herself'. The child sees itself in the mirror, but the image is reversed. Identity is a mere outer skin that constantly distorts one's relations with others. When the fragmented body gives way to the armour of the subject – and to its identity, already alienating by definition – the 'ego' is formed.

The moment of self-identification is crucial because it represents a permanent tendency of the individual: the tendency that leads him or her throughout life to seek and foster the imaginary wholeness of an 'ideal ego'. The unity invented at these moments, and the ego that is the product of successive inventions, are both spurious; they are attempts to find a way around certain inescapable factors of lack, absence and incompleteness in human living.

Lacan writes how the child proceeds in a fictional direction; that is to say, he resorts to phantasy to overcome his alienation from his own reality. Like a graph that approaches zero, but never reaches it, the child's self-concept will never match up to his own being. The *gestalt* that he has picked out in the mirror is both smaller and more stable than he is and is something outside him that is having an effect upon him without his understanding it. It gives him the *illusion* that he has control over his body when he has not.

Lacan's account of subjectivity was developed with reference to the idea of a fiction. His concept of the mirror phase took the child's mirror image as the model and basis for its future identifications. This image is a fiction because it conceals, or freezes, the infant's lack of motor co-ordination, and the fragmentation of its drives. Nevertheless, it gives the child a sense of a coherent identity in which it can recognise itself. This moment has meaning only in relation to the presence and the look of the mother who guarantees its reality for the child. The mirror image is central to Lacan's account of subjectivity, because its apparent smoothness and totality is a myth. The image in which we first recognise ourselves is a *misrecognition*.

Lacan's point is that the ego is constituted by an identification with another whole object, an imaginary projection, an idealisation ('Ideal-1') which does not match the child's feebleness. The ego is thus not an agent of strength, but the victim of an illusion of strength, a fixed character-armour, which needs constant re-inforcement. This alienated relationship of the self to its own image is what Lacan calls the domain of the Imaginary. The Imaginary is the world, the register, of *images*, conscious or unconscious, perceived or imagined. It is the pre-linguistic, pre-Oedipal domain in which the specular image traps the subject in an illusory ideal of completeness. The Imaginary is to be understood as both a stage in human genesis, and a permanent level of the human psyche.

Hegel: Need, demand, and desire (1946)

Just after the Second World War, in 1946, a Russian émigré, Alexandre Kojève, gave a series of lectures that greatly influenced the French intelligentsia. At the lectures were writers like Raymond Queneau, Jean Hyppolite (the translator into French of Hegel's *Phenomenology of Spirit*), Georges Bataille and Jacques Lacan. From attendance at these lectures Lacan became acutely aware that there is a difference between our relation to things and to people. With people we have to ask: what does the Other want? Combining Freud's notion of wish and Hegel's idea of recognition, Lacan began to talk of desire. What is desire? And what is the difference between need, demand and desire? But, first, some remarks about Freud's notion of wish and Hegel's notion of recognition.

Freud's German term '*Wunsch*' is usually translated as 'wish'. The German and English words are limited to individual, isolated acts of wishing, while the French '*désir*' has the much stronger implication of a continuous force. In Freud, unconscious wishes can be fulfilled even though only in a distorted way in dreams or in the symptom (through a chain of condensations and displacements which keeps them repressed). Freud states that need derives from a state of internal tension and achieves satisfaction through the specific action which obtains the object (food, for example). Wishes, on the other hand, are indissolubly bound to 'memory-traces'. He believed that a deep unconscious wish was required to provide the motive force for the dream and that all such wishes were infantile and sexual. And what does Hegel mean by recognition? This term means more than simply that one is aware of the other's existence. Recognition means being recognised *as a person*, and for Hegel this means being recognised as an *independent and autonomous agent*.

For Lacan, the story begins at birth. Birth entails trauma – a separation. At birth the baby separates from a part of itself. Wholeness is lost and s/he will desire it always. Of course, the baby does not know what is missing; the baby cannot articulate its lack. The baby cries. We ask what does the cry mean? What is its demand? The mother has to interpret what the baby wants. She gives the baby her breast. *Need is biological; it can be satisfied.* But the baby needs more than the milk – what is this 'more'?

If a mother offers 'too much' satisfaction, the child will never feel hunger and, therefore, will never know the pleasure of assuaging its hunger. Similarly, when the mother anticipates the child's hunger and stuffs it, the child will cease to eat. When the child asks something of its mother, there is a loss that will persist over and above anything which she can possibly give, or say, in reply. The demands of the child are answered by the satisfaction of its needs – but there is always something left over.

Demand is always transitive, for it is always directed to an other (usually the mother). While need aims at an object which satisfies it, demand appeals to an other in such a way that even if the demanded object is given, there can be no satisfaction. This is because the demand is really for something else. For the next thing the other can give, for the thing that will 'prove' the other's love.

The child addresses a series of demands to the mother. She may respond to them with a variety of specified objects, but none will satisfy the child's wants. One demanded toy, for example, is rapidly replaced by another, and the entire list of substitute objects is ultimately unsatisfying. The child wants to be filled by the other, to be the other, which is why no determinate thing will do. It demands a love that paradoxically entails its own annihilation, for it demands a fullness of the other to stop up the lack that conditions its existence as a subject.

The demand for food is not simply the demand for satisfaction of nutritive need. It is also a demand for love. The demand operates in the interplay of the demanded object, and the other who, in delivering up the object, affirms the subject as loved.

Freud described how the baby can be observed to hallucinate the milk that has been withdrawn from it and the infant to play throwing-away games to overcome the trauma of its mother's necessary departures. This game is called the fort-da game. Freud observed his eighteen-month-old grandson who had a cotton reel with a piece of string tied to it. Holding the string, he would throw the reel over the edge of his cot and utter sounds that Freud interpreted as being an attempt at the German '*fort*', meaning 'gone' or 'away'. He would then pull the reel back into his field of vision, greeting its reappearance with a joyful '*da*' ('there').[7] By this game the child was learning to control his feelings about the presence and absence of the loved object, the mother. In the fort-da game one can see the beginnings of language, what Lacan calls the Symbolic.

But the main point is this: Lacan uses the example of the game to show that the object that is longed for comes into existence as an object only when it is lost to the infant. Thus any satisfaction that might subsequently be attained will always contain this loss within it. The baby's *need* can be met, its *demand* responded to, but its *desire* exists only because of the initial failure of satisfaction. Desire persists as an effect of a primordial absence.

The concept of desire is crucial to Lacan's account of sexuality. It has been said that if we fail to grasp this Hegelian concept there is danger of a reduction of sexuality back into the order of a (satisfiable) need.[8] Need always tends to become 'demand', 'new needs'. Desire is seen in Lacan as that need which is 'unable to be articulated in demand'. Need is satisfiable, desire is insatiable.

I believe that Lacan says many profound things about desire. Consider the following: 'I always find my desire outside of me because what I desire is always something that I lack, that is other to me.' That is to say, demand is for an object, whereas desire is for a lack.

Lacan says that all demands are ultimately demands for love. But one can never be sure of what the Other wants or whether the Other is satisfied. And he suggests that one ought to sustain desire, and not seek an object that will gratify it and thereby erase it.

Focusing on the role of desire, Lacan drew attention to the nostalgia binding the subject to the lost object (for example, the breast/the mother), and how the subject made repetitive attempts to find the lost object. But Lacan did not believe that there was a simple relation between desire and an object that will satisfy it. He tried to show that desire is linked with the desire of the Other. Hegel had already brought up this latter notion in the master–slave story in which both master and slave strive for recognition. Lacan argued that it was Freud who had brought to light the notion of unconscious desire. In Lacan's view, the object of human desire is always the desire of the Other – it is both the desire for the Other's desire and desire for the Other. Thus as the subject's desire is at first unknown to him, he looks for it in the Other, and his desire becomes the Other's desire.

I have tried to show the meanings of desire, but how does it arise, what unleashes it? The '*objet-petit-a*' represents the little machine that unleashes desire. It is really Lacan's formula for the lost object which underpins symbolisation, cause of, and 'stand in', for desire. The '*objet-petit-a*' is found wherever there is a passage-way on the body linking the interior to the exterior. Desire takes place in a specific place. All the objects have some relation to separation. The breast, for example, is something that the infant will one day lose. The penis is another such object because it is imagined to be detachable or severable. The breath, the voice, a song, all of these things can be objects of desire. Even a glance can be an '*objet-petit-a*'.

One of the most enigmatic objects in the list of '*objets-petit-a*' that Lacan gives is the pound of flesh desired by Shylock in *The Merchant of Venice*. As is well known, if the judgment were awarded and Shylock were to get his pound of flesh, the young Christian in his debt would die. Lacan sees this as one of the possible figures of the '*objet-petit-a*': an object that is part of something else from which it cannot be separated, an inaccessible part of a larger whole.

I mentioned separation just now. The separation of the mother from the child and of the child from its image is paradigmatic of all separation. Perhaps, as Freud suggested, in every human being, there is a fundamental cleavage or 'split'. Lacan refers to the story told by Aristophanes, in Plato's *Symposium*, of the androgynous, four-legged creature who is split in two by an angry Zeus. Since that time the two parts of the creature have been struggling to rejoin one another and to reconstitute the original spherical whole. Each half holds fast to any object it thinks might be its lost counterpart.[9]

This is a phantasy. (A phantasy is an imaginary scene in which the subject is a protagonist, representing the fulfilment of a wish. Sometimes it is not clear whether a phantasy is conscious, pre-conscious or unconscious. The 'ph' spelling is used to indicate that the process is unconscious.) We all have our own authentic phantasies, belonging to ourselves and no one else. There are as many phantasies as there are subjects. The essence of phantasy is its impossibility. Though imaginary, phantasy is a structure absolutely necessary to the subject. Phantasy is for each individual a private stage on which the subject's relationship to the object of its desire is played out, and this relationship is impossible in the real.

I will conclude this section by telling you a story. The story, which fascinated Lacan, is by Marguerite Duras and is called *The Ravishing of Lol. V. Stein*.[10] The story illustrates some of Lacan's life-long interests: mad women, lovers, hysterics; the scopic drive (the pleasure in looking) and the gaze. It is about desire and lack, how this dialectical opposition is present in every visual recognition. Love, says Lacan, is the self-image in which you are wrapped by the other, and which leaves you when it is stolen away . . . Lacan's interest in the novel focuses on the ambiguity of *ravisse-ment*, which means 'rapture' in both an abstract and passive sense, being enraptured and ravished away. Very briefly, the novel is about an American woman called Lola Valerie Stein. On the night her engagement was being celebrated the man she loved walked out before her very eyes with a woman in black with whom he had danced in an intimate manner. Lola was struck dumb and re-mained so for some time. She changed her name then to Lol. V., as though it had become necessary to amputate her true name. She lived a quiet life but the embers of madness smouldered beneath the ashes. She then conceives a strange passion: she arranges for another couple to make love and watches them. When the man tries to bring things to a head by seeking out Lol. she becomes mad on the actual spot where her reason was stolen from her by the fiancé and the woman in black some years earlier.

Lacan saw the novel as being about 'scopophilia', the location of the object of desire in the act of looking itself. The plot turns on a gaze. Every gaze designates, and it designates the person who is looking. Lol., by forcing the couple to be looked at, also forced them to look at her. She did not 'see' them, but their love depended on her gaze. She can find herself only in the other couple. At the end of the novel Lol. sinks into madness – she could be touched by love only at a distance.

The ego and the id (1953–64)

Against ego-psychology

In 1963 Lacan was expelled from the International Psychoanalytic Association. The story is a complicated one.[11] The Société Psychanalytique de Paris, founded in 1926, was active until the Second World War. After losing many members in the conflict, it resumed its activities in 1946. Two years later Lacan became a member of the 'committee on teaching'. In 1953 it was proposed to found an Institute of Psychoanalysis. Only physicians were to be permitted to become members. Understandably, psychoanalysts who were not physicians raised a protest against these proposals. After a short period of time, Lacan resigned from his influential position as director and, together with a few friends, founded a new Société Française de Psychanalyse.

The new society asked to be affiliated to the International Psychoanalytic Association (IPA). The IPA demanded Lacan's expulsion. Lacan was expelled, finally excommunicated by the International, and his teaching was condemned. In 1963 the IPA permitted him to practise analysis but not to teach or train candidates. In 1964 Lacan went on to found his own school, L'Ecole Freudienne de Paris.

Why was Lacan expelled? It is generally held that there were important theoretical issues in question, especially concerning Lacan's attacks on the theory of ego-psychology and his practice of the short session. Let us look at these two issues.

Lacan never missed an opportunity to criticise American ego-psychology. Founded by European immigrants, this sort of psychoanalysis overemphasised adjustment and adaptation of the individual to existing social conditions. In the view of the American analysts the ego is to be protected, the job of analysis is to reinforce the ego against the demands made on it by the double call of the superego and the id. Ego-psychologists, like Heinz Hartmann, Ernst Kris and Rudolph Loewenstein, asserted that the ego had an aspect that was not tied up with the individual's neurotic conflicts. There was a conflict-free zone (the 'autonomous ego'), which seemed free to act and choose, independent of constraints. In their view the analyst's role was to become the ally of the 'healthy' ego forces in their struggle to dominate instincts and drives. It was said that the patient, in order to strengthen his or her 'autonomous ego', should identify with the ego of the psychoanalyst. Hence it was the analyst's job to develop a powerful ego.

Lacan attacks this position with many arguments. First, he criticises the ego-psychologists' concept of a 'healthy part' of the ego. How, asks Lacan, can they know which 'part' is 'healthy'? Does this not assume that the purpose of analysis is achieved by an identification with the analyst's ego? Is the goal of psychoanalysis to bring the patient to see the world as the analyst sees it? Lacan traces most of ego-psychology's problems and contradictions to the idea that there is an 'objective', 'knowable' reality.

For Lacan, the ego is the enemy. The origin of the ego is in the mirror phase. The mirror, held by the mother, proffers the developmentally half-formed and muscularly uncontrolled child its first idea of itself as a stable unified appearance. As we have seen, the ego is constituted by 'alienating identifications'. Lacan's own conception of the ego suggests that it must be profoundly distrusted because it is unable to discriminate the subject's own desires from the desires of others. According to Lacan, the ego is not autonomous, but subordinated and alienated to the people and images with which it has identified during its development. He thought that an analysis had failed if it ended with the analysand (I prefer to use this term rather than the word patient, which has negative connotations) identifying with the analyst. At the conclusion of therapy what should have disappeared is the armour of the ego, the glass cage of narcissistic illusions.

There is a famous remark of Freud's about the continuing work of analysis: 'Where id was, there ego shall be. It is a work of culture – not unlike the draining of the Zuider Zee.' In the original the first sentence is: '*Wo Es war, soll Ich werden.*' This is usually translated: 'Where id was, there ego shall be'. Of course, most ego-psychologists like this translation because it prioritises the ego; the 'primitive' id develops into the 'rational' (well-adjusted) ego. For Lacan the ego represents false identification. Lacan observes that Freud used the pronouns without articles; he did not write '*das Ich*' but merely '*Ich*'. Nor did he write '*das Es*', so he is not writing about the id. Lacan therefore translates the sentence quite literally: 'Where it was, there must I come to be.'[12] One of the main concerns of psychoanalysis is to find a way of moving between the repressed material in the unconscious ('Where it was') and a subject free of all defensive dependency ('I must come to be'). Other translations by Lacan include: 'Where it was, there ought I to become.' Or, 'Where it used to be, it is my duty that I come to be.' Lacan contends in each of these reformulations that the realm of unconscious energy, far from requiring even firmer custodianship and control from the ego, has unsuspected bounty to offer: it is the proper site for the subject, a repository of truth.

For the variable session

Some people say that Lacan was expelled because he was experimenting with analytical sessions of variable duration. The conventional length of a session was an invariable fifty-minute hour. Lacan came to the conclusion that the length of the session should be adjusted according to what the patient was saying: some long, some short. He argued that the psychoanalyst attends not so much to the meaning of the analysand's words as to their form. In his view the ritual ending of the session after a predetermined fixed length of time was 'a merely chronometric stopping place'. By contrast, he wanted to find for each session a stopping place suited to what the patient was saying. He believed that nothing in theory warrants the fifty-minute session. Rather, the adjustment of the length of the session should become one of the tools of psychoanalysis.

Lacan antagonised many people by putting the length of the psychoanalytic session into question. The difference between the fifty-minute hour and the 'short' session is a difference between two concepts of time. On the one side, time is filled with precision; on the other, it is approximate and variable. In the normal psycho-analytic hour it is the clock that decides the ending of the session.

Lacan argued that some analysands, knowing that they were guaranteed fifty minutes no matter what, used their sessions to discuss things that did not interest them in the least. Lacan reasoned that such analysands were using the fifty-minute hour as a resistance, as an excuse to waste the analyst's time, to make him or her wait for them: 'We know how the patient reckons the passage of time and adjusts his story to the clock, how he contrives to be saved by the clock. We know how he anticipates the end of the hour . . . keeping an eye on the clock as on a shelter looming in the distance.'[13]

One argument in favour of the variable session is that it prevents boredom. Many patients come to know when the analyst is going to end. If the analyst cuts off quickly, sessions cannot become an empty ritual. The analyst can thus use the element of surprise to open up new pathways. Lacan's view was that if the patient could be dismissed in the middle of a sentence or a dream or an interval of silence it would provoke the patient to make a clear revelation of that s/he had been hesitant to disclose.

In analysis, associations emerge in a rather disconnected way in a series or chain. It is presupposed that the last element in the series or chain will link the others that could not have been grasped before this last element emerges. This is another way of saying that we do not know the meaning of a sentence until the final term is pronounced and until the punctuation is placed.[14]

Usually free association takes place *within* the analytic session. With Lacan, the variable, or 'short' sessions act as a stimulus to new thoughts or associations that take place *between* sessions. This means that the most relevant associations are not likely to be the ones produced within the session but the ones produced between the sessions.[15] The combined pressure of the shortness of the sessions and the unpredictability of their cessation creates a condition that greatly enhances one's tendencies to free associate. Through the experience of short/variable sessions the analysand learns first to get right to the point and second, to say as much as possible quickly.

Some people believe that psychoanalysis has the medical model of treatment and cure. The social acceptance of analysis seems to be based on the idea that it can provide cures. If this is the case it is part of medicine. In contrast, Lacan tried to introduce a break between psychoanalysis and medicine. He said that his theorisation had nothing whatever to do with medicine or even with natural science. Psychoanalysis did not have as its goal curing patients; if people in analysis did get better, it was a welcome side-effect. If the goal of analysis is not cure, what is it? Lacan believed that the direction of analysis ought to lead towards a verbalisation of the unconscious.

The unconscious: 'The discourse of the Other'

Traditionally, the main characteristics of the unconscious appear in the descriptions of the id, but it should be remembered that the ego and the superego also have unconscious portions. The unconscious insists on being heard in our dreams, forgettings, misrememberings, slips of the tongue, jokes and our symptoms. But it is always speaking in the face of censorship and repression. For Lacan, Freud's essential insight was not that the unconscious exists, but that it has a *structure*, and this structure affects in innumerable ways what human subjects say and do and thus, in betraying itself, it becomes accessible to analysis.

Lacan conceives the unconscious as a 'language which escapes the subject in its operation and in its effects'. For Lacan the unconscious is a self and not a series of disorganised drives. He repudiates any conception of the unconscious as linked with the instinctual, the archaic or the regressive, as the place of the divinities of the night. In his view the key to understanding the unconscious is to realise that it is structured logically. For Lacan knowledge is something that is written as logic. He wanted to formalise the structures of psychoanalysis. By this he meant writing them in the kind of letters that have been the hallmark of formal logic since the time of Aristotle. Certainly such a project could not cover the entirety of the field, nor was it intended to.

The basic argument is that knowledge should be writable. Freud had declared in *The Ego and the Id* that the materials of the unconscious could not be present to consciousness without passing through preconscious word-representations. If the thing-representations in the unconscious are ultimately readable as letters, as forming letters, these letters can become clear to consciousness only when they are part of words. As such they gain a meaning that is the meaning of the words, and consciousness will latch on to those words as the content of the unconscious. Here is an example: a child sees a woman's legs in the form of a M or a V, and if the experience makes a large enough impression, this letter will run through the child's history as a thread linking the names of people and places, each of which will take on a certain meaning for consciousness.[16]

Let us now consider what is happening when an element from the unconscious finds its way into a spoken sentence. Freud's concept of 'negation' ('*Die Verneinung*') is discussed by Lacan in *Ecrits*. Freud argued that the subject matter of a repressed image or thought can make its way into consciousness on condition that it is *denied*. Here are two well-known examples: 'You may think that I mean to say something insulting, but, really I've no such intention.' This means: 'I want to insult you.' 'I saw someone in my dream. It was certainly not my mother.' This means: 'It was my mother.' Negation, then, is a way of taking account of what is repressed. It is always a sort of admission. In short, this phenomenon of *Verneinung* (translated as negation or denegation) permits the speaking of unconscious material that would otherwise be censored by the ego.

From a Lacanian perspective, denegation affirms the existence of an Other with whom the subject wishes to maintain his or her difference. The subject who uses a denegation says that what the Other is supposed to be thinking is wrong. Not only is the Other different from the subject, but it is wrong. In short, whatever is negated in the sentence is the unconscious material. The subject experiences the unconscious as what Lacan called 'the discourse of the Other'.[17] You may have heard people say: 'Someone keeps putting words in my mouth, words that are not mine.'

Lacan believes that the concept unconscious has become fixed and essentialised. His view of the unconscious challenges libertarian–Freudian attempts to speak about the unconscious as a universal substratum of vital energy, to be merged with or plugged into. Lacan is also critical of the practice of referring to an 'individual's unconscious' as if it were a particular possession. In his view we do not own our unconscious. We do not control it. It is not a prior or inferior emanation of ourselves that we can somehow school or train. The unconscious is Other.

I should point out that Lacan's Other is polysemic. Like many other Lacanian concepts, the meaning of the Other depends upon the context in which it is used. It can refer to the Subject–Other encounter ('the first object of desire is to be recognised by the other'), the Father or the Mother, the site of the inter-subjectivity of analysand and analyst and sometimes, the unconscious. When Lacan says that 'the unconscious is the discourse of the Other' he is knotting together several suppositions: the human subject is divided; the unconscious has a linguistic structure; the subject is inhabited by the Other; psychoanalysis is a variety of speech. There is a hint too that there is a kinship between the structure of language and the structure of the subject; both are articulations of difference; neither has a centre; both involve endless displacement; neither has a point of plenitude or stasis.

Lacan argues that there is a split between the conscious and the unconscious. This is a daily experience. (I have castration anxiety at the same time as I regard it as impossible.) Moreover, he says that to grasp the unconscious is, at the same time, to fail to grasp it. Lacan remarks that 'twice-lost Eurydice is the most striking image we can give, in terms of myth, of the relation between Orpheus the analyst and the unconscious'.[18] Let us now turn to the analyst and some problems about interpretation.

On interpretation (1953)

While many ego-psychologists ask, what is the patient doing? What is s/he saying and to whom? Lacan argues that we need to know where the subject is. From where is the subject speaking?

Some Kleinian analysts believe that they can give complete, non-contradictory interpretations to their patients.[19] They often give a little interpretation in each session. This implies that when the analysis is concluded, all the little pieces of mosaic add up to one whole, coherent picture. Their assumption is, of course, that there can be a complete interpretation. In contrast, Lacan believes that there can never be a complete interpretation; meaning, like a dream, is always slipping away. We can never know the whole truth – only a half-truth. Furthermore, it could be said that the interpretations of Kleinians are often literal; for example, a tunnel represents a vagina, a train equals a penis. Against such a view, Lacan argues that interpretation works only through equivocation.

Lacan makes some interesting points about interpretation, about speaking and listening, in his paper *Variations on the Standard Treatment* (1953). He emphasises the role of speech in psychoanalysis and argues against the idea of speech as a mere vehicle or a tool. He stresses the constituting power of speech, its structuring aspect. We have to listen not only to the intention of the speaker but also to what the discourse tells us about the speaker. There is often ambiguity, but there is a point at which ambiguity stops. The listener can always ask: what does s/he want to say? We can deduce from this that the speaker does not say what s/he wants to say. There is a well-known distinction between what a speaker means by his or her words and what the speaker's words mean. It should also be noted that there is a difference between speaking *to* someone and speaking *with* someone.

The speaker and listener are linked; this is what Lacan means by inter-subjectivity. But there is always the point at which *the listener decides* what the speaker wants to say. The meaning of the speaker's discourse depends on who hears it. In contrast to the usual view that the speaker reveals the true meaning, Lacan writes of 'the discretionary power of the listener'. The stress is on the responsibility of the listener. Lacan argues that truth does not exist before the interpretation. Interpretation creates the truth – it is an inter-subjective process. The analyst has to decide what the analysand is saying but – whether s/he speaks or remains silent – s/he cannot escape ethical problems because so much depends on the interpretation.

Antigone: A model of ethical action (1959)

Lacan was deeply interested in ethics. In one of his essays, 'Kant avec Sade' (1962–3), the attempt to construct a rationally coherent system of ethics by Kant is discredited by a structural analogy with the delirious rationality of Sade. It is argued that by attempting to universalise ethics and to establish the criteria for universally binding ethical laws which are not dependent on the logic of the individual situation, Kant merely succeeds in separating pleasurability from the notion of the good.

An important theme in one of his seminars, *The Ethics of Psychoanalysis* (1959), is the desire for death. Lacan believes that there are two deaths. He suggests that there is a difference between biological death and symbolic death. In Sophocles's play, Antigone is excluded from the community; in other words her symbolic death precedes her natural death. In Shakespeare's play the ghost of Hamlet's father represents the opposite case: natural death unaccompanied by symbolic death. In the above seminar Lacan comments on the tragedy of Antigone, in a play which clearly expresses human beings' relation and debt to the dead.

For Lacan, Antigone is a model of ethical conduct. But, first, let us remind ourselves of the story. The sons of Oedipus, brothers of Antigone, Eteocles and Polynices, have killed each other in battle. Eteocles was fighting on the side of the state, Thebes, and Polynices was attacking it. The ruler of Thebes, Creon, brother of Jocasta, decrees that the corpse of Eteocles be buried with full honours and that the corpse of Polynices be left to be ripped apart by dogs and birds. Wilfully disobedient, Antigone performs the proper funeral rites for Polynices. She takes full responsibility for her actions. Creon sentences her to be walled up in a cave with just enough food to relieve his guilt for her death. Antigone chooses to die: she hangs herself. As a consequence, Creon's son Haemon, fiancé of Antigone, also kills himself, and so does Creon's wife, Eurydice. For having declared himself and the state as mightier than the gods, Creon loses everything.

Creon represents what we could call a strong ego. He cannot tolerate a defiance of his authority, especially from a woman. On the other hand, Antigone's action is ethical. She is not in flight from responsibility and is not afraid of desire. Her act is disinterested; she does not consider the claims of her ego for happiness. She does not procrastinate about something she knows she must do. Antigone represents a principle of ethical conduct: she acts according to her desire and that desire is the desire of the Other.

CHAPTER | *Lacan's* Ecrits: *A review*
SIX

Reading as the production of meaning

In this chapter I want to draw all the threads of the previous chapters together. I will do this by giving an exposition of some of the key themes contained in Lacan's *Ecrits*.[1] As this chapter contains many ideas already discussed in earlier sections of the book, it provides an opportunity for revision and a reconsideration of important topics such as: the significance of the mirror phase; the nature of the id and the ego; reasons for the rejection of ego-psychology; the meaning of the terms signifier and signified, metaphor and metonymy; and Lacan's concept of desire.

The first point to note about these writings is that they were almost all given as 'speeches', addresses to meetings of psycho-analysts. In them Lacan is trying to persuade the experts to listen to him. Lacan's seminars, on the other hand, although presented orally, aim at teaching students how to read the text of Freud.[2] Second, it should be noted that *Ecrits*, a collection of 'articles', is not theoretically or epistemologically homogeneous. Almost one thousand pages in the original French, the product of some thirty years of research, it has a monolithic reputation.

The book is extraordinarily difficult to read for many reasons.

It is said that these 'writings' are a rebus. A rebus, like a dream, is a sort of picture-puzzle which looks like nonsense but, when separated into elements and interpreted, makes sense. Lacan's writings are a rebus because his style mimics the subject matter. He not only explicates the unconscious but strives to imitate it. The unconscious becomes not only the subject matter but, in the grammatical sense, the subject, the speaker of the discourse. Lacan believes that language speaks the subject, that the speaker is subjected to language rather than master of it.

When I am reading *Ecrits*, Roland Barthes's distinction between the readerly (*lisible*) and the writerly (*scriptible*) text often comes to mind.[3] Barthes makes a distinction between two sorts of writers. The lesser sort is the *écrivant*, for whom language is the means to some extra-linguistic end. S/he is a transitive writer in that s/he has a direct object. The other sort of writer, the *écrivain*, writes intransitively in so far as s/he devotes attention to the means, which is language, instead of the end. While the *écrivant* produces a Work, the *écrivain* produces a Text. Texts are *scriptible* because the reader, as it were, rewrites them as s/he reads. Works, on the other hand, are *lisible* or readable; we do not rewrite them but simply read them from start to finish. We proceed horizontally through a Work, but vertically, if that is possible, through a Text. In short, the readable (*lisible*) text is merchandise to be consumed; such a text moves inevitably and irreversibly to an end, to the disclosure of what has been concealed. The writable (*scriptible*) text requires the production of meanings, the active participation of the reader. Barthes has said that the goal of literary work is to make the reader no longer a consumer but a producer of the text. It seems to me that when we are reading *Ecrits* we can no longer be passive consumers. We must contribute something; we must produce meaning.

It could be argued that Lacan is to some extent working within a French literary tradition. His debt to the surrealist movement is particularly noticeable. Lacan's style, as I said earlier, owes much to André Breton, one of the leaders of surrealism. The style is further convoluted by the use of punning and, in the later work, there are many Joycean puns which are untranslatable. It has been said that his texts are so organised as to prevent skim-reading.

There are other difficulties. The architecture of *Ecrits* is such that it almost impossible to trace the development or history of the concepts deployed; chronology is in effect abolished. *Ecrits* contains an *index raisonné* compiled by Jacques-Alain Miller, in which the user is instructed to look, not for words, but for concepts, the implication being that they remain theoretically (and epistemologically) the same from 1936 to 1966. And so the concepts of the 1960s appear to exist in texts written before the Second World War. In other words, a fundamental assumption of unity and systematicity transforms *Ecrits* into a conceptually homogeneous text rather than a collection of papers written over a considerable period of time, with all the shifts and modifications that implies.[4]

Somebody once said the *Ecrits* seem to put the reader through an experience analogous to analysis: complete with passion, desire to know, transference. The *Ecrits* seem designed to force the reader into a perpetual struggle. An analysis terminates only when the patient realises it could go on for ever. Perhaps the reader of Lacan's work should be prepared for an unending struggle rather like the analytic patient's?

The mirror phase (1936)

The first text in the English edition of *Ecrits* is called 'The mirror stage as formative of the function of the I as revealed in psychoanalytic experience'. The essay is about the formation of identity, the moment of constitution of the self.

Lacan begins his account – as it has been discussed in Chapter 5 I will be concise – with the first months of the infant's life. The infant is relatively unco-ordinated, helpless and dependent. Between the age of six and eighteen months the infant becomes aware, through seeing its image in the mirror, of its own body as a totality. The human infant seems to go through an initial stage of confusing the image with reality, and may try to grasp hold of the image behind the mirror, or seize hold of the supporting adult. Then comes the discovery of the existence of an image with its own properties. Finally, there is the realisation that the image is its own – when it moves, its image moves, and so on. The mirror image is held together, it can come and go with a slight change of the infant's position, and the infant's mastery of the image fills it with triumph and joy.

The mirror image anticipates the mastery of its body that the infant has not yet objectively achieved. In other words, the infant's *imaginary* mastery of its body anticipates its biological mastery. Lacan believes that the formation of the ego commences at the point of alienation and fascination with one's own image. The image is the first organised form in which the individual identifies him- or herself, so the ego takes its form from, and is formed by, the organising and constitutive qualities of this image.

I want to stress the point that the ego is formed on the basis of an imaginary relationship of the subject with his or her own body. The ego has the illusion of autonomy, but it is only an illusion, and the subject moves from fragmentation and insufficiency to illusory unity. Even though the infant is its own rival before being a rival of another, it is captured from very early on by the human form and conditioned by the other's look, for example, by the face and gaze of the mother. The mirror phase inaugurates an indentification with other human images and with the world the subject shares with them.

In the mirror phase one can see evidence of transitivism: the child who strikes another says that he or she has been struck; when one child is punished the other also cries. In both cases, the identity of the one remains indistinct from, confused with, the other. Transitivism occurs when the borders separating them are affirmed and simultaneously confused. Like Melanie Klein, Lacan considers that the roots of primordial aggressivity can be seen in the earliest months of life. Aggressivity and narcissism appear to be tightly bound to one another. Lacan argues, in short, that the ego is not present from birth; it is something that develops. He believes that Freud put too much stress on the ego's adaptive functions, and that there was not enough emphasis on the ego's refusal to acknowledge thoughts and feelings from the unconscious.

Let me summarise the main points. The mirror phase is a moment of self-delusion, of captivation by an illusory image. Both future and past are thus rooted in an illusion. The mirror phase is the founding moment of the imaginary mode. It represents the first instance of what, according to Lacan, is the basic function of the ego: misrecognition (*méconnaissance*). The ego's function then is purely imaginary, and through its function the subject tends to become alienated. The ego 'neglects, scotomises, misconstrues'.[5] It is an agency that constantly misreads the truth that comes to the subject from the unconscious.

In Lacan's view, the ego's mastery of the environment is always an illusory mastery as a result of the way it is formed at the mirror phase. Human subjects continue throughout life to look for an imaginary 'wholeness' and 'unity'. These quests, controlled by the ego, are quite futile.[6] The mistake that many people make is that they confuse the human subject with the ego. The ego might give a feeling of permanence and stability to the subject, but this is an illusion. And we must remember that the subject is neither unified nor stable.

Lacan is, therefore, fundamentally opposed to any idea that one should help the analysand to strengthen his or her ego, or to help him or her adjust to society in any way. He is hostile to those who say that the aim of psychoanalysis is to produce healthy, well-adjusted individuals who know what 'reality' is. Lacan stresses the workings of the unconscious and the role of unconscious impulses. In his view there is a basic 'lack of being' at the heart of the human subject. The subject comes to feel an illusory unity at the time of the mirror phase, but with the introduction of language, s/he has the possibility of at least representing his or her thoughts and feelings.

The function and field of speech and language in psychoanalysis (1953)

This paper, often called the 'Rome Report' or the 'Rome Discourse', marked Lacan's break with the analytic establishment and the formation of his own school of psychoanalytic thought. The paper, the founding statement of Lacanian theory, defines psychoanalysis as a practice of speech and a theory of the speaking subject.[7] It is in this text, written in 1953, that Lacan begins to talk like Lacan. Psychoanalysis, he asserts, is distinguished from other disciplines in that the analyst works on the subject's speech. He points out that Freud often referred to language, particularly when he was focusing on the unconscious. After all, language is the 'talking cure'.

The theory of the three interacting orders, the Symbolic, the Imaginary and the Real, first appears in detail in this paper. I will briefly explain these concepts here, but will leave a fuller discussion of them till the next chapter. These orders can be conceived as different planes of existence which, though interconnected, are independent realities, each order being concerned with different functions. At any moment each may be implicated in the redefinition of the others.

The Imaginary order includes the field of phantasies and images. It evolves out of the mirror phase, but extends into the adult subject's relationships with others. The prototype of the typical imaginary relationship is the infant before the mirror, fascinated with its image. The Imaginary order also seems to include pre-verbal structures, for example, the various 'primitive' phantasies of children, psychotic and perverse patients.

The Symbolic order is concerned with the function of symbols and symbolic systems. Language belongs to the Symbolic order and, in Lacan's view, it is through language that the subject can represent desires and feelings. It is through the Symbolic order that the subject is constituted.

The Real order is the most elusive of these categories, and is linked to the dimensions of sexuality and death. It seems to be a domain outside the subject. The Real is the domain of the inexpressible, of what cannot be spoken about, for it does not belong to language. It is the order where the subject meets with inexpressible enjoyment and death.

In the 'Rome Discourse' Lacan's main emphasis is on the function and independence of the Symbolic order. Lacan illustrates the early insertion into the Symbolic order by the story Freud tells of his eighteen-month-old grandson playing the 'fort-da' game. (The child had a cotton reel on a piece of string which he alternatively threw away and pulled back.) Freud said that the game was related to the disappearance and appearance of the mother.[8] He suggested that by the repetition of this game of presence and absence the child seemed to cope with his mother's comings and goings, and tried to 'wean' himself from her. Freud noted that the child had turned a passive experience into an active one.

Lacan stresses the point that speech is the dimension by which the subject's desires are expressed and articulated. It is only when articulated and named before the other (for example, the analyst) that desires are recognised. It is also only with speech that subjects can fully recognise their histories. With the introduction of the language system, individuals can put themselves and their pasts in question. Subjects can restructure events after they have occurred. Indeed, it is well known that all of us are constantly rearranging our memories, histories and identities.

Let us examine the relationship between the imaginary and the symbolic. The imaginary is made up of imagos. An imago is an unconscious image or cliché which orients the way in which the subject apprehends other people. In the imaginary mode (or register), one's understanding of other people is shaped by one's own imagos. The perceived other is actually, at least in part, a projection. Psychoanalysis is an attempt to recognise the subject's imagos in order to ascertain the deforming effect upon the subject's understanding of his or her relationships. The point is not to give up the imagos, which is an impossible task, nor to create better ones. In the symbolic register, the subject understands these imagos as structuring projections.

Lacan condemns ego-psychology as hopelessly mired in the imaginary because it promotes an identification between the analysand's ego and the analyst's. The ego, for Lacan, is an imago. The enterprise of ego-psychology reshapes the analysand's imagos into ones that better correspond to 'reality' – that is, the analyst's imagos. *Ecrits* is full of attacks on ego-psychology because he regards it as a betrayal of psychoanalysis, a repression of the unconscious, and a manipulation of patients. One of his main criticisms is that it never gets beyond 'the language of the ego'.

Lacan describes two types of speech: on the one hand the speech which takes its orders from the ego (empty speech) and is addressed to the other (with a little o), the imaginary counterpart, through whom the subject is alienated. On the other hand, there is full speech, addressed to the Other, which is beyond the language ordered by the ego. The subject of this speech is the subject of the unconscious. Thus, Lacan can say: the unconscious is the discourse of the Other.

For Lacan, the subject's truth is not to be found in the ego. Instead it is to be found in another place, which Lacan called the place or 'locus' of the Other (with a capital O) at another level. Even if the patient lies, or is silent, or remembers nothing, what s/he cannot say or remember can be rediscovered elsewhere, in another locality. This was, after all, Freud's basic discovery: the subject speaks most truthfully, or the truth anyway slips out, when the ego's censorship is reduced, for example through dreams, jokes, slips of the tongue or pen.

In contrast with the practice of ego-psychologists, Lacan suggests that the analyst should be a mirror (but not a mirror stage). S/he can serve as a screen for the analysand's personality or values or knowledge. It is not the analyst's ego but his or her neutrality that should mirror the analysand. And obviously, the analyst should be able to distinguish the two registers in the patient's speech. The analyst is addressed both as the other through whom the patient's desire is alienated, and as the Other, to whom the analysand's true speech is addressed.

The Freudian thing (1955)

'The Freudian thing' was a commemorative oration delivered at the Viennese neuro-psychiatric clinic in 1955, and in it Lacan repeatedly taunts his clinical audience with a contrast between Freud's intellectual heroism and the alleged pusillanimity of most clinicians. The lecture could have been entitled: the unconscious, language and the tasks of the analyst. Many of the themes discussed so far in the book are to be found in this lecture.

Lacan begins by referring to Freud's revolution in knowledge: the discovery that the centre of the human being was no longer at the place assigned to it by the humanist tradition. He states that the meaning of a return to Freud is a return to the meaning of Freud. Truth, he says, belongs to the unconscious – it is found in dreams, jokes, nonsense, word play. In what could the unconscious be better recognised, in fact, than in the defences that are set up in the subject against it? The most innocent intention is disconcerted at being unable to conceal the fact that one's unsuccessful acts are the most successful and that one's failure fulfils one's most secret wish.

Lacan then links the topic of the unconscious with language. It is language that distinguishes human society from animal society; language is constituted by laws. If you want to know more, he says, read Saussure, the founder of modern linguistics. Lacan launches an attack on ego-psychology and its connections with 'the American way of life'. He is antagonistic to ego-psychology with its reference to 'the healthy part of the subject's ego', its stress on 'adaptation to reality', and its belief that the purpose of analysis is achieved through 'identification with the analyst's ego'.

In his view it is the ego-psychologists who support the translation of Freud's phrase '*Wo Es war, soll Ich werden*' as 'Where the id was, there the ego shall be.' Lacan argues that this is false, a mistranslation. He believes that there is a fundamental distinction between the true subject of the unconscious and the ego as constituted in its nucleus by a series of alienating identifications. The correct translation of the German emphasises not the ego but the unconscious: 'Where the subject was, there ought I to become.' Or, alternatively, 'There where it was, it is my duty that I should come into being.'

The third theme of the lecture is the task of the analyst. It is important, Lacan says, that the analyst should know why s/he intervenes, at what moment the opportunity presents itself and how to seize it. For this to occur the analyst must fully understand the difference between the Other to which his or her speech must be addressed, and that second other who is the individual he sees before him or her. The Other (capital O) is the locus in which is constituted the I who speaks to him/her who hears . . . Lacan believes that in the analytical situation there are not only two subjects present but two subjects each provided with two objects, the ego and the other (*autre*), the unconscious. This then is a game for four players.

It is in this paper that Lacan discusses two important phenomena in psychoanalysis – the return of the repressed and transference – in the context of recognition. Both these phenomena are forms of repetition, types of return. We know, for example, that the victims of traumas return to the traumatic scene in their dreams, and the infant repeats the painful scene of its mother's departure. Lacan believes that a desire must insistently repeat itself until it be recognised. Repetition is the effect not so much of the frustration of a desire but of the lack of recognition of a desire. Indeed, Lacan sees the psychoanalytic situation as a context conducive to the subject's recognition of his or her desires.

But how do subjects come to recognise their desires? What the analyst must do is to reply to what s/he hears. That reply sends back to the subject in inverted form what s/he was saying that s/he could never hear if s/he did not hear it returning from the analyst. Thus is accomplished the recognition that is the goal of analysis, the recognition by the subject. The subject must come to recognise his or her own drives, which are insisting, unbeknownst to him or her, in his or her discourse and actions. That recognition is reached through the mediation of the analyst. The analyst returns to the subject what the subject was saying so that the subject can recognise it and stop saying it.

Although the analyst is the one who is 'supposed to know' the truth, s/he really has to give up the power associated with his or her position in order to encourage the encounter with the Other. The analyst, according to Lacan, should not identify with the Other, but only encourage the analysand to encounter his or her own Other.

Lacan mentions the fact that Freud regarded the study of literature, art, languages and institutions as necessary to an understanding of (the text of) our experience. In Lacan's view there should be an initiation into the methods of the linguist, the historian and the mathematician. Psychoanalysis can be sustained only by constant communication with other disciplines that form the 'sciences of inter-subjectivity' or the 'conjectural sciences'.

In the concluding section of 'The Freudian thing' there is a moving reference to the Actaeon myth: 'Actaeon, too guilty to hunt the goddess, the prey in which is caught, O huntsman, the shadow that you become, let the pack pass by without hastening your step, Diana will recognise the hounds for what they are . . .' (*Ecrits*, p. 145). Actaeon was guilty of having surprised the chaste goddess Diana in her bath. Taken aback, the goddess transformed him into a stag, and then his own dogs hunted and devoured him. This Ovidian parable can be interpreted in many ways. We know that Lacan stressed the insistent power of repression and that the discovery of the unconscious is itself subject to repression. Freud's discovery was a terrifying one, even to Freud himself. We also know that Freud's thoughts have become codified; ego-psychologists and others have domesticated and/or repressed the unconscious. Is Freud a new Actaeon turned upon and savaged by his own thoughts for having unveiled the goddess of the unconscious? Or is, perhaps, Actaeon Lacan himself?

The agency of the letter: Reason since Freud (1957)

Lacan is always telling us that we should listen to what the unconscious says. The subtitle of the essay, 'Reason since Freud', is a reference to a debate about knowledge. Lacan argues that we have to abandon the idea of reason as belonging to the positive sciences; nor does it belong to conscious logical or philosophical reason, but to the unconscious. Reason is the insistence of a meaning, the primacy or authority of a letter which insists on being expressed or heard. He reminds us that the subject is implicated in language, even before his or her birth; that is to say there is a place assigned to him or her by a discourse which pre-existed his or her birth.

During the 1950s Lacan began to make use of Saussure's concepts but, as I said in Chapter 4 on language, he adapted them in important ways. For Saussure the linguistic sign is a unification of a sound-image (the signifier) with a concept (the signified). The signifier and the signified are like two sides of a sheet of paper. While Saussure put the signifier and the signified in an ellipse which indicates the structural unity of the sign, Lacan removed it. Lacan wanted to emphasise that the signifier and signified are two distinct and *separate* orders. He therefore introduced what he called a 'cut' (*coupure*) into the Saussurean sign with the introduction of a new emphasis on the bar, as a formula of separateness rather than reciprocity of signifier and signified. This move calls into question any theory of correspondence between words and things.

Lacan writes that the algorithm that is the foundation of modern linguistics is S/s. While Saussure formulated the signified on top, Lacan puts the signifier on top – to give it pre-eminence.[9] He argued that signifiers are combined in a signifying chain. Meaning does not arise in the individual signifier but in the connection between signifiers. Saussure had admitted that there can occur a shift or sliding (*glissement*) in the relationship between the signifier and signified. In contrast, Lacan argues not only that the two realms of signifier and signified are never united, but that there is an incessant sliding of the signified under the signifier. This does not mean that there are no moments of stability at all. Lacan suggests that there are 'anchoring points' (*points de capiton*); these are certain 'nodal points' which stop the sliding signifiers and fix their meaning. (Sometimes, it is said that 'the floating signifiers' are 'quilted'.)[10]

After every quilting of the signifying chain, which retroactively fixes its meaning, there always remains the persistence of a gap between utterance and its enunciation: you're saying this, but what are you really telling me?

One of the most important functions of speech is that a subject uses it to signify something quite other than what s/he says. The meaning is always veering off, or being displaced. One must not think that speech masks one's thoughts. The subject produces through his or her speech a truth which s/he does not know about. Truth resides, as it were, in the spaces between one signifier and another, in the holes of the chain.

The linguistic concepts of metaphor and metonymy occupy an important place in Lacanian theory. I will make only one basic point here as I discussed these concepts in Chapter 4, 'The functions of language'. To put it simply, a metaphor is based on a proposed similarity, or analogy; Lacan defines it as 'one word for another'. He defines metonymy as the relation 'word by word'. It is the relation between two signifiers along the line of any concrete discourse. This is linear because only one word is pronounced or written at a time. In the metonymic dimension, the signifier can receive its complete signification only by deferred action.

The main point is this: Lacan inserts Saussurean linguistics into Freud's notion of condensation and displacement and links it with Jakobson's analysis of the two poles of language: metaphor and metonymy. Lacan connects metaphor with condensation and metonymy with displacement. (I should remind readers that Freud argued that condensation and displacement were the two processes basically responsible for the form assumed by dreams.[11] He believed that they were the basic unconscious mechanisms at work in, for instance, symptom formation and the production of jokes and slips of the tongue.) Lacan describes condensation as the 'superimposition of signifiers' and compares it to his notion of metaphor, where one word is substituted by another. He considered that in displacement one could see a 'veering off of signification' which is similar to his notion of metonymy. It seems to me that Lacan has a preference for metaphor and tends to privilege it. In metaphor a signifier substitutes for another signifier only in order to articulate what cannot be said, that is the signified. It is in metaphor that desire finds a pathway for expression.

The significance of the phallus (1958)

It is in this paper that Lacan uses the term 'masquerade'. The term is not in Freud but it appears in a famous paper by Joan Rivière, 'Womanliness as a masquerade' (1929).[12] Her paper is important because of the debate around the construction and representation

of sexual identity. Rivière's paper is concerned with 'women who
wish for masculinity' and who may then put on 'a mask of
womanliness' as a defence, to avert anxiety and retribution feared
from men.

The particular case Rivière discusses involves a successful intellectual woman who seeks reassurance from men after her public
engagements.

> Analysis of her behaviour after her performances showed that she was
> attempting to obtain sexual advances from the particular type of men
> by means of flirting and coquetting with them in a more or less veiled
> manner. The extraordinary incongruity of this attitude with her
> haughty impersonal and objective attitude during her intellectual per-
> formance, which it succeeded so rapidly, was a problem.[13]

Rivière suggests that the problem can be solved by reference to
Oedipal rivalry: in her successful professional career the woman
rivals and takes the place of the father; in her acknowledgement
nevertheless of womanliness, the flirting and coquetting, she pla-
cates him: '. . . it was an unconscious attempt to ward off the
anxiety which would ensue on account of the reprisals she antici-
pated from the father-figures after her intellectual performance'.[14]

A woman identifies as a man – takes on masculine identity – and
then identifies herself after all as a woman – takes up a feminine
identity. Masquerade, 'the mask of womanliness' seems quite
simple but there are some puzzling questions: where does Rivière
draw the line between genuine womanliness and 'masquerade'? If
there is a mask, then there is a behind-the-mask – and we need to
know what is behind. In Stephen Heath's view, by collapsing
genuine womanliness and the masquerade together, Rivière under-
mines the integrity of the former with the artifice of the latter.[15]

What is the Lacanian interpretation of the patient described in
Rivière's paper? In 'The signification of the phallus' Lacan writes:

> Paradoxical as this formulation may seem, I would say that it is in
> order to be the phallus, that is to say the signifier of the desire of the
> Other, that the woman will reject an essential part of her femininity,
> notably all its attributes through masquerade. It is for what she is not
> that she expects to be desired as well as loved.[16]

In other words, the game being played is that of being the phallus. With the mother as initial object, the child seeks to be the phallus she wants. Now, according to Lacan, no one has the phallus, it is a signifier, the initial signifier of the lack-in-being that determines the subject's relation to the signifier. The subject is constituted in lack and the woman represents lack.

Lacan credits Rivière with pinpointing in the masquerade 'the feminine sexual attitude'. The masquerade serves to show what she does not have, a penis, by showing – the adornment, the putting on – something else, the phallus she becomes, as woman to man, sustaining his identity and an order of exchange of which she is the object. Lacan remarks: 'Such is the woman concealed behind her veil: it is the absence of the penis that turns her into the phallus, object of desire.'[17] Adornment *is* the woman, she exists veiled; only thus can she represent lack, be what is wanted: lack is never presented other than as a reflection on a veil.

I think I should mention that at the time Lacan gave his paper on the meaning of the phallus (1958), he wanted to emphasise the place of the Symbolic order in the determination of human subjectivity. (He argued that the contemporary science of linguistics was unavailable to Freud.) In the paper Lacan returns to some of the debates of the 1920s and 1930s and criticises what he sees as a reduction of the phallus to an object of primitive oral aggression, belonging in the realm of the instinct. Instead he places the phallus within the Symbolic order and argues that it can be understood as a *signifier* only in the linguistic sense of the term.

Lacan has often been accused of phallocentrism. And it is true that he has asserted that 'the phallus is the privileged signifier'. The meaning of the term phallus, however, has often been misunderstood. The term phallus must be distinguished from the term penis. The penis is an organ of the body; the phallus is signifier, function or metaphor. Lacan says explicitly that the phallus is not a fantasy, not an object, but least of all an organ, a penis. The phallus symbolises the penis and the clitoris. It is a signifier. In short, Lacan's distinction between the penis and the phallus enables Freud's biologistic account of male superiority and women's penis-envy to be explained in linguistic and symbolic, and thus historical terms.

Lacan's paper contains a discussion about desire and the difficulties of the sexual relation, especially for the woman, whose relationship to the phallic term is described in terms of masquerade. Let me recapitulate some of the key points: the drama of the subject in language is the experience of its lack in being, and that experience is a movement of desire. Desire is a relation of being to lack. Nothing can make up division, no object can satisfy desire – what is *wanting* is always wanting, division is the condition of subjectivity.

The phallus, with its status as potentially absent, comes to stand in for the necessarily *missing* object of desire at the level of sexual division. That no one has the phallus is an expression of its reality as signifier of lack: if division cannot be made up, desire satisfied, then the phallus is not an end, not some final truth but, paradoxically, the supreme signifier of an impossible identity.

Pre-Oedipally, both sexes have a masculine relation to the mother seeking to be the phallus she wants. The prohibition of the mother under the law of the father, the recognition of castration, inaugurates the Oedipus complex for the girl, she now shifting her object love to the father who seems to have the phallus and identifying with the mother who, to her fury, does not: henceforth the girl will desire to have the phallus.

The phallus is the signifier of lack marking castration. It signifies what men (think they) *have* and what women (are considered to) *lack*. The woman does not *have* the phallus, the object of desire for another. The phallus is the signifier of signifiers, the representative of signification and language. The phallus is the crucial signifier in the distribution of authority and power. It also designates the object of desire.

Lacan writes about the castration complex in the masculine unconscious and *penisneid* in the woman's unconscious. Man is threatened with loss, woman is deprived. Because she feels deprived, her (structural) attitude is one of envy. In an interesting paragraph, Lacan does not use the more usual word deprivation or envy, he uses the word nostalgia.[18] The dictionary definitions of 'nostalgie' – homesickness and regret for something past – are useful in understanding Lacan's text. But there is a third definition which is also helpful in understanding Lacanian theory: unsatisfied desire. The Lacanian subject is castrated, that is to say, deprived of the phallus, and therefore can never satisfy desire.

Now, one might say that desire does not know its object, has no (conscious) idea of its object, because of repression. Of course, the repressed was once conscious and so the desire is for a return to an object whose knowledge is only contingently unavailable to the subject. But what if the object of desire was an indefinable something, the result of primary repression? The primary repressed was never present to consciousness; it is primordially and structurally excluded. There is no past state that was once present to which one could return, even in phantasy. The returned cannot be imagined because one does not know the object. (Saint-Exupery defines nostalgia as the desire for what cannot be defined.) What Lacan calls desire is precisely the result of this primary repression and yields up a nostalgia beyond the drive to return, a desire constitutively unsatisfied and unsatisfiable because its 'object' simply cannot ever be defined. In short, primary repression is that part of needs which is left out in the articulation of a demand, and which we experience as desire.

The subversion of the subject and the dialectic of desire in the Freudian unconscious (1960)

Lacan's work, like psychoanalysis generally, draws heavily on literature. Gradually, however, his writings seem to move in the direction of science: first, linguistics, and later, mathematics. This paper is full of algorithms and graphs and exemplifies the drive towards 'science'.

The paper examines the way in which Freud's notion of the unconscious has overturned the traditional concept of the subject. Lacan claims that because of the dominating role of the signifier (language) in the constitution of the human subject, one can no longer think of the subject in terms of positivist scientific thought. The subject cannot be conceived as an objectively knowable thing (a signified). Instead, Lacan argues, one has to think in terms of a different kind of knowledge, for the subject arises in relation to desire which is unknown to him or her.

Lacan's concept of truth can be related to his view of psychoanalytic knowledge. In his view truth is essentially disturbing and, as Freud demonstrated, expresses itself in the unconscious. The apparently unknown knowledge in the unconscious speaks. It says what it knows, while the subject does not know it. For Lacan, the unconscious is the language, or form, through which this knowledge about truth is always and exclusively represented.

Lacan made an interesting distinction between linguistics, the science concerned with the formalisation of knowledge, and *La Linguisterie*, concerned with the side of language that linguistics had left unformalised. *La Linguisterie* is the language with which the unconscious is concerned, and which psychoanalysis can decipher at the moments when the ordinary language structure is interrupted, or breaks down as in jokes, dreams and parapraxes. *La Linguisterie* speaks about what cannot be consciously known. Unconscious truth often appears unacceptable, stupid, marginal or unacceptable.

Lacan placed the function and structure of language in the forefront of his theory. The logic of the unconscious appears, for example, in the analytic relationship when the analyst finds her- or himself listening to different orders in a discourse. Suppose an analysand says 'I think I do not exist.' What is happening here? The first 'I' indicates the subject of the enunciation (*énonciation*, the act of uttering the words) but does not signify the subject's existence, which is considered in the 'I' of the statement (*énoncé*, the actual words uttered), 'I do not exist.' One is faced here with what Lacan called a cut (*coupure*) between different orders of discourse – where, on the one hand, the subject enunciates his or her symbolic existence as the 'I' who speaks and thinks, but then denies this existence at the level of the statement, 'I do not exist.'

It should be emphasised that the Lacanian view of the unconscious revolves around the question of lack, the lack of being that results from the subject's dependence on the Other. One can see certain similarities between the Lacanian concept of lack of being and the Freudian theory of the death drive (which aims to bring the living being back to the inorganic state).

Lacan illustrated the relationship between the subject and his death with a dream referred to by Freud. Freud argued that dreams do not differentiate between what is wished and what is real. For instance, a man who had nursed his father during his last illness and had been deeply grieved by his death, had the following dream: 'His father was again alive and he was talking to him as of old. But as he did so he felt it exceedingly painful that his father was nevertheless dead, only did not know it.'[19]

Freud wrote that, at bottom, dreams are nothing other than a particular form of thinking, made possible by the conditions of the state of sleep. We must not focus on the 'hidden meaning', the latent content, but centre our attention on the form itself, on the dream-work. We must ask: why does this content assume this particular form? We should remember that there are always three elements at work: the manifest dream-text, the latent dream-content or thought, and the unconscious desire. This desire attaches itself to the dream, it intercalates itself in the interspace between the latent thought and the manifest text.

According to Freud, dreams function to the pleasure principle, that is, according to the dreamer's wish. The pleasure principle is the reign of wishes, unbridled by reality. The father was dead, only did not know that the dreamer wished it. Freud remarks: 'It is thus a matter of the familiar case of self-reproaches after the loss of a loved person, and in this case the reproach goes back to the infantile significance of the death-wish against the father.'

In *Beyond the Pleasure Principle* Freud explained that the repetition of painful experiences in dreams and children's play is an attempt to master an exceedingly painful event by taking over the position of author of this event. The dream, described above, is an illustration of the repetition compulsion and the death drive that are beyond the pleasure principle.

In Lacan's view, the dead father dream expresses not only the Oedipal desire for the father's death but also a more radical death drive or 'death desire'.[20] The Oedipal wish is not only a wish for the father's death, but also and as centrally a wish to be in the father's place. If one tries to think at one and the same time the desire to be in the father's place, one risks facing the desire for one's own death.

In considering the dream, Lacan focuses on the topic of knowledge and he makes a distinction between *savoir* and *connaissance*, which runs through the first part of this paper. The two words can both be translated as 'knowledge'. Lacan distinguishes between a biological instinct which is a *connaissance* without *savoir*, and what we find in Freud, which is a *savoir* without *connaissance*.[21] *Connaissance* in this paper is associated with psychology and its perception of the person as a unified whole with natural developmental states. *Savoir* is associated with Hegel, language, unconscious knowledge and desire. Underlying Lacan's theory of desire is the concept of drive. His notion of drive implies the 'drifting' movement of desire. There is a sense in which the subject does not know where the current is going and so does not have what is called *connaissance*.

Lacan then focuses on the nature of the subject's being. He argues that the subject has a basic dependence on the Other. In a way, the Other is the real witness and guarantor of the subject's existence. The subject's basic dependence on the Other is clear when we think of the mother's role in relation to the infant. She looks after the infant, calls it by a name and tells it who it is. She is the M-Other who created it. The Other is the 'place' where the subject is born. The Other was there before the subject's birth, but the mother is also a subject, itself based on a lack of being. The mother's love cannot be absolute as she cannot fulfil this absolute demand for love made by the infant. No matter how much she gives it and how much its needs are satisfied, the mother can never fill the void she shares with her child. *The demand for love goes beyond the objects that satisfy need.* As Lacan says, Desire takes shape in the margin in which demand is torn apart from need.[22]

But what is the object which unchains desire? The object a, *objet (a)utre*, is the object of desire permeated and mobilised by lack. The *objet a* represents the lacking or lost object. It is the object of desire on its way to becoming the cause and condition of desire as well. It always escapes the subject. The *objet a* may be an orifice, a breast; it has something to do with an edge or cut: 'The lips, the enclosure formed by the teeth, the rim of the anus, the tip of the penis, the vagina, the slit formed by the eyelids . . .' To this list Lacan adds the phoneme, the gaze, the voice.[23]

Perhaps it would be best to describe *objet a* as the cause of desire. In a sense it is the phallus which the child wishes to be in order to complete its mother, the symbolic complement of its own lack. It is the object of the radical lack lived by the child who is separated at birth from its mother. It is the first image to fill in the crack of separation. In short, the *objet a* (sometimes called the *objet-petit-a*) is the signifier of desire.

I mentioned just now the lack of being of the mother. This is represented, according to Lacan, by the signifier of the phallus, which she does not have and which she desires. The infant identifies with the phallus, as the object lacking to, and desired by, the mother; and hence how s/he links her- or himself to her lack of being through the phallus. But however strong the dual imaginary mother–child relationship is, a third term intervenes – the Other, the father. The father brings back the mother to her own lack of a phallus, that is to say, to her castration. The mother looks for what she does not have, by receiving the phallus from the father, or by identifying it with her child. The child identifies with the phallus in order to satisfy its mother's desire. The phallus also signifies the law of symbolic castration for it belongs to the father, the Other who forbids the enjoyment of the mother–child 'symbiosis'.

The phallus signifies sexual difference. It is what splits human beings into what Lacan called 'sexed partial beings'. In Aristophanes's famous myth, described in Plato's *Symposium*, each sexual half is looking desperately for the other complementary half; Lacan believes that the subject's search for his or her sexual complement is replaced by the search for that part of her- or himself that is lost for ever, owing to the fact that he or she is a sexed partial being.

One effect of Lacan's concern with desire is the displacement of the concept libido (the word Freud used to describe the force of the 'sexual desire'). Lacan always uses the term libido sparingly – it is ousted by 'desire'. In later years, in Lacan's own writings, desire tends to be eclipsed gradually by *jouissance*.

What is *jouissance*? The human subject is confronted by the unconscious which is striving to express what is really forbidden to the speaking subject – *jouissance* and death. In *Beyond the Pleasure Principle* Freud said that 'there exists in the mind a strong tendency towards the pleasure principle, but that tendency is opposed by certain other forces or circumstances'. Lacan makes an important distinction between *plaisir* (pleasure) and *jouissance*, a term which signifies the ecstatic or orgasmic enjoyment – and exquisite pain – of something or someone. *Jouissance* goes beyond *plaisir*. In French, *jouissance* includes the enjoyment of rights and property, but also the slang verb, *jouir*, to come, and so is related to the pleasure of the sexual act. But it also refers to those moments when too much pleasure is pain.

Jouissance, then, is not pleasure in pain – that is masochism. *Jouissance* is unconscious, it is unconscious pleasure which becomes pain. An example: while listening to music the other day I burst out crying without knowing why. *Jouissance* begins where pleasure ends. When *jouissance* becomes conscious it is no longer *jouissance*, it is merely pleasure. *Jouissance* occurs when physical pain becomes unphysical pleasure. Now, *plaisir* is bound to desire as a defence against *jouissance*. *Jouissance*, like death, represents something whose limits cannot be overcome.

The Imaginary, the Symbolic and the Real

Introduction: Lacan's changing concepts

It may be helpful to think of Lacan's work as consisting of three main periods: in the first period, 1932–48 (the dates are approximate) the main idea is the domination of the human being by the image (the imago). In the second period, 1948–60, the function of the image is subordinated and the dominant field of knowledge in his thinking is linguistics. Lacan argues that this form of explanation (a theory of the signifier) was not available to Freud. In the third period, 1960–80, the key idea is that of the three 'orders' or 'registers': the Imaginary, the Symbolic and the Real. When Lacan moved from the psychiatric hospital to the university, in 1963, he began to concentrate on the formalisation of psychoanalysis by the use of logic and mathematics. These topics are the main themes of this chapter.

The Imaginary

One of the difficulties in understanding Lacan is that his concepts are in constant flux. Between the 1950s and the 1970s there were many changes in his conceptualisation of the Imaginary, Symbolic, and the Real. Some Lacanians refer to the three orders as RSI (which, amusingly, sounds like the word 'heresy'). But this is not the sequence in which the concepts were developed. At the beginning of his teaching Lacan focused on the Imaginary.

The Imaginary grows from the infant's experience of its 'specular ego'. It arises with the mirror phase but extends far into the adult individual's experience of others and of the external world.[1] Wherever a false identification is to be found – within the subject,

or between one subject and another or between subject and thing –
there the Imaginary holds sway. It can be thought of as a kind of
garment, the first layer of which is armour. The Imaginary performs the function of *méconnaissance* (misrecognition) and is to be
distinguished from knowledge (*connaissance*).

Lacan's concept of the Imaginary first appeared in his 1936
paper 'The mirror stage'. A major reference point of this paper is
Freud's 1914 essay 'On narcissism – an introduction', the myth of
Narcissus being especially apt to describe that moment in which an
apparent reciprocity reveals itself as no more than the return of an
image to itself. The concept of the mirror phase draws our attention to the *interdependency* of image, identity and identification.
One of the main features of the mirror phase is that the child is in a
state of nursling dependency and relative motor inco-ordination
and yet the image returned to the child is fixed and stable. The
basic relation, then, is between a fragmented or inco-ordinate subject and its totalising image.

I want to stress the paradox that the subject finds or recognises
itself through an image which simultaneously alienates it, and
hence, potentially confronts it. This is the basis of the close relationship between narcissism and aggressivity. (The child expels
objects which it fears as dangerous.) There are, then, two factors to
be noted: first, the factor of aggression, rivalry, the image as alienating, and second, the fundamental misrecognition which is the
foundation of subjectivity.

Freud maintains that for the subject there are four alternative
narcissistic object choices:

(a) what he himself is,
(b) what he himself was,
(c) what he himself would like to be,
(d) someone who was once part of himself.[2]

Now the important distinction for us is between ideal ego and
ego ideal. Ideal ego is usually defined as an ideal of narcissistic
omnipotence constructed on the model of infantile narcissism. Ego
ideal is an agency of the personality resulting from the coming
together of narcissism (idealisation of the ego) and identification
with parents, or with their substitutes. The ideal ego corresponds
to what 'he himself was', and the ego ideal to what 'he himself

would like to be'. The ideal ego would (therefore) be a projected image with which the subject identifies and is related to the mirror phase, the ego ideal would be a secondary introjection. For Lacan the ideal ego is an essentially narcissistic formation, originating in the mirror phase and belonging to the Imaginary.

Let us now consider the relation between imaginary and symbolic identification, between the ideal ego and the ego ideal. Imaginary identification is identification with the image in which we appear likeable to ourselves, with the image representing 'what we would like to be', and symbolic identification, identification with the very place from where we are being observed, from where we look at ourselves so that we appear to ourselves likeable, worthy of love. (We must remember that the trait on the basis of which we identify with someone is usually hidden, and is not necessarily a positive feature).

Imaginary identification is always identification on behalf of a certain gaze in the Other. We should always ask: for whom is the subject enacting this role? This gap between the way I see myself and the point from which I am being observed to appear likeable to myself is crucial for grasping hysteria. The hysterical neurotic is experiencing her- or himself as somebody who is enacting a role for the other. In short, the difference between how we see ourselves and the point from which we are being observed is the difference between imaginary and symbolic identification.

The Symbolic and the Real

In the early 1950s Lacan shifted the emphasis from the captivating image to language, the Symbolic. Drawing on the work of Saussure, Lévi-Strauss and Jakobson, Lacan said that the Imaginary is determined by signifiers. He argued that language is crucial in the construction of identity. Consider the possible effects of the words in a casual remark by a mother to her little child: 'You are just like your father!' Lacan stresses the fact that meaning is constructed retroactively, and that listeners have power because it is they who interpret. When, for example, a child needs something, its requests have to be interpreted – its demands are always refracted through language.

At this stage of Lacan's work the Symbolic consists of a mixture of concepts. There are certain structural, anthropological notions and there is the important Hegelian idea (passed on through Kojève) of recognition. Desire is the desire for recognition. If a person says 'You are my master' the implication is 'I am your slave'. If one says 'You are my wife' the implication is 'I am your husband'. This relation between the Subject and the Other is called the dialectic of recognition. We all want to be validated, to be recognised. Sometimes we do hear recognition being given: 'You are such a wonderful mother', or 'You've been such a thoughtful daughter'. But we also hear painful cries when recognition has been denied: 'Couldn't he have found *one* nice thing to say?'

About 1957/8 there is a change in Lacan's concept of the Symbolic: it becomes an autonomous structure. This means that the human subject is absent from the signifying chain; the subject is 'abolished'. Instead of recognition of the subject there is a lack of recognition: a want to be. There is a 'lack of being'. This shift from the realm of the Hegelian dialectic of recognition to that of representation (language) is really the effect of a new discourse: structuralism. In structuralist thought there is little place for the human subject. One of its slogans is: 'the subject is dead'.

It was about 1955/6 that Lacan developed the view that the Real resists symbolisation. The Real is 'the impossible to symbolise'. The analytical notion of impossibility was influenced by the work of Alexandre Koyré, who asserted that that which exists is always in relation to the impossible.[3] For Lacan explanation of the Real is always in terms of the impossible. The Real is that which is outside the Imaginary and the Symbolic. The Real is that which is excluded, the impossible to bear. Lacan's notion of the Real has little to do with any assumptions about the nature of the world, with 'reality'. The Real is a concept that cannot exist without the barrier of the Symbolic, which predates the birth of the subject.

It can happen that a subject in the grip of madness hallucinates the Real where it does not exist and thinks that it is 'seeing'. This shows the way in which the Real is impossible to see, or to hear since, in any case, it is 'always-already-there'. The Lacanian concept of the Real harks back to the Freudian id; it is associated with the sudden, the disconcerting and the unpredictable.[4]

I have already said that what happens in an analysis is constituted through a discourse; psychoanalysis, a dialectical experience, deals solely with words. Lacan did not conceptualise his role as that of the interpreter, offering meanings for each dream and symptom. Basically he waited for patients to be able to connect things up for themselves.[5] Like most analysts, he listened to something other than what was being said. What the analyst focuses on is the discourse of the Other, the unconscious that slides through the gaps in intentionality.

Lacan defined the objective of analysis as the breaking of any Imaginary relationship between analysand and analyst through the intervention of a third term which throws them on to the axis of the Symbolic. The intervention of a third term is the precondition of language (the use of the three basic pronouns 'I'/'you'/'he-she-it'). What matters here is that the Symbolic sets a limit to the 'Imaginary' of the analytic situation. Both analyst and analysand must come to see how they are constituted by an order which goes beyond their interaction as such. Lacan believes that the subject and the analytic process must break out of the Imaginary dyad which blinds them to what is happening outside.

The Symbolic and the name-of-the-father

I have said something about the order of language (the Symbolic), and of the ego and its identifications (the Imaginary). The Imaginary and the Symbolic are not successive stages but are intertwined. The Real comes close to meaning 'the ineffable' or 'the impossible' in Lacan's thought. It serves to remind human subjects that their Symbolic and Imaginary constructions take place in a world which exceeds them.

It should also be noted that the 'orders' are not stable concepts; at each moment each may be implicated in the redefinition of the others. Although the Imaginary and the Symbolic are distinct and opposed, the Symbolic encroaches upon the Imaginary, organises it, and gives it direction. Even before it is born, the child has a place in a family. Lacan points out that the human subject, as s/he acquires speech, is inserting her- or himself in a pre-existing Symbolic order and thereby submitting his or her desire to the systemic pressures of that order: in adopting language s/he allows his or her 'free' instinctual energies to be operated upon and organised.

Lacan believed that it was the failure to grasp the concept of the Symbolic (the order of language) which had led psychoanalysis to concentrate increasingly on the adequacies and inadequacies of the mother–child relationship, an emphasis which tends to be complicit with the idea of maternal role (the concept of mothering).

In contrast, Lacan emphasised the concept of castration because of the reference which it always contains to paternal law. He argued for a return to the concept of the father, but this concept is now defined in relation to that of desire. The phallus forbids the child the satisfaction of his or her own desire, which is the desire to be the exclusive desire of the mother. The duality of the relation between mother and child must be broken; the phallus stands for that moment of rupture. It refers mother and child to the dimension of the symbolic which is figured by the father's place. The phallus breaks the two-term relation and initiates the order of exchange.

It is to emphasise the position and law of the father that Lacan uses the term 'paternal metaphor'. He insists that the father stands for a place and function which is not reducible to the presence or absence of the real father as such. That is to say, an Oedipus complex can be constituted even if the father is not there. Note that the father is a function and refers to a law, and that by breaking the imaginary dyad, the phallus represents a moment of division.

The Symbolic function is associated not only with the father but also with Lacan's expression the name-of-the-father. Lacan worked out the theory of the name-of-the-father in reconsidering the case of Judge Schreber.[6] This man came from a distinguished Prussian family. His father had a reputation as an educator who stressed the value of physical training and the use of various kinds of corrective apparatus. Judge Schreber became psychotic; he believed he had a mission to redeem the world. This, however, he could do only if he were first transformed from a man into a woman. He began to dress before a mirror in women's clothing. He was obsessed by the fear of God, whom he expected to impregnate him as though he were an immaculate Virgin.

What had happened? According to Lacan, Schreber's psychosis did not result from a real absence of the father. Rather, it had to do with the 'bankruptcy' resulting from a distortion in what Lacan calls the 'paternal metaphor'.[7] The paternal metaphor establishes the correlation between the family name – necessarily the father's name – and the subject coming into the world. If the father, present or not, fails to occupy the position assigned to him by our culture, disaster ensues.

Unable to find himself in his father, Schreber had turned instead to his mother. But the 'place' of the father, the source of his own name, his family identity, and therefore his insertion into the world of human relations, remained empty. It did not disappear: it simply remained vacant. Lacan called this mechanism 'foreclosure'. Foreclosure is a legal term implying a forfeiture of a right not exercised within the prescribed limits. The father is there, but paternal authority can nevertheless be lost in various ways, so that the father forfeits his symbolic right, to the great detriment of the child. To put it in another way, foreclosure refers to the exclusion of a certain key signifier, the name-of-the-father, from the Symbolic order.[8] This often triggers psychosis.

On psychosis

The Aimée case, which I related in Chapters 2 and 5, gave the reader some idea of the world of the psychotic. The study of psychosis sheds light on the nature of human reality. Freud's 1911 study, an analysis of Schreber's *Memoirs of My Nervous Illness*, is a landmark in the development of his concern with psychosis. The link between paranoia and homosexuality, the importance of narcissism and projection, have been key elements in Freudian analysis ever since. In his work on psychosis Freud noted the psychotic's altered relation to reality, and how the 'Imaginary external world' of a psychosis attempts to put itself in place of the 'external world'. On the psychotic's relation to reality, Freud wrote:

> A fair number of analyses have taught us that the delusion is found applied like a patch over the place where originally a rent had appeared in the ego's relation to the external world . . . neurosis is the result of a conflict between the ego and its id, whereas psychosis is the analogous outcome of a similar disturbance in the relations between the ego and the external world.[9]

He added that there was no sharp distinction between neurosis and psychosis; in both cases what is important is not only the *loss of reality* but the *substitute for reality*.

One of Lacan's seminars (held in 1955 and published in 1981) deals with the question of psychosis largely through a commentary on Freud's analysis of Schreber's *Memoirs*. The question is important to Lacan, partly because he wants to prove that psychoanalysis can deal with psychosis, but also because it extends his own early work on paranoia (his doctoral thesis and the articles he wrote in the surrealist journal *Minotaure*).

Lacan's analysis, like Freud's, hinges on a conception of language. In a Freudian perspective, he asserts, man is nothing but the subject caught in and tortured by language. Our psychic reality is interwoven with signifiers. The Oedipus complex and the threat of castration are myths evolved by Freud to describe the process whereby the subject is caught up by the signifier. There are, according to Lacan, basic signifiers without which no world of human signification can be built: the phallus, as signifier of the difference of the sexes, is one of them. Psychosis occurs when those basic signifiers disappear, when the relation between the subject and the signifier is perturbed.

The normal process of access to subjectivity is usually described through a sewing metaphor, the aformentioned '*points de capiton*', or the 'upholstery buttons'. The subject attaches significance, it 'anchors itself' to certain signifiers; these signifiers, like upholstery buttons, pin down the floating mass of signification, by attaching it to the system of signifiers. If they fail, the correspondence is no longer achieved, words no longer carry meaning and communication, or inter-subjectivity, fails. Psychosis is caused by a gap in the chain of basic signifiers. In the case of Schreber, the missing signifier is 'being a father', the basic signifier which constitutes a man.

In Lacan's view, the father introduces the principle of law, in particular the law of the language system. When this law breaks down, or if it has never been acquired, then the subject may suffer from psychosis. In order to escape the all-powerful imaginary relationship with the mother, and to enable the constitution of the subject, it is essential to have acquired the 'name-of-the-father'. This is a structure which lays down the basis of the subject's 'law', in particular the law of the language system. And I should add that in terms of Lacan's three orders, name-of-the-father refers not to the real father, nor to the imaginary father, but to the symbolic father.

Lacan states, echoing Freud, that in studying psychosis the problem lies not in the reality that is lost, but in that which takes its place. He emphasises the rent or gap (*béance*) that appears in the relation of the psychotic subject to the world, and the nature of the 'patch' which the psychotic subject applies over this gap. Lacan suggests that when there is a gap in the Symbolic order and the place of the Other is deleted or seriously disordered, a gap opens in the Imaginary order, leading to various imaginary distortions, and also new phenomena in the Real order such as voices (auditory hallucinations). The Real order is the domain that subsists outside symbolisation. It is what is outside the subject; in the case of hallucination, it is what has been expelled or foreclosed by the subject. The altered structure of the psychotic subject coincides with his or her using language in various ways: the symbolic moorings of speech may be dislocated and s/he may speak in a round-about, fragmented, confused or in an excessively stylised way.

Lacan's concept of foreclosure (*Verwerfung* in German, *forclusion* in French) is held to be the origin of psychotic phenomena. Lacan points out that Freud used the word *Verwerfung* to mean a rejection of something as if it did not exist, which is quite different from a repression. There is an important distinction between foreclosure and repression. Where foreclosure seeks to expel a given notion, thought, memory or signifier from the unconscious, repression seeks to confine it there. Repression belongs to the ordinary functioning of the mind and in certain conditions may produce disabling neurotic effects; foreclosure, however, is a violent refusal of symbolisation and its effects are catastrophic. It is an operation that gives psychosis a structure distinct from that of neurosis. Psychosis is a disastrous disturbance in the symbolic order.

The difference between neurotic repression and psychotic foreclosure has been summarised in this way:

> If we imagine common experience to be like a tissue, literally a piece of material made up of criss-crossing threads, we could say repression would figure in it as a rent or tear, which none the less could still be repaired; while foreclosure would figure in it as a gap due to the

weaving itself, a primal hole which would never again be able to find its substance since it would never have been anything other than the substance of a hole, and could only be filled, and even then imperfectly, by a patch, to use Freud's term.[10]

From Lacan's comments on Judge Schreber's illness it is clear that psychosis involves 'the foreclosure of the name-of-the-father in the place of the Other and . . . the failure of the paternal metaphor'.[11] For psychosis to be triggered off, the name-of-the-father has to be foreclosed. With foreclosure of the name-of-the-father, and an absence of the representation of the subject by the phallic image, the relation between the Imaginary, Symbolic and Real orders is put out of alignment. As Bice Benvenuto has said, the study of psychosis sheds light on the nature of human reality, which in Lacan's opinion is a function of interactions between the Real, Imaginary and Symbolic orders.[12]

Jameson's view of the three orders

Some insightful points about these orders and their relation to society have been made by the leading American critic, Fredric Jameson. I will give a brief précis of his article, 'Imaginary and symbolic in Lacan', because it is of great interest: apart from summarising the topic, it emphasises the similarities between psychoanalytic and Marxist approaches.

Jameson has argued that orthodox Freudianism has tended to remain locked within the categories of the individual and individual experience. In his view there is need for a model which is not locked into the classical opposition between the individual and the collective, but is rather able to think these discontinuities in a radically different way. He thinks that Lacan's conception of the three orders, the Imaginary, the Symbolic and the Real, may provide a useful model.[13]

The Imaginary order, a kind of pre-verbal register whose logic is essentially visual, is a stage in the development of the psyche. Its moment of formation has been named the 'mirror phase' by Lacan. It occurs between six and eighteen months, when the child demonstrably 'recognises' his or her image in the mirror. It marks a fundamental gap between the subject and its own self or imago which can never be bridged. It is from Melanie Klein's pioneering psychoanalysis of children that the basic features of the Lacanian Imaginary are drawn.[14] The mirror phase, which is the precondition for primary narcissism, is also, owing to the equally irreducible gap it opens between the infant and its fellows, the very source of human aggressivity. One of the original features of Lacan's early teaching is its insistence on the inextricable association of these two drives: narcissism and aggressivity. This phase, then, is already an alienation, the subject having been captivated by his or her specular image.

The next phase of psychic development is the Symbolic order. Why did Lacan emphasise the function of language? The linguistic materials are not intended to be substituted for the sexual ones; rather we must understand the Lacanian notion of the Symbolic order as an attempt to create mediations between libidinal analyses and the linguistic categories, to provide, in other words, a transcoding scheme which allows us to speak of both within a common conceptual framework. The Oedipus complex, for example, is transliterated by Lacan into a linguistic phenomenon which he designates as the discovery by the subject of the name-of-the-father. (This refers to the father's role as the possessor of the mother and the place of the Law.) The accession of the child to speech and the Symbolic is accompanied by an increase, rather than a lessening, of anxiety. The Symbolic order is a further alienation of the subject; the alienating function of language is arrested by the palpable impossibility of returning to an archaic, pre-verbal stage of the psyche itself.

Jameson reminds us that Lacan stresses the naming function of language. The acquisition of a name results in a thoroughgoing transformation of the position of the subject: 'If we must define that moment in which man [*sic*] becomes human, we would say that it is at that instant when, as minimally as you like, he enters into a symbolic relationship.' Second, we should bear in mind the significance of the bar which divides signifier from signified in the semiotic fraction: the pronoun, the first person, results in a division of the subject which drives the 'real subject' as it were underground, and leaves a 'representative' – the ego – in its place.

Third, Lacan's belief in the determination of the subject by language results in a rewriting of the classical Freudian Unconscious in terms of language: 'the Unconscious is the discourse of the Other'.[15] The Unconscious is the 'treasure house of the signifier'.

Fourth, there is a relationship between language and sexuality. Lacan makes a distinction between need, which is a biological phenomenon, and demand, an interpersonal phenomenon, conceivable only after the emergence of language. And then there is Desire. With *'plaisir'* there is a momentary reduction of a purely physical tension, but this is not the case with desire. Desire can never be fulfilled.

But what is the 'Real'? The Real is what resists symbolisation absolutely. Jameson writes, 'Nevertheless, it is not terribly difficult to say what is meant by the Real in Lacan. It is simply History itself.'[16] In Jameson's view both psychoanalysis and Marxism depend fundamentally on history, in its sense as story and storytelling. To say that psychoanalysis and Marxism are materialisms is simply to assert that each reveals an area in which human consciousness is not 'master in its own house': only the areas decentred by each are the quite different ones of sexuality and of the class dynamics of social history.

Jameson believes that psychoanalysis and Marxism, each one essentially a hermeneutic (the art, or theory of interpretation, of understanding the significance of human actions, utterances, products and institutions), have much to teach each other in the way of method. Marxism and psychoanalysis indeed present a number of striking analogies of structure with each other, as a checklist of their major themes can testify: the relation of theory and practice; the relation of 'false consciousness' and the problem as to its opposite; the role and risks of the concept of a 'midwife' of truth, whether analyst or vanguard party; the question of desire and value and of the nature of 'false desire' and so forth. Jameson can see that, in Marxism as well as in psychoanalysis, there is a problem – even a crisis – of the subject. He is concerned about the subject and the status it ought to have in Marxism today, and is sympathetic to the Lacanian view of the decentred subject.

Models and mathemes

I turn now to the models and mathemes that were Lacan's concern during the last decade of his life. It is significant that in his early work Lacan often selected visual images to express the operation of the psyche; he used, for example, figures such as anamorphosis and the Gordian knot.[17] In the last ten years of his life Lacan increasingly began to use number theory, topology, logic, and there are references to mathemes, to quantum physics and so on. Why is this?

I think that it can be shown that Lacan used geometrical models of every kind throughout his life. The earliest were zig-zag models that looked like large Zs. Then there were what mathematicians call Klein bottles. There were also the famous Möbius strips.[18] And, finally, there was the period of the Borromean knots. It should be noted that the earlier representations, lines, arrows, symbols, gave way to three-dimensional models. Lacan's mathematical objects gave him the means to represent forms without boundaries or simple separations. He wanted to show that the unconscious is a structure with neither an outside nor an inside. Lacan argued that many people's thinking is based on the concept of an enclosed space, for example, a sphere. People use that space to make a primary differentiation between what is inside and what is outside. People even divide things up into an inner world and an outer reality. Lacan believed that, generally speaking, psychoanalytic theory is stuck in this spherical way of conceptualising things. People are always being advised to integrate things or parts of the self, as in: 'Pull yourself together!'

Lacan thought that the Euclidian geometry of planes, lines, solids and spheres had ignored a crucial element, the ring, which is the most elementary form of knot. Once the base structure is the ring instead of the sphere, things change. A ring is not a container. Any point in the centre of the ring (by which I mean not a circle but a three-dimensional object) can be considered to be either inside or outside the ring. With the ring the dualism of inside/outside loses its force. But if the containing capacity of the sphere is eliminated, what makes things hold together psychically? His answer was that the elements of mental life are organised according to the structure of the chain or knot.

Lacan used the concept or image of the knot quite frequently. In the mid-1970s he tried to theorise the interrelation of the Symbolic, the Imaginary and the Real in terms of the topology of knots. In his view these orders are tied together in the form of a 'Borromean knot'. (He introduced the idea in 1975.) The

Borromean knot is a linkage of three 'string rings' in such a way that no two rings intersect.[19] The structure of the knot is such that the cutting of any one ring will liberate all of the others. Lacan used the theory of knots to stress the relations which bind or link the Imaginary, Symbolic and Real, and the subject to each, in a way which avoids any notion of hierarchy, or any priority of any one of the three terms. The emphasis is on the intricate and inextricable nature of the ties which make the subject both subject *of* and *to* the unconscious.

Beginning in 1973, Lacan took a new interest in teaching psychoanalysis in the university as his conviction grew that the future of psychoanalysis lay in its formalisation into mathematical statements (mathemes). When Lacan talks about the possibility of mathemes, he is suggesting that there is a psychoanalytic science that is deeply rooted in other scientific disciplines and that they can be formalised and transmitted apart from going through the process of a personal analysis. In short, Lacan's general position is that psychoanalytic research *can* be the province of the non-analyst.

In 1974 Lacan seemed to decide that the intellectual home for psychoanalysis had to be the university. Mathematicians, philosophers, linguists began to take a larger and larger part in the Lacanian programme at the University of Paris at Vincennes. The Vincennes Department of Psychoanalysis was renamed 'Le Champ Freudien'. The department was refounded on new principles that stressed the psychoanalytic matheme and the necessity for research.

Lacan's stated ideal is not to mathematise the whole of his work or to provide a formal mapping of the entire analytic process, but simply to isolate a 'mathematisable minimum'. The theory of mathematical formalisation is probably derived from the contemporary French philosophy of science, with its stress on rationalist epistemology. Lacan came to believe that mathematics, with its purification of discourse through the gradual expulsion of the Real and its formalisation, was the most appropriate form for scientific discourse. Formulae obviate the need for long, discursive expositions. After all, everything that has been produced as science is non-verbal.

Lacan's use of mathematics has long been controversial, and some people believe that mathemes and references to mathematisation are only illustrative and metaphorical. Many of the graphs and formulae are no more than mnemonics with a fairly basic pedagogic purpose. They provide no more than a restatement of a point which can be made verbally and introduce no real formalisation or abstraction. They are really devices for thinking.

On the other hand, some people argue against the above view; they assert that there is a parallelism between the structure of mathematics and the structure of psychopathology. Mathematics can shed light on psychopathology. The mind can be explained by mathematics. For example there is the fascinating case of Georg Cantor, the mathematician who was responsible for the development of modern set theory. He was a manic depressive and some theorists claim that his theory of sets was influenced by his unconscious and that there is an homology between his mathematics and his mental state. In other words, Cantor's delusional problems had elements in common with his work on set theory.

Is Lacan's idea of the matheme to be interpreted literally or metaphorically? Jacques-Alain Miller takes the literal point of view. He sees the mathemes as equational and describes them by analogy to a book on symbolic logic. In such a book some things do not need translation because they stay constant in all languages; these latter, claims Miller, are analogous to the mathemes. For Miller, without the mathemes psychoanalysis would only be able to form a society of initiates guarding a secret. In his view, if there are no mathemes, the fundamentals of psychoanalysis will remain ineffable.

On the other hand, Serge Leclaire has declared that the psychoanalytic act is an affair of speech, and in relation to this speech, the mathemes, important though they might be, are best seen as 'graffiti'. They are traces, testimonies, but still *written* expressions of an essentially *verbal* act of rage, or passion, or pain, or pleasure.[20]

There are also some analysts who are sympathetic to the mathemes taken as a metaphor for new and higher aspirations for their discipline. François Roustang, for example, believes that a high gulf separates what Lacan means by the mathemes from what his disciples have understood him to mean. Miller and his circle see mathemes as formulae that need to be discovered. When and if they are discovered, psychoanalysis will become scientific. Lacan, on the other hand, first posed the problem of the matheme as a

question: is a psychoanalytic matheme possible? Roustang argues
that all such interrogatives are necessary in order to situate, define
and elaborate psychoanalysis in relation to science.

One of the main problems with mathemes is that though analysts make mathematical symbols, they cannot get anything from
them because, in contrast to the use of such symbols in physics or
even in economics, they are not using them to reach mathematical
conclusions.

I must admit I am often puzzled by Lacan's graphs, mathematical devices and equations. Why did he use them? Were 'mathemes'
an attempt to mathematise the subject? Why did he want to formulate analytical experience as a structure? Was he influenced by
Lévi-Strauss's view that without formalisation there is no theory?
Was he a poet who wanted to be a mathematician? Or, is it possible
that these strings, knots and little letters were attempts to defend
himself against his own poetic language?[21] Sometimes it seems
that Lacan wants to be a poet; at other times, he wants to capture
some aspect of the mind through mathematisation, what he calls a
'mathematisable minimum', but he is not willing to filter out the
rest, even temporally.

It is clear that Lacan is struggling to articulate a new way of
thinking about the interrelationship among psychoanalysis, mathematics, science and poetry. Perhaps the mathematisation of
psychoanalysis will never really be complete, but its presence as an
aspiration is used to keep psychoanalysis working in a positive
relation to science. It could be said that in trying to place Lacan on
one side or another of the line that divides science from poetry, the
line itself comes into question. I agree with Sherry Turkle's view
that Lacan seems to assert the need for equational science among
those who he feels use poetic justifications to avoid the hard and
vigorous work ahead and asserts the need for poetry among others
who may be allowing scientific rigour to narrow their field of
vision.[22]

Some criticisms of Lacan

I wish now to outline a few points on which a critique of Lacan
might focus. First of all, his writing style – Lacan's attempt to
impede the facile transmission of his ideas often appears as a

calculated effort to be unreadable. It could be said that Lacan's style disallows any distinction between descriptive and prescriptive writing. As we read Lacan, we can feel his arguments being traversed by unargued personal predilections. For example, one of his tendencies (rather like the Engels of *Anti-Duhring*) is to see true freedom as residing in the recognition of necessity.[23]

The work of Lacan places emphasis on the priority of the text, or what he calls the 'primacy of the symbolic'. But, as we have seen, the symbolic is merely one of three orders, to be set alongside the imaginary and the real. This means that he cannot be regarded in any sense a linguistic idealist. Nevertheless, Lacan attributes talismanic power to the word; he seems to suggest that the pact of speech alone can put an end to the oscillating antagonism of the relation between ego and other.[24]

Lacan's main focus is consistently on the abstract otherness of an impersonal symbolic order; he pays little attention to concrete others, that is individuals exchanging reactions and emotions. Richard Wollheim has remarked that Lacanian theory has no room for individual experience, and is accordingly very poor, by Freudian standards, in case histories.[25]

Many people agree that Lacan 'Saussureanised' psychoanalysis by decreeing that the unconscious is structured like a language. But Emile Benveniste has argued that there are many important *differences* between the unconscious and language. First, unlike the unconscious, language is something that is learned. Second, whereas the linguistic sign is essentially 'arbitrary', that is unmotivated, Freudian 'symbols' are by definition deeply motivated. Third, the unconscious is one and universal – its dreams and neuroses are made up of a vocabulary common to every individual in all cultures – while language, precisely as system, is articulated into several different natural languages.[26]

It has been suggested by J.G. Merquior that Lacan's celebrated dictum was a prop in a bold move to get rid of the positivism and the biologism of classical Freudian thought. Lacan's 'return to Freud' was, perhaps, an attempt to break with the outmoded epistemologies of the nineteenth century.[27]

I mentioned (in Chapter 4 on language) that Lacan favours metaphor. Metaphor is more apparent than metonymy, so it is given greater consideration. Luce Irigaray, in an article called 'The mechanics of fluids', is critical of the privilege of metaphor (quasi-

solid) over metonymy (which has much to do with fluids). She
complains that science has studied solids and neglected fluids. She
then links this to the neglect of feminine sexuality in psychoanalysis, by means of assertions that the feminine is fluid. Irigaray
connects the privilege of metaphor over metonymy with the
phallocentric neglect of femininity. I mention this because her
article is a critique of Lacan, whom she accuses of neglecting
fluids, and thus women, in favour of the solidity of the phallus.[28]

Lacan is frequently accused of phallocentrism, an accusation
easy to level at a theorist who proclaims that the phallus is the
privileged signifier. For example, one of Luce Irigaray's criticisms
of Lacan is that psychoanalysis remains trapped in phallocentrism,
from which it claims to construct universal and eternal values.
Against Lacan's idea of the phallus as privileged signifier, the
constant and final meaning of symbolic exchange, for men and for
women, Irigaray claims the female body as the site of an alternative
symbolic. She stresses the multiplicity of female desires and argues
for an alternative female unconscious. (I will be considering
Irigaray's work in the next chapter.) Lacan's defenders do not
deny the privilege of the phallus in his system, but they argue that
his attackers misunderstand the meaning of the term. Feminists
influenced by Lacan argue that both sexes can take up the masculine and feminine places; these shift and slide – no one has the
phallus.

Lacan asserts that culture is always patriarchal, that it is in the
exchange structures described by Lévi-Strauss that the essential
order of the Symbolic can be found. The law of the Father is seen
as being identical with the law of language. Lacan's theory implies
that the array of meanings available to each person are fixed by the
cultural order, that each person's desire is structured in accordance
with an overarching, symbolic presence. The determinism here is
striking: the individual subject is reduced to a cipher apparently
produced entirely by outside forces. Moreover, Lacan suggests
that the law of the Father is to be identified with culture, *per se*,
that is that all cultures are patriarchal. This idea is at odds with the
notion of the arbitrariness of the organisation of desire: if meanings are always fixed in the same way, always patriarchal, then
some thing must be determining this fixity.[29]

Many writers have pointed out the closeness with which Lacan
follows Lévi-Strauss's account of the social as constituted by

relations of communication and symbolic exchange. It is well known that Lévi-Strauss's analysis of primitive societies leaves relations of power and domination almost entirely out of account. Peter Dews has said that in Lacan's adaptation of Lévi-Strauss there is a neglect of the possibility of systems of meaning promoting or masking relations of force. Moreover, in his fusion of the Lévi-Straussian concept of exchange with the Hegelian dialectic of recognition, Lacan neglects the view of both Hegel and Kojève, that this dialectic is intertwined with that of labour and struggle.[30]

Peter Dews believes that Lacan's theoretical reconstruction of psychoanalysis lacks the potential for a critique of modern society and culture which was built into Freud's original model. Lacan's interpretation of psychoanalysis returns it to a historical and political vacuum. And so it is not surprising that during the early 1970s, in the wake of the political upheavals of the late 1960s, new conceptions of the unconscious arose in France (Lyotard, Deleuze and Guattari) which stress the heterogeneity of desire and language, and emphasise the capacity of desire to dislocate and disrupt symbolic and social order.[31] Against some of these criticisms it could be argued that Lacan's ideas have been put to work. There are many independent-minded followers, such as Jean Laplanche, J.B. Pontalis, Serge Leclaire, Maud and Octave Mannoni, who have extended and refashioned Lacan's concepts (without attempting to imitate his literary manner). It is clear from their work that Lacan is the originator of a coherent and continuing tradition of psychoanalytic enquiry.

So far I have provided a general introduction to the work of Lacan, and a few criticisms of it. To show the importance and wide application of his thought to other fields, I would now like to discuss, in the chapters that follow, his work in relation to three discourses: feminism, film studies and literature.

| *Sexuality, love and
feminism*

The Oedipus and castration complexes

Before I consider feminism and Lacanian psychoanalysis, I think it would be useful to focus on Freud's view of the Oedipus and castration complexes and on Lacan's linguistic reinterpretation of them. This is followed by a discussion on feminine sexuality, romantic love and the phantasy of oneness. Finally, there is a consideration of post-Lacanian French feminism and there is a brief exposition of the key ideas of Cixous, Irigaray and Kristeva.

Let us begin with the question of sexual difference. According to Freud the little boy and the little girl initially share the same sexual history, which he terms 'masculine'. They start by desiring their first object. In phantasy this means having the phallus which is the object of the mother's desire (the phallic phase). This position is forbidden (the castration complex) and the differentiation of the sexes occurs. The castration complex ends the boy's Oedipus complex (his love for his mother) and inaugurates for the girl the one that is specifically hers. She will transfer her object love to her father who seems to have the phallus and identify with her mother who, to the girl's fury, has not. Henceforth the girl will desire to have the phallus and the boy will desire to represent it.[1]

In Freud's early work (1890s to about 1919) the particular ways in which the Oedipus complex appears and is resolved characterise different types of normality and pathology. In this early work the Oedipus complex is a simple set of relationships in which the child desires the parent of the opposite sex and feels hostile rivalry for the one of the same sex as itself. Freud assumed that there was a natural and normative heterosexual attraction.

But running counter to this view there is the argument of the *Three Essays on the Theory of Sexuality* (1905).[2] This is the revolutionary work in which Freud argues that for the sexual drive there is no natural, automatic object; it has no fixed aim. The sexual drive is polymorphous; its aim is variable, its object contingent. This argument eroded any idea of normative sexuality. If no heterosexual attraction is ordained in nature there can be no genderised sex; there cannot at the outset be a male or female person in a psychological sense. In short, Freud's position during this first period is contradictory: his discovery of the Oedipus complex led him to assume a natural heterosexuality. On the other hand, the rest of his work argued against this possibility.

According to Freud, the peak period for the experience of the Oedipus complex is about three to five years of age. The complex has positive and negative versions. In the so-called 'positive' Oedipus complex the child desires the death of its rival, the parent of the same sex, while harbouring sexual desires for the parent of the opposite sex. In the so-called 'negative' Oedipus complex, the child loves the parent of the same sex, and hates the parent of the opposite sex.

By 1924 Freud realised the central importance of the castration complex. Before this complex was given its full significance, it seems that the Oedipus complex dissolved naturally, a passing developmental stage. Once the castration complex is postulated it is this alone that shatters the Oedipus complex. The castration complex institutes the superego as its representative. The Oedipus and castration complexes govern the position of each person in the triangle of father, mother and child.

In Freud's theory it is the father who already possesses the mother, who metaphorically says 'no' to the child's desires. The prohibition only comes to be meaningful to the child because there are females who have been castrated in the sense that they are without the phallus. It is only through 'deferred action' that previous experiences such as the sight of female genitals become significant.

Freud writes that the boy's castration complex arises from the penis being given significance from the father's prohibition, but he also suggests that, sometimes, the girl's penis-envy comes from a simple perception that she makes: she sees the actual penis, realises that it is bigger and better and wants one. Freud's account, then, is retroactive; fearing phallic castration, the child may 'recollect' previous losses; castration gives them their relevance.

Lacan developed his views on the Oedipus complex, which have a very different emphasis from those of Freud, from the mid-1950s to the early 1960s. Lacan argues that subjectivity and sexuality are socially produced, not the effects of nature or development. The mirror phase initiates a process which culminates in the Oedipus process or paternal metaphor. The child submits to the Law of the Father. The paternal figure serves to separate the child from an all-encompassing relation with the mother. The father intervenes into this imaginary dyad and represents the Law. The Father embodies the power of the phallus and the threat of castration. Accepting his authority and phallic status is the precondition of the child's having a place within the socio-symbolic order, a name and a speaking position. The phallus is the pivotal term around which the social production of both sexes is oriented. The phallus subjects both sexes to the Symbolic.

In connection with the Oedipus complex Lacan often uses the term 'paternal metaphor'. This refers to the prohibition of the father. The father stands for a place and a function which is not reducible to the presence or absence of the real father as such. In other words, an Oedipus complex can be constituted perfectly well even if the father is not there. Lacan argues that in order to escape the all-powerful, imaginary relationship with the mother, and to enable the constitution of the subject, it is essential to have acquired what he calls the 'name-of-the-father'. The father introduces the principle of law, in particular the law of the language system. As I pointed out in the last chapter, when this law breaks down, or if it has never been acquired, then the subject may suffer from psychosis.[3]

One of the reasons why Lacan's work is valuable is that he has described the mechanisms by which gender becomes organised under patriarchy. Two aspects of this have generated a great deal of interest (and abuse) among feminists: the castration complex and the use of the phallus as the signifier of desire.

As I have mentioned earlier, subjectivity, for Lacan, arises only through experiences of lack and absence; the human subject is created in the context of division, the principal one being that of castration. Castration operates retrospectively by giving meaning to all other experiences of division and separation. Lacan's interpretation of the Freudian idea of the phallus is also important, for it centres on a view of its symbolic function as the creator and sustainer of difference based on a power that is itself illusory.

Let me make this clearer. The phallus is *not* the penis; the former is not physical but symbolic. At the time of the castration complex the phallus subjugates both boys and girls; to the boys it holds out the hope that accession to its power may become possible. But the castration complex also solidifies an awareness of lack for both girls (an awareness of an absence which results in penis-envy) and boys (the discovery of the impossibility of Oedipal union with the mother). All sexuality is created in this lack, leaving male and female as partial beings full of desire. Because sexuality as division is incomplete, the phallus comes to represent that which stands outside it, that which is whole and which can repair the damage produced by castration and instituted by the Law of the Father.

The imagined phallus of the Father is introduced as the third term to break up the mother–child relationship and, in doing this, it structures human relationships, it subjugates and marginalises women. It should be remembered, however, that the phallus is not in the possession of any living male. The phallus, in one sense, is material: it implies the dominance of the patriarchal order and the Law of the Father. But, in another sense, it is also illusory.

In some ways the phallus represents the human predicament that desire is always unattainable, it is that which has been lost and never can be found. In fact, Lacan refers to the barring of the Other (O), the notion that the Symbolic order is premised on the recognition of the unattainability of desire. It is an important element in Lacan's theory that no complete unity or Otherness is possible; there is only the search for the Other that reflects and constructs the absences each individual feels inside and which are phantasised as fulfilling the desires that have had to be repressed.

Feminine sexuality

Lacan writes about love, sexual relationships and feminine sexuality in his twentieth seminar *Encore* (1972–3). He argues that there is an ever-increasing demand for love made by the infant to the mother, who in turn tries to satisfy the baby's needs. In the analyst–analysand relationship also, just as in the mother–child relationship, there is an unfulfilled and unutterable demand for love. There is something which language cannot express, but which demands recognition.

Lacan suggests that the object of psychoanalysis is not sexuality itself, but its effects and the problem it constitutes for the person who speaks (or, to use Lacan's term, the 'speaking being'). After birth the visible world dominates and one can say that sight guarantees the existence of things over what cannot be seen. Thus the visibility of the phallus predominates over the black hole of the female genitals. The woman functions as a part which has to be integrated into a whole; she is 'not all'.

In his early work Lacan's use of the term symbolic relies heavily on Lévi-Strauss's notion of kinship in which women are defined as objects of exchange. In the later work Lacan shifted the emphasis away from the process of exchange (women as objects) to the construction of woman as a category within language (woman as *the* object). Lacan's concepts are continually changing. And I must restate another key concept in Lacan's later work: *'objet a'*. This is his term for the lost object which underpins symbolisation, cause of and 'stand in' for desire. What the man relates to is this object and the 'whole of his realisation in the sexual relation comes down to phantasy'.[4]

I think that Lacan's seminar contains many thought-provoking remarks. Here are a few examples. One: there are no certain, innate and natural characteristics associated with femininity and masculinity. Two: all speaking beings must line themselves on one side or the other of the sexual division, but anyone can cross over and inscribe themselves on the opposite side from that to which they are anatomically destined. Three: as the place on to which lack is projected and through which it is simultaneously disavowed, woman is a 'symptom' for the man.[5] Four: *the* woman can be written only with *the* crossed through. There is no such thing as *the* woman, where the definite article stands for the universal.[6]

Lacan engages in a sharp critique of the universalism espoused by some feminist groups. He thinks that the concept 'woman' had been essentialised and so he put his emphasis on the 'not all' (*pas-toute*) of woman as a universal sexual category. The force of *pas-toute* is not only to militate against the idea that all women, by virtue of a common biology, can be represented by one common term, but also to suggest that references to particular or personal experience cannot be presented as if they were natural and unproblematic reflections of a universal sexual essence.

To put it briefly, Lacan challenges our 'common-sense' notions of knowledge and belief. He often discusses the claim of a subject to know, the claim to know oneself as subject. For Lacan the analysand's unconscious reveals a fragmented subject of shifting and uncertain sexual identity. To be human is to be subjected to a law which decentres and divides: sexuality is created in a division, the subject is split; but an ideological world conceals this from the conscious subject who is supposed to feel whole and certain of sexual identity. Lacan's work contains a trenchant critique of oneness but before we consider that let us ask: what have Freud and Lacan to say about romantic love?

Love: the phantasy of oneness

Freud divides adult love relations into two broad categories; those modelled on 'anaclitic' attachments, and those modelled on narcissistic ones. The anaclitic type includes those who love persons who are concerned with the child's feeding, care and protection (in the first instance, its mother or a substitute for her). The narcissistic type consists in those who are plainly seeking themselves as a love object. Both types, however, find a common origin in the infantile phase of primary narcissism.

Although each position is available to either sex, Freud suggests that there is a tendency for men to occupy the more anaclitic position, and for women to occupy the more feminine, narcissistic position. To recapitulate, anaclisis is an active masculine form, modelled on loving another who resembles the subject's infantile nurturers; the feminine form involves the passive aim of being loved.

Freud argues that the anaclitic lover tends to overevaluate the love object. The type conforms most readily to the stereotyped image of romantic love, a love based on putting the love object on a pedestal and abjecting the self. It is often the case that a lover transfers narcissistic self-regard on to the love object and is thus able to love himself, as it were, in loving the other.

For the narcissistic woman, the strength of the other's love for her is the measure of her own value and worth. Moreover, in loving her child, she is both loving herself (a biological extension of herself) and another who is like her. She extends her self-love through maternal love. Such a woman needs subjects to affirm her, and her lovers are a testimony of her value.

According to Lacan, it is only by means of the other that one's possession of, or identity with, the phallus can be confirmed. Through a man, a woman can become the phallus (his object of desire); through sexual relations with a woman, a man can be affirmed as having a phallus. However, this ideal, like demand itself, is impossible. The demands of each make the satisfaction both seek impossible. Lacan suggests that love consists in a series of (non-symmetrical) demands for the proof of the other's commitment. The proofs sought from the other are impossible, imaginary, tests of love.

In a sense, a woman never receives the affirmation of her subjectivity she desires. At best, the man's desire for her affirms her as a sexual being but not as a unique specific subject. In the sexual act, for example, she finds her demand for affirmation frustrated, she is homogenised to the category of passive object.

The man also finds his expression of romantic love frustrated. Sexual intercourse is both the affirmation of his possession of the phallus and a reminder of the possibility of castration. In the process of 'taking' the woman the man is reminded of her lack. He is thus reminded of the possibility of his own. (It is, of course, a residue of the castration threat that lies behind the paranoid phantasy of the sexually insatiable woman who exhausts men and depletes them of their sexual powers.)

The man proclaims his love for the woman, but when she takes him as her sexual object his desire is reduced to the sexual performance, and thus the phallus is reduced to the penis. In this sense, he cannot satisfy the woman's desire. The woman desires the phallus but she receives the penis. In her sexual relations with him, she loses her place as desirable subject in order to become sexual object. The aims of neither are satisfied.

Why is this? Love relations involve an unresolved tension between demand and desire. When the woman functions in the register of demand, it is to the man, his capacity to reflect her and give her identity, that her demands are addressed. But when she functions in the register of desire, she desires (to be) the phallus. This entails that she be treated as a sexual object by the other, undermining her demand for recognition as a subject. Women are left with a disjunctive choice: either demand or desire, either narcissistic affirmation of the ego, or affirmation as a sexual being, either love or sex.

A woman can be a man's object of desire in so far as she 'veils' the 'mysteries' for which he searches, only, that is, in so far as her 'lack' is veiled or hidden. If the man's conquest is successful, its mystery vanishes and the object loses its fascination. The nearer satisfaction comes, the more impossible is its attainment. The imaginary vacillation between a yearning for, and fear of, incorporation by the other provides the structural framework within which his phantasies and practices are developed. He is enticed by his own narcissistic phantasies of wholeness and perfection.

Even if a man distinguishes two types of women, one, an alter ego he respects but who holds no mystery for him, the other a phallus, object of fascination and desire, the latter collapses into the former after a period of close familiarity. His sexual partner becomes more an object of affection than of desire after sustained intimacy. Then his desire diverges to another woman, and the cycle starts again.

I said earlier that Lacan's work contains a trenchant critique of oneness. He says that the principles of singleness, unity and indivisibility have become an ideology. The sexual relation hangs on a phantasy of oneness which women have come to support. We must 'make one' out of two separate beings (the married couple), 'make one' in the form of a child, 'make one' out of all the potential meanings of a term, 'make one' out of all the diversity of human groups. And so the pleasure in being together becomes duty. The imperative of marriage is: 'two become one'. The imperative of *'faire un'*, of making two into one, rules every aspect of human life. We have all come to believe in phantasied unity. Lacan writes: *'We are as one.* Of course everyone knows that it has never happened for two to make one, but still *we are as one*. That's what the idea of love starts out from . . . the problem then being how on earth there could be love for another.'[7] For Lacan the ideology of oneness and completion closes off the gap of human desire.

Most human subjects hold the view that somewhere there is a point of certainty, of knowledge and of truth. Notions of identity and wholeness remain at the level of phantasy. When the subject addresses its demand outside itself to another, this other becomes the phantasied place of just such a knowledge or certainty. Lacan calls this the Other – the site of language. The Other appears to hold the 'truth' of the subject and the power to make good its loss – but this is a phantasy.

Lacan has made us aware of the instability of language. He argues that sexuality too is unstable; each sex coming to stand, mythically and exclusively, for that which could satisfy and complete the other. Lacan argues that psychoanalysis should not try to produce 'male' and 'female' as complementary entities, sure of each other and of their own identity, but should expose the phantasy on which this notion rests.

The traditional view will be familiar: every man seeks, in a woman he chooses as his sexual partner, a substitute for his mother. A man falls in love with a woman when some feature of her reminds him of his mother. But we should also remember the negative dimension; in phantasy, mother is reduced to a limited set of symbolic features; as soon as an object too close to the Mother appears in the phantasy frame, the desire is suffocated in incestuous claustrophobia. Phantasy is a construction enabling us to seek maternal substitutes, but at the same time a screen shielding us from getting too close to the maternal thing. Phantasy, then, provides the co-ordinates of our desire. It constructs the frame enabling us to desire something. In the phantasy-scene desire is not satisfied or fulfilled but is constituted. In short it is through phantasy that we learn to desire.

It is emphasised by Lacan that 'romantic', passionate love is love in the imaginary order, it is bondage. We all experience this type of love from time to time. He suggests that when one is in love one is really saying: 'I am what is lacking in you, with my devotion to you, with my sacrifice for you, I will fill you out, I will complete you.' The operation of love is therefore double: the subject fills in his own lack by offering himself to the other as the object filling out the lack in the Other.

Every desire, even the apparently purest of desires, is a desire to have oneself recognised by the other, and a desire to impose oneself in some way upon the other. (This is, of course, an aspect of the master–slave story.) But every object of desire is necessarily ephemeral and destined to be supplanted because it is incapable of stopping up the lack inscribed in the subject.

Love, then, is always narcissistic in so far it is a desire for unreachable unity. Sex also implies a lack of unity, and a wish to be whole – but it is impossible to be part of a whole being. For Lacan the phallus is the symbol of external communal power, which forms the basis for the authority of the Symbolic order, in both men and women. But the phallus is also the symbolic and idealised substitute for the missing sexual unity, or oneness.

For Lacan, love is always structured with reference to the phallus. The subject demands a wholeness, unity, and completion which it imagines the other can bestow on it. Lacan is emphatic that this demand for Oneness is a demand for an impossible harmony and complementarity between the sexes. It is impossible, he asserts, because the relation to the other is always mediated by the Other. The Other always intervenes between the subject and the other. There is, therefore, no direct, unmediated relation between the sexes.

One of Lacan's more startling statements in *Encore* is that 'there is no sexual relation'. No sexual relation does not mean no relation to a sex. As I said earlier, Lacan believes that men and women are not complementary to one another. They are not two halves that could be joined in union. There is no sexual relation because there is no one, no two together, man and woman given complementarity. Language constitutes the subject in relation to the Other, not to anyone. We should try and understand that 'the desire of man is the desire of the Other'. Desire passes through, is in relation to the Other, not through or to some 'partner'.

Lacan states his views bluntly: love is like psychosis. As in the saying 'love is madness': 'Love rarely comes true, as each of us knows, and it only lasts for a time. For what is love other than banging one's head against a wall, since there is no sexual relation?'[8]

Lacan traces that phantasy through a sustained critique of courtly, religious and ethical discourse. Courtly love 'is an altogether refined way of making up for the absence of sexual relation by pretending that it is we who put an obstacle to it'.[9] Courtly love is a love of the impossible, a love for the obstacle which forever thwarts love – an elegant way of coming to terms with the absence of sexual relations.

One of Lacan's main concerns in *Encore* is the question of female *jouissance*. *Jouissance* is a notoriously polysemic term in Lacan. It denotes both the possession-enjoyment of rights, privileges or property, and the possession-enjoyment of an object capable of giving pleasure. In popular registers it means 'orgasm', with *jouir* as the equivalent of 'to come'. But *jouir* can antiphrastically (use of a word to imply the exact opposite of its normal meaning) come to refer to the experience of exquisite pain which occasions a momentary loss of consciousness. It can also comprise an element of horror, a highly erotocised death drive that goes far beyond the pleasure principle.

Lacan has made striking use of a sculpture of St Teresa to illustrate his concept of *jouissance*. He refers to this statue by Bernini in Rome as the model for another *jouissance* – the woman as mystic. Here is a well-known passage from St Teresa's writings:

> In his hands I saw a long golden spear and at the end of the iron tip I seemed to see a point of fire. With this he seemed to pierce my heart several times so that it penetrated to my entrails. When he drew it out I thought he was drawing them out with it and he left me completely afire with a great love for God. The pain was so sharp that it made me utter several moans; and so excessive was the sweetness caused me by this intense pain that one can never wish to lose it, nor will one's soul be content with anything less than God. It is not bodily pain, but spiritual, though the body has a share in it – indeed, a great share. So sweet are the colloquies of love which pass between the soul and God that if anyone thinks I am lying I beseech God, in His goodness, to give him the same experience.[10]

Many writers have commented on the tension, which runs through Lacan's writings on feminine sexuality, between his critique of the forms of mystification latent to the category Woman, and the repeated question as to what her 'otherness' might be. This tension is clear in Lacan's comments on St Teresa, whose statue he took as the model for the woman as mystic.

Of religious love Lacan writes:

> The first being of which we are aware is that of our own being, and everything which is for our own good will, by dint of that fact, be *jouissance* of the supreme Being, that is, of God. In short, in loving God it is ourselves we love, and by first loving ourselves – a convenient charity as they say – we render to God the appropriate homage.[11]

Lacan is highly critical of those people (at the end of the last century) who attempted 'to reduce the mystical to questions of fucking'.[12] Mysticism, in his view, is one of the available forms of expression where such 'otherness' in sexuality utters its most forceful complaint: 'The mystical is by no means that which is not political. It is something serious a few people teach us about, and most often women . . . [mystics] sense that there must be a *jouissance* which goes beyond.'[13] Lacan states that the enjoyment of the woman can be compared to the culminating moment of a relationship with God:

> It is as it was for St Teresa – you have only to go to Rome and see Bernini's statue to understand at once that she is, without doubt, in the act of enjoying. And what does she enjoy? It is clear that the essential testimony of mystics consists in saying that they experience it, but do not know anything about it.[14]

Having discussed the Oedipus and castration complexes, the concept of *jouissance* and the phantasy of oneness, the desire for unreachable unity, let us turn, first, to the relationship between psychoanalysis and feminism and, then, to the ideas of some French feminists who are heavily indebted to Lacan's reading of Freud.

Between psychoanalysis and feminism

It is clear that psychoanalysis and feminism have a great deal in common: they are both concerned with female subjectivity and female sexuality. But there are also some differences. The reasons why many feminists are distrustful of psychoanalysis are well known: there is the Freudian dogma of female anatomical inferiority and penis-envy, and the attendant privileging of the male model in the Oedipal drama. And, in Lacanian theory, there is the status of the phallus as privileged signifier as well as the crucial importance accorded to the paternal function in the Symbolic register, with an accompanying disparagement of the Imaginary, the pre-Oedipal, and the maternal.

Obviously, there are some enormously complex issues in this area: the nature of sexual difference, and of difference itself, as well as the status of conscious action ('demand') which is always undermined by unconscious 'desire'.

The main feminist positions have been schematically outlined, in family terms, as debate and struggle between the founding Father(s) and the theoretical daughters.[15] In the first position we encounter Freud (and Lacan). Freud's view is now familiar: all libido is masculine, and the child's first desire is directed towards the mother. When the child discovers her anatomical inferiority, her love for the mother turns to resentment. The girl child then takes her father as love object, in the hope of having a child, preferably a boy, who will compensate and substitute for her missing penis. In this version, the clitoris is an inferior organ, desire is masculine, vaginal sexuality is normal; active, aggressive sexual behaviour on the part of the woman is homosexual, and woman herself is an inferior moral and sexual being. Lacan, it could be said, has created a *linguistic* version of this scenario. His theory gives prominence to the paternal function in initiating the Subject into the Symbolic Order, and considers the phallus to be the privileged signifier of human desire.

One feminist response to the centrality of the male term in the doctrine of the Father(s) has been that of the Father's 'dutiful daughter'. Examples include Jane Gallop, Barbara Johnson, Juliet Mitchell, Jacqueline Rose – they all attempt to defend Freud. They point out Freud's own discomfort with rigid notions of masculine and feminine, and his equation of these terms with the notion of active and passive. These 'dutiful' daughters can be criticised, however, for supporting the notion of the castration complex, and the privileged place of phallus as signifier.

In the debate over female subjectivity besides the Father and the Father's daughter, there is the 'Mother's daughter'. The Mother's daughter rejects the views of the Father (Freud/Lacan) and the Father's daughter. She often repudiates the authority of paternal law altogether by contesting the importance of the paternal function in the Symbolic Order. The Mother's daughter, in a kind of 'affirmative' action, seeks to rehabilitate the pre-Oedipal, the Imaginary, and the maternal. In her revolt against paternal law, the Mother's daughter often models herself on Antigone (see Chapter 5) rather than Oedipus.

Perhaps the best-known proponent of this view is Luce Irigaray. She proposes a new 'fluid' language, free from phallic logic, a m(other) tongue, characterised by openness rather than closure. Rather than repressing difference, the m(other) tongue is by nature heterogeneous, plural, open. Irigaray, Kristeva (in her concept of the semiotic) and Cixous all to some extent participate in this vision of female expression which represents the 'other' of phallic or monologic systems.

French feminism: The responses of Cixous, Irigaray and Kristeva

It is sometimes said that while Anglo-American feminism is characterised by the belief that women are equal, French feminism is about the insistence that women are different, and is a challenge to phallogocentric thinking and patriarchal structures of language. Whereas American feminists of the 1960s had started by vigorously denouncing Freud, the French took it for granted that psychoanalysis could provide an emancipatory theory of the personal. French theory has contributed powerfully to the feminist debate about the nature of women's oppression, the construction of sexual difference and the issue of women's relations to language and writing.[16] In the following brief exposition of some aspects of French feminist theory, I will focus on the work of Hélène Cixous, Luce Irigaray and Julia Kristeva.

One of Hélène Cixous's main concerns is the relation between categories of thought and structures of oppression. She argues that it is the organisation of language, the dual hierarchised oppositions that structure philosophical thought and narrative language, that provide the rationale for, and the means of, the oppression of women. The categories of thought that serve to privilege particular terms and concepts and to repress others include, for example, the following oppositions: Activity/Passivity, Sun/Moon, Culture/Nature, Day/Night, Father/Mother, Head/Emotions, Intelligible/Sensitive, Logos/Pathos.[17] Cixous argues that these binary oppositions are inextricably involved in the patriarchal value system. Each opposition can be analysed as a hierarchy where the feminine side is always seen as the negative, powerless instance. In the struggle for signifying supremacy, victory is always equated with activity (male) and defeat with passivity (female). She denounces the equation of femininity with passivity and death as leaving no positive space for woman. Her criticism is really of a system of thought that seeks to repress difference. Cixous examines the operation of this murderous system, as the support of both colonialism and patriarchy.

For Cixous woman is a cultural construct: a category with definable attributes, which have been massively reinforced by myth, legend and literature. On the basis of a close reading of Greek,

Shakespearean and contemporary literature, she argues that woman has been consistently relegated to the margins of narrative and history. Her concentration on fiction is a response to the power of legend and myth to structure our categories of thought, to offer us models of social and sexual relations. Cixous wants to challenge the forms of *representation* that serve to produce, and to legitimate, power relations.

The 'feminine' is used by Cixous to refer to forms of writing, and of thought that exceed the binary oppositions which have structured Western thought and supported patriarchy. The 'feminine' is what Cixous describes as excessive, as disruptive. The feminine is that which has been 'repressed', which returns as disruption through the mechanisms of the unconscious.

Cixous believes that writing should subvert the accepted conventions of narrative, should steal fragments of discourse and put them to scandalous use. She advocates a writing that reproduces the pleasure of song, reintroduces the materiality of the voice, and re-explores the body.[18] In 'writing the body' women must explore the possibility of new images, new ways of representing sexuality and materiality. She greatly admires Clarice Lispector, a left-wing Brazilian, modernist writer, who uses language in non-coercive, non-categorical, and therefore emancipatory ways.

It is, of course, women that have most interest in the deconstruction of the dual hierarchised oppositions that structure language and thought. In her most recent work, her plays, Cixous is concerned with the construction of new sorts of identity which cut across the oppositions. This move, from painful marginality to new sorts of unity which respect the facts of difference, is represented as possible, but is infinitely fragile. In her view theatre is uniquely placed to construct such identities, which do not repeat the dominant, the hierarchical system of difference. Theatre offers recognition and new identification, an inter-subjectivity that is elsewhere impossible.[19]

Some post-Lacanian feminists, like Cixous and Irigaray, have tried to express a vision of an alternative female order. These theorists often conceptualise the female body in a new way; they believe that the rhythms and sensations of femininity present a subversive alternative to the dominance of the name-of-the-father. They argue that patriarchy is associated with an insistence on the dominance of the phallus, on a 'oneness', one way of speaking, one mode of sexuality. In contrast, female opposition is expressed in the form of heterogeneity, multiple meanings, multiple sexuality. Among these feminist writers there is a profound interest in women's relationship to language. In opposition to Lacan, claims are made for the existence of a women's language, suppressed under patriarchy.

Some of the more common arguments for an *écriture feminine* are: first, the woman is more naturally a writer because she is close to the mother-tongue, close to creation. Second, the woman is close to the body. A woman does not write like a man, because she speaks with the body; writing is of the body.

Cixous contends that feminine texts are texts that attempt to split open the closure of the binary opposition, undermine the dominant phallogocentric opposition, and revel in the pleasures of feminine writing.[20] She passionately believes in *écriture feminine*, but denies the possibility of ever defining it. Cixous's work contains a lyrical, euphoric evocation of the essential bond between feminine writing and the mother as source and origin of the voice to be heard in female texts. In these texts the emphasis is on *the voice* as against the look. She believes that all feminist texts are close to the voice. The mother's voice, her breast, milk, honey and female waters are all involved as parts of an eternally present space surrounding her and her readers. It is not, apparently, the empirical sex of the author that matters, but the kind of writing. We must not confuse the sex of the author with the 'sex' of the writing he or she produces. Cixous believes that, in France, only Colette, Marguerite Duras, and Jean Genet really qualify as feminine writers.

I will now turn to Irigaray and Kristeva, two practising psychoanalysts who share Lacan's broad anti-humanism, his commitment to the primacy of language in psychical life, and his understanding of the necessarily sexualised position assumed by the subject in the Symbolic.

Luce Irigaray has made a detailed study of Freud's views on femininity. Her doctoral thesis, *Speculum of the Other Woman*, (a speculum is an instrument with a concave mirror gynaecologists use to inspect the 'cavities' of the female body) led to her immediate expulsion from Lacan's *Ecole Freudienne*.[21]

Luce Irigaray argues that there are many representations of mother/son relationships but that mother/daughter are unsymbolised, that is to say, there is an absence of linguistic, social, cultural representations of that relationship. Unsymbolised mother/daughter relationships hinder women from having an identity in the symbolic order (that is distinct from the maternal function). Women, in the absence of symbolisation (being outside the symbolic order), are in a state of dereliction, of being abandoned. And so the practical question for feminism, as Irigaray sees it, is how to construct a female sociality, a female symbolic, and a female social contract: a horizontal relation between women so that women are no longer left in the state of dereliction.

As women do not have access to culture and society, they are prey to the interminable rivalry between themselves; they often become agents of their own oppression. Hate, envy or rivalry might be both operative and inescapable in relations between women because a way of negotiating them symbolically is not available. In short, women suffer from 'drives without any possible representatives or representations', which is another way of saying that the relation between mother and daughter is unsymbolised.

This brings us to the question of individuation. It is said that at an unconscious level women often do not separate sufficiently from their mother; their identity never becomes distinct from that of their mother, and they remain in a state of fusion in which it is impossible for them to distinguish between their own feelings and those of their mother.[22] Now, Irigaray accepts the clinical view that women have difficulty in separating from their mothers, that they tend to form relationships in which identity is merged, and in which the boundaries between self and other are not clear. Irigaray argues that the clinical picture also applies to Western metaphysics; in metaphysics, too, women are not individuated: there is only the place of the mother, or the maternal function.

Irigaray goes on to suggest that Freud's thought is governed by the terms of classical philosophy, what Derrida refers to as the metaphysics of presence. Western representation privileges seeing; what you can see (presence) is privileged over what cannot be seen (absence) and guarantees Being, hence the privilege of the penis which is elevated to a phallus: '*Nothing to be seen is equivalent to having no thing. No being and no truth.*'[23]

Irigaray argues that the Freudian theory of sexual difference is based on the visibility of difference; it is the eye that decides what is clearly true and what is not. Thus the basic fact of sexual difference for Freud is that the male has an obvious sex organ, the penis, and the female has not; when he looks at the woman, Freud apparently sees nothing. The female difference is perceived as an absence or negation of the male norm.

Freud's argument is familiar: there is no sexual difference in the pre-Oedipal stage; through the oral, anal and phallic phases the little girl is no different from the little boy. It is at the moment of Oedipal crisis that the crucial change in the little girl's orientation occurs: whereas the little boy continues to take his mother as his object, the little girl has to turn from her pre-Oedipal attachment to the mother and take her father as love object instead. This shift is difficult to accomplish; in fact Freud doubted whether most women really manage wholly to relinquish their pre-Oedipal attachment and develop a fully 'mature' femininity.

Irigaray believes that Freud was forced into this incoherent and misogynist theory of femininity by his unwitting subservience to the misogynist rules of the Western philosophical tradition. To hold that the woman first sees her clitoris as a small penis and then decides that she has already been castrated, can be read as a projection of the male fear of castration. As long as the woman is thought to envy the man's penis, he can rest secure in the knowledge that he must have it after all. In other words, the function of female penis-envy is to bolster up the male psyche. Woman is man's Other: his negative or mirror image. This is why Irigaray claims that patriarchal discourse situates woman outside representation: she is absence, negativity, the dark continent.

Irigaray makes some interesting remarks on the importance of the look, or gaze, in Freudian theory. Freud's own texts, particularly 'The uncanny' theorise the gaze as a phallic activity linked to the anal desire for sadistic mastery of the object.[24] His argument is that the gaze enacts the voyeur's desire for sadistic power in which the object of the gaze is cast as its passive, masochistic feminine victim. As long as the master's scopophilia ('love of looking') remains satisfied, his domination is secure.

Irigaray is also noted for her exaltation of mysticism. Her argument is this: the mystical experience is an experience of the loss of subjecthood, of the disappearance of the subject–object opposition. Mysticism holds a particular appeal to women whose subjectivity is being denied and repressed by patriarchal discourse. Though not all mystics were women, mysticism, nevertheless, seems to have been the one area of high spiritual endeavour under patriarchy where women could and did excel more frequently than men. Irigaray is not claiming that all women are mystics at heart, but rather that under patriarchy, mysticism offers women a real, if limited, possibility of discovering some aspects of pleasure.

Male pleasure, she claims, is seen as monolithically unified, represented as analogous with the phallus, and it is this mode that is forcibly imposed upon women. Woman's sex, however, is not one; her sexual organs are composed of many different elements (lips, vagina, clitoris, cervix, uterus, breasts) and her *jouissance* is therefore multiple, non-unified, endless. She finds pleasure more in touch than in sight. According to Irigaray, the 'otherness' of woman resides in her inconstancy, her multiplicity and flux, which functions subversively to undermine masculine attempts at control.

Irigaray believes that the subject of science is male, meaning that male language, the epistemology of the sciences, knowledge which leads to control, mastery and domination, are all subtended by the male imaginary, whatever the actual sex of the knower. Female language on the other hand, like the language of the psychoanalyst, should be language which has an effect: a language that reintroduces the values of desire, pain, joy and the body.

Irigaray's project has been thoughtfully summarised in this way:

In psychoanalysing the philosophers, she claims to have discovered that the order of discourse in the west, its rationality and epistemology, are supported by an imaginary that is in effect governed unconsciously by one of the 'sexual theories of children', the phantasy that there is only one sex, that that sex is male, and that therefore women are really men, in a defective, castrated version. In this imaginary, the mother is at best only a function.[25]

Irigaray suggests that symbolising the mother/daughter relationship, creating externally located and durable representation of this prototypical relation between women, is an urgent necessity, if women are to achieve ontological status in this society. She argues that the only way in which the status of women could be fundamentally altered is by the creation of a powerful female symbolic to represent the other against the omnipresent effects of the male imaginary.

Broadly speaking, socialist feminists believe that changes in the symbolic follow from changes in the material: if you work to bring about changes in women's social status and social institutions, then masculinity and femininity will come to have quite different meanings or perhaps will disappear altogether as sexual stereotypes. Irigaray contends that women's symbolic status cannot be altered in this way. One cannot easily change symbolic meanings, because they have an imaginary foundation which persists despite material changes. Instead of working towards undermining the masculine/feminine distinction, she wants to strengthen the feminine side of the pair through the creation of a female world, a female symbolic which would act a counterweight to the male one. She argues that if the feminine is not supported by specifically feminine institutions then it will always be swallowed up again by the masculine. Women need to be able to *represent* their difference.

Let us now turn to the work of Julia Kristeva. In her famous essay 'Women's time' Kristeva writes that feminism has developed in three broad stages: the first stage is that in which women demand equal access to the patriarchal, symbolic order, desiring equality rather than subjugation. The problem with this approach is that women are seen as no different from men; women are 'to become men'.[26] This approach leads to a complete surrender to patriarchy and its values. It assumes that women must replace being defined by the phallus with her identification *with* the phallus.

The second type of feminism is that in which women reject the male symbolic order in the name of difference, resulting in radical feminism (for example, the work of Irigaray). Femininity is not only celebrated by radical feminism but also seen as better and essentially different.

The third type of feminism is that in which women reject the dichotomy between masculine and feminine as metaphysical and aim at transcendence of the categories of sexual difference – or at least recognition of their cultural construction. In this stage scholars analyse the symbolic systems through which we communicate and organise our lives so as to understand how it is that we learn to be what our culture calls 'women' as against what are called 'men'.

Kristeva's account of the three types of feminism relies on Lacan's theories of the way the subject is constructed in a patriarchal language order, the Symbolic, and in which woman is normally relegated to the position of absence, or lack. Lacan's distinction between the Imaginary and the Symbolic is central to the different kinds of feminism being discussed here. For Lacan, the Imaginary proper lacks gender specificity – or rather, it brings both genders into the feminine through the illusory sense of being merged with the mother. The 'mirror phase', the moment when the child first sets up a relationship to its image in the mirror, marks an awareness that the sense of oneness with the mother is illusory. The child begins to be aware of the mother as an object distinct from itself.

This recognition of the mother as the Other is a universal experience and one that is essential for the human-to-be to become human. The mother–child dyad must be interrupted by the language order if the child's development is to move beyond the Imaginary. The mirror phase thus prepares the child for its subsequent entry into the realm of the Symbolic, in which the child takes up its position as a 'sexed' being (it recognises various subject positions such as 'he', 'she', 'you', 'it'). Because signifying systems are organised around the phallus as the prime signifier, the woman occupies the place of lack or absence. The boy and girl thus find themselves in vastly different positions vis à vis the dominant order once they enter the realm of the Symbolic.

The problem for the girl is in being positioned so as to identify with the mother, which means desiring what the mother desires – the phallus. This desire has nothing to do with anything essential or biological but everything to do with the way that the Symbolic is organised. It has been said that Lacan's system, particularly as used by Kristeva, frees us from the tyranny of the biological. It also enables us to see that some conventions that people thought of as due to 'nature' are in fact socially constructed.

This brings us to Kristeva's theory of language. She sees the ideological and philosophical basis of modern linguistics as fundamentally authoritarian and oppressive: in her view there has to be a shift away from the Saussurean concept of *langue* towards a re-establishment of the *speaking subject* as an object for linguistics. This would move linguistics away from its fascination with language as a monolithic structure and towards an interest in language as a heterogeneous process. Her theory of language as a complex signifying process located in and between subjects suggests that we should study language as specific *discourse* rather than universal *language*. She adds that we must avoid defining the 'speaking subject' as a Cartesian ego. The speaking subject must instead be constructed in the field of thought developed after Marx, Freud and Nietzsche; it should be seen as divided, de-centred, a subject in process.[27]

Kristeva displaces Lacan's distinction between the Imaginary and the Symbolic into a distinction between the semiotic and the symbolic. The interaction between these two terms then constitutes the signifying process. The semiotic is linked to the pre-Oedipal primary processes, the basic pulsions (or drives) of which Kristeva sees as predominantly anal and oral. The world of the semiotic, then, is close to the world of the unconscious: we can imagine it in the cry, the sounds, the gestures of the baby. In adult discourse, the semiotic functions as rhythm, prosody, word game, the no-sense of sense, laughter.

Kristeva develops a notion of signifying practice, 'significance', that covers both the symbolic order of rational language and the marginal, repressed feminine discourses of poetry, irrationality, art and so on, which draw directly on repressed, unconscious thought and which she calls 'semiotic'. All signifying practice involves both aspects of 'significance' but, depending on the type of discourse, one side or the other will predominate. Thus, for example, rational discourse is predominantly symbolic, whereas poetic discourse is governed by the semiotic side of language and draws on repressed signifiers which, under patriarchy, are predominantly feminine in character.

Kristeva calls the unconscious basis of language the 'semiotic *chora*'. It results from the organisation of the drives prior to the acquisition of language. Kristeva follows Lacan in positing the mirror phase as the first step that opens the way for the constitu-tion of all objects which from now on will be detached from the semiotic *chora*, and the Oedipal phase with its threat of castration as the moment in which the process of separation or splitting is fully achieved. Once the subject has entered into the Symbolic order, the *chora* will be more or less successfully repressed and can be perceived only as pulsional *pressure* on symbolic language: as contradictions, meaninglessness, disruption, silences and absences in the language. The *chora* is a rhythmic pulsion rather than a new language. It constitutes, in other words, the heterogeneous, dis-ruptive dimension of language, that which can never be caught up in the closure of traditional linguistics theory.

The semiotic challenge to symbolic relations occurs on the site of the individual subject. After entry into language, subjectivity is not constituted as fixed and conscious to itself once and for all. It is constantly in process and is differentially reconstituted within language every time an individual speaks.

We should remember that the fluid motility of the semiotic is associated with the pre-Oedipal phase and therefore with the pre-Oedipal mother, but Kristeva makes it quite clear that (like Freud) she sees the pre-Oedipal mother as a figure that encompasses both masculinity and femininity. This fantasmatic figure, which looms as large for baby boys as for baby girls, cannot be reduced to an example of femininity, for the simple reason that the opposition between feminine and masculine does not exist in pre-Oedipality. The semiotic, in short, is not to be associated with the feminine. Any strengthening of the semiotic (which knows no sexual difference) must therefore lead to a weakening of traditional gender divisions.

How does Kristeva define 'woman'? 'I understand by "woman",' she writes, as 'that which cannot be represented, that which is not spoken, that which remains outside naming and ideologies.' She contends that 'woman as such does not exist'. 'I favour an understanding of femininity that would have as many "feminines" as there are women.'[28] Kristeva has also said that she sees 'femininity' as 'that which is marginalised by the patriarchal symbolic order'. This 'relational' view allows her to argue that men can also be constructed as marginal by the Symbolic order, as her analyses of male avant-garde artists (Céline, for example) have shown.

Kristeva's emphasis on femininity as a patriarchal construct enables feminists to counter all forms of biologistic attacks from the defenders of phallocentrism. However, her deep suspicions of identity lead her to reject any idea of an *écriture féminine* that would be inherently feminine or female. She believes that the revolutionary subject, whether masculine or feminine, is a subject that is able to allow the *jouissance* of semiotic motility to disrupt the strict symbolic order. One of the best examples of this kind of 'revolutionary' activity is to be found in the writings of late-nineteenth-century avant-garde poets. Kristeva is fascinated by the avant-garde texts of Mallarmé, Lautréamont, Artaud, Joyce, Schoenberg, Stockhausen, Cage and even Giotto and Bellini.

These texts (whether they are written, dramatic, musical, visual or auditory) are disturbing because they provide a more direct expression of the semiotic than is usually possible in more conventional symbolic representational systems. Kristeva believes that by transgressing the boundaries of the symbolic order, the avant-garde creates upheavals and ruptures which may enable what is usually unspoken to be articulated. In her triad of subversive forces, Kristeva specifies: 'madness, holiness, and poetry'.

It has been suggested above that Kristeva's theory of the constitution of the subject and the signifying process is largely concerned with developments in the pre-Oedipal phase where sexual difference does not exist (the *chora* is a pre-Oedipal phenomenon). The question of difference becomes relevant only at the point of entry into the Symbolic order. Kristeva discusses the situation for little girls at this point in her book *About Chinese Women*. Kristeva points out that since the semiotic *chora* is pre-Oedipal, it is linked to the mother, whereas the Symbolic is dominated by the Law-of-the-Father. Faced with this situation, the little girl has to make a choice: 'either she identifies with her mother, or she raises herself to the symbolic stature of her father. In the first case, the pre-Oedipal phases (oral and anal eroticism) are intensified.' If on the other hand the little girl identifies with her father, 'the access she gains to the symbolic dominance [will] censor the pre-Oedipal phase and wipe out the last traces of dependence on the body of the mother'.[29] Kristeva thus outlines two different options for women: mother-identification, which will intensify the pre-Oedipal components of the woman's psyche, or father-identification, which will create a woman who will derive her identity from the same symbolic order.

Though Kristeva has done a lot of independent research, Lacanian psychoanalysis remains the fundamental methodological and conceptual grid upon which she relies. Her earliest works are based on Lacan's notion of the mirror phase and the castration complex. For her, these two moments provide the necessary conditions for the subject's acquisition of a speaking position. However, there are some differences. Kristeva suggests that Lacan concentrates too heavily or exclusively on verbal language at the expense of other modes of signification. Second, in contrast to Lacan, for whom the imaginary order functions in a visual register, Kristeva stresses all the senses. Third, while Lacan insists on a definitive break between the imaginary and the symbolic, Kristeva posits more of a continuity.

Let me now summarise the main points. Kristeva's approach differs from that of Irigaray by its acceptance of the phallic order: language and the Symbolic are necessary to create a division between child and mother. Kristeva denies that the phallic attributes of language are necessarily male; the phallic mother is more powerful than the phallic father, because more veiled and obscured. She believes that the phallus is not necessarily male, but is available to women too; equally the feminine attributes of the semiotic are available to all with bodies to feel. For the semiotic is a particularly physical system, dealing with those aspects of language that are not simply concerned with representation but with rhythm, tone, slips and colour. The semiotic operates to subvert the Symbolic order, holding out the possibility of a radical break. The semiotic is clearly expressed in certain forms of art, hence the importance of art for Kristeva.[30]

While some writers like Cixous validate the specifically feminine, others, like Kristeva, take femininity as representative of potentials that lie within every individual. She believes that people of either gender can be 'feminised' in a revolutionary fashion. Nevertheless, she can be criticised for allowing the images of femininity and motherhood to merge, placing immense emphasis on the role of the pre-Oedipal mother and romanticising her.[31]

Kristeva's approach valorises the mother–child relation, female language and creativity. But, inevitably, there are some problems with it. It could be argued that such theorising, at worst, risks a fetishisation of the female body, a privileging of maternity at the expense of non-productive sexuality, or even an equation of feminine creativity with maternity. Indeed, the privileging of the Imaginary may neglect the Symbolic altogether, promoting a new fiction of unified subjectivity, experienced in a golden semiotic age of infant fusion with the mother. Some of the women writers that support this approach fail to recognise the importance of history and political struggle.

It seems that much of feminist psychoanalytic theory seems to propose a choice between Father and Mother, system and silence, rigid structure and anarchy. Many feminists are in the awkward position between a 'phallocratic' theory which either disparages woman or effaces her, and perhaps equally authoritarian feminist doctrine, which, at its worst, threatens to deny the specificity of woman in the name of equality. In one sense, as Jane Gallop has remarked, feminism has been seduced by psychoanalysis (the father) and is forced to confront the issue of sexuality. In another sense, psychoanalysis has been seduced by feminism (the daughter) and is forced to confront delusions of mastery.[32]

CHAPTER NINE | Lacan and film

Introduction

Drawing on the work of Christian Metz, it is argued in this chapter that the cinema involves us in the (Lacanian) Imaginary. A child looking at the mirror is compared with the spectator looking at the screen. There is an exploration of the similarities and differences between film and dream, and there is an exposition of how it is through shot relationships that meaning emerges and a subject position is constructed for the viewer. The chapter concludes with a discussion about castration anxiety, the male gaze, voyeurism and fetishism in the cinema.

Cinema: The imaginary signifier

Psychoanalytic studies of the cinema are of various kinds. First, there is the nosographic approach; this treats films as symptoms from which it is possible to 'work back' to the neurosis of the film-maker. What interests the analyst in this approach is not the film but the film-maker. In other words, biographism remains intact, and with it an indifference to the filmic text as such.

Second, there is the approach that studies film scripts. The script is one aspect, among others, in the textual system. To study the script from a psychoanalytic viewpoint is to constitute it as a signifier. Echoing Lacan, Metz remarks:

> It is easy to forget that every signifier itself needs to be a signified, and that every signified, in turn, can but be a signifier. This constant back and forth is precisely the work of the symbolic; it is not possible to constitute some elements as 'pure' signifiers and others as 'pure' signifieds.[1]

A third approach focuses on the textual system and its inter-pretation. Metz likes to see film as a whole, as a signifier, and is sympathetic to this approach. Metz believes that, more than the other arts, or in a unique way, the cinema involves us in the Imaginary. He reminds us about the mirror phase – the moment when a child first perceives its own image.[2] In discussing the mirror phase Metz compares the child looking at the mirror with the spectator looking at the screen:

What the child sees in the mirror, what he sees as an other, who turns into 'I', is after all the image of his own body; so it is still an identification with something *seen*. But in traditional cinema the spectator is identifying only with something *seeing*: his own image does not appear on the screen; the primary identification is no longer constructed around a subject-object, but around a pure, all-seeing and invisible subject, the vanishing point of the monocular perspective which cinema has taken over from painting.[3]

When we watch a film we are like a child, in a hyper-perceptive state, susceptible to the imaginary. Really to understand film we must perceive the photographed object as absent, its photograph as present, and the presence of this absence as signifying. The film spectator must first of all have undergone the mirror phase. But as the latter instituted the ego largely in the imaginary, the second mirror of the screen, a symbolic apparatus, itself in turn depends on reflection and lack.

Film viewing and dreaming

Before I outline the principles of psychoanalytic criticism as they have developed in film studies I would like to recapitulate some basic points about the unconscious and dreams which will help to explain what happens when we watch a film.

As I have explained in earlier chapters, the workings of the un-conscious find no *direct* expression in conscious life. However, the complicated pathways between conscious activity and unconscious desire are made evident through the vehicle of language. As slips of the tongue, failures of memory, jokes and puns, dreams and neuroses indicate, unconscious wishes and desires underlie even the most apparently 'innocent' activity. This fact implies that there can never be a one-to-one relationship between language and the world. Meaning always exceeds its surface, and things do not always 'mean' what they appear to mean. We can never say with any certainty that the speaking subject says exactly what it means or means what it says. We can never possess the 'full' meaning of any of our actions.

In his writings on language Lacan has suggested that there can be no anchoring of particular signifiers to particular signifieds – that meaning emerges only through discourse, as a consequence of displacements along a signifying chain. Moreover, he insists upon the commutability of the signified, upon its capacity to function in turn as a signifier. Finally, by defining the signifier as that which 'represents the subject for another signifier', Lacan indicates that signification (meaning) cannot be considered apart from the subject. Although it constitutes itself through speaking, the Lacanian subject is always simultaneously spoken. It inherits its language and its desire from the Other.

The practice of the cinema is possible only through the perceptual passions: the desire to see (the scopic drive, scopophilia, voyeurism). There is also, of course, the invocatory drive. These two sexual drives are distinguished from the others in that they are more dependent on a lack. Purely organic instincts or needs can be satisfied. Hunger, for example, can be satisfied only by food, but food is quite certain to satisfy it. Sexual drives remain more or less unsatisfied, even when the object has been attained. Desire is very quickly reborn; it has its own rhythms, often quite independent of those of the pleasure obtained; the lack is what it wishes to fill, and at the same time what it is always careful to leave gaping, in order to survive as desire. In the end, perhaps, it has no real object (though there are numerous, interchangeable substitutes); desire pursues an imaginary object, an object that has always been lost and is always desired as such.

Let us now turn to the question: what happens when we watch a film? There exists a complex psychoanalytic theory of film spectatorship. Theorists, such as Christian Metz and others, discuss the unconscious structures that underlie our experience of film, and note how the powerful impression of reality in cinema is first and foremost an illusion. They also explore the similarities and differences between film and dream. Psychoanalytic film theory, which is largely based on the work of Lacan, discusses film spectatorship in terms of the circulation of desire. More than any other form, the cinema is capable of reproducing the structure and logic of dreams and the unconscious.[4] Remember that Freud believed that dreams are the 'royal road to the unconscious'.

Freud wrote that dreams are nothing more than a particular form of thinking made possible by the conditions of the state of sleep. It is the *dream-work* which creates that form. The dream-work is completely different from waking thought; it does not think, calculate or judge in any way at all, it restricts itself to giving things a new form.

Freud enumerated four operations: condensation, displacement, conditions of representability, in which it becomes possible for certain thoughts to be represented by visual images, and secondary revision in which a logical, narrative coherence is imposed on the stream of images. Freud writes that the function of secondary revision is to expunge from the dream the absurd incoherent fashion in which it was produced by the three prior operations left to themselves. Its function is to make a daydream of the dream, to construct the dream's 'façade', to make the dream conform to the laws of intelligibility.

Conditions of representability are sometimes called 'considerations of figurability'. This mechanism has two objectives: to illustrate an initial text, but also to replace certain portions of it by figures or images.[5] Freud gives the following example: he thought of having to revise an uneven passage in an essay. What came to mind? He saw himself planing a piece of wood!

The important point is this: drawing on the structural linguistics of Roman Jakobson, Lacan sees the principle of metaphor in condensation, and the principle of metonymy in displacement.[6] Displacement is the replacing of one particular idea by another in some way closely associated with it. In displacement the psychical charge is transferred entirely from one representation to another. One of the characteristics of displacement is that it encourages condensation and even enables it to occur. Displacement is a more general, more permanent operation, of which condensation is, in a sense, a particular case. In short, dreams are symbolic fulfilments of unconscious wishes, and the essential function of both condensation and displacement is, of course, to deceive the censor.

Metz believes that there is a set of differences, and partial resemblances, between fiction films and dreams. He suggests that they arise from the difference between waking and sleep. The principal difference is this: the dreamer does not know that s/he is dreaming; the film spectator knows that s/he is at the cinema.

Another point is that the fiction film is a real perception, there are real images; dreams occur within the psychic apparatus. A film is not really hallucinatory, it rests on true perceptions which the subject cannot fashion to his or her liking. The dream, however, responds to the wish. In other words, while the dream state is more strongly bound to the pleasure principle, the filmic state is based, to a greater extent, on the reality principle. The filmic situation brings with it certain elements of motor inhibition, and it is in this respect a kind of sleep in miniature, a waking sleep. Spectators are relatively immobile; they are plunged into darkness, and feel in a kind of daze.

The fiction film is, in general, considerably more 'logical' and 'constructed' than the dream. It rarely happens that we find in film narrative that impression of true absurdity which we commonly experience when we remember our own dreams. (Metz makes the point that if the manifest content of a dream were transposed to the screen, it would make an unintelligible film.) In the dream what is astonishing does not astonish and, consequently, nothing is absurd.

Another difference that must be considered is the story. The film story is a told story; there is an action of narration. The dream-story, however, is without an act of narration; it is a story from nowhere, which nobody tells to nobody.

Psychoanalytic film theory focuses on the ways in which the viewer is positioned, by means of a series of 'lures', as the desiring producer of the cinematic fiction. According to this idea, when we watch a film we are somehow dreaming it as well; our unconscious desires work in tandem with those that generated the film-dream. The spectator, then, is a central part of the entire cinema-machine, what has been called the 'cinematic apparatus'. This is a complex, interlocking structure. Some of the technological and libidinal/erotic components which intersect to form the cinematic apparatus include: the technical base (for example, specific effects produced by the camera, light, etc.); the conditions of film projection (the darkened theatre, etc.); the film itself as a 'text'; and the spectator as a desiring subject.

Metz has argued that the spectator has a capacity for belief, and that this belief in the film involves a basic process of disavowal. (The process of disavowal is a primal defence mechanism for dealing with external reality. For example, a person may hold two incompatible positions at the same time. S/he may simultaneously disavow and acknowledge.) Behind every incredulous spectator (who *knows* the events taking place on the screen are fictional) lies a credulous one (who nevertheless *believes* these events to be true); the spectators thus disavow what they know in order to maintain the cinematic illusion.[7] The whole effect of the film-viewing situation turns on the continual back and forth of knowledge and belief; this split is the consciousness of the spectator. The spectator is, in a sense, a double-spectator, whose division of the self is like that between conscious and unconscious. So even at the very basic level of belief in the cinematic fiction, something akin to unconscious desire is at work.

It is important to realise that film theory sees the viewer not as an individual person, but as an artificial construct, produced and activated by the cinematic apparatus. The spectator is conceptualised as a 'space' that is both 'productive' (as in the production of the dream-work) and 'empty' (anyone can occupy it). The cinema, in some sense, constructs its spectator through what is called the 'fiction-effect'. There are certain conditions that make film viewing similar to dreaming: we are in a darkened room, our visual perception is heightened to compensate for our lack of physical movement. Because of this the film spectator enters a 'regime of belief' (where everything is accepted as real) that is like the condition of the dreamer.

The construction of the viewer

Psychoanalytic film theory goes to great lengths to distinguish between the real person and the film-viewer, drawing on operations of the unconscious for its description. Three elements go into the psychoanalytic construction of the viewer: regression, primary identification, and the concealment of those 'marks of enunciation' that stamp the film with authorship.

Regression

Some writers believe that the conditions of the dream state produce a state of artificial regression. The totalising, womblike effects of the film-viewing situation represent, for him or her, the activation of an unconscious desire to return to an earlier state of psychic development, one before the formation of the ego, in which the divisions between self and other, internal and external, have not yet taken place. This condition is like the earliest forms of satisfaction of the infant in which the boundaries between itself and the world are confused.

Primary identification

Metz defines primary cinematic identification as the spectator's identification with the act of looking itself. This type of identification is considered primary because it is what makes all secondary identifications with characters and events on the screen possible. This process is at once constructed and directed by the look of the camera; the spectator is given that illusory capacity to be everywhere at once.[8] It has been argued that this type of identification is possible because the viewer has already undergone that formative psychic process called the mirror phase.

The film-viewer's fictional participation in the unfolding of events is made possible by this first experience of the subject, that early moment in the formation of the ego when the small infant begins to distinguish objects as different from itself. What links this process to the cinema is the fact that it occurs in terms of visual images; what the child sees at this point (a unified image that is distanced and objectified) forms how s/he will interact with others at later stages in life. The fictive aspect is also crucial here; the perception of that 'other' as a more perfect self is also a misperception. We should remember that the notion of the self as fully conscious, coherent and in command of its meanings is a fictional construct – the unconscious tells us this is so.

The concealment of those 'marks of enunciation' that stamp the film with authorship

The third element in the construction of the cinematic viewer has to do with 'authorship' and its effacement. It was stated earlier that a number of conditions combine to give the spectator the impression that it is s/he who is dreaming the images and situations that appear on the screen. Dreams and phantasy have this in common with fiction: they are all imaginary productions that have their source in unconscious desire. Unconscious desire, of both film-maker and spectator, is but one element in the complex operations of technology and text. But something must happen to hide the author of the film from view. The viewer must be made to forget that a fiction is being watched, a fiction which has, in a sense, come from another source of desire.

Film theory uses the term enunciation, a concept borrowed from structural linguistics, to refer to the fact that in every verbal exchange there is both the statement (what is said, the language itself) and the process that produces the statement (how something is said, from what position).[9] Now, film theory applies this concept to the cinema. It is argued that in every film there is always a place of enunciation, a place from which the cinematic discourse proceeds. This is theorised as a position and is not to be confused with the actual film-maker.

There is a connection between the process of enunciation and voyeurism, the erotic component of seeing that founds the cinema.[10] Freud believed that there was a libidinal investment in looking to see, in seeing. The libido for looking is present in everyone in two forms, active and passive, male and female. The pleasure in looking is in relation to knowledge which makes use of it, the looking to see, to know the other body. There is, then, a sexual pleasure in looking, a libidinal investment in the eye as phallus.

In psychoanalytical terms voyeurism applies to any kind of sexual gratification obtained from vision, and is usually associated with a hidden vantage point. (Freud gives the example of Peeping Tom, the man who looked through the shutters at Lady Godiva and was punished by going blind.) Metz argues that in order for the cinematic fiction both to produce and maintain its fascinating hold on the spectator, it must appear as if the screen images are the expressions of the spectator's own desire. He draws attention to the process by which every film-maker chooses the series of images, organises the image flow, etc. He maintains that what distinguishes the classical narrative film is the effacement or hiding of these marks of enunciation which point to this work of selecting and arranging shots. In other words, the work of production is concealed; the source of enunciation is hidden – this is the famous 'invisible editing' of Hollywood cinema.[11] Let us now look at some of the procedures by means of which a subject position is constructed for the film-viewer.

The meaning of suture

In the cinema (a combination of images and linguistic sounds) subjectivity is constantly reactivated by the imaginary and symbolic registers. The name given to the techniques by means of which cinematic texts confer subjectivity upon their viewers is suture. Jacques-Alain Miller defines suture as that moment when the subject inserts itself into the symbolic register in the guise of a signifier, and in so doing gains meaning at the expense of being. Suture closely resembles the subject's inauguration into language illustrated by Lacan, with the 'fort-da' game. French thinkers have taken the concept into film studies, where it has been used to think about questions such as: what is the cinematic equivalent for language in the literary text? What is cinematic syntax?

Some theorists argue that shot relationships in films are the equivalent of syntactic ones in linguistic discourse. *It is through shot relationships that meaning emerges and a subject position is constructed for the viewer.* One particular arrangement of shots is very important in the operations of suture and that is the shot/reverse shot formation. To put it simply, in the shot/reverse shot formation the second shot shows the field from which the first shot is assumed to have been taken. There is a convention in film making that the camera should not cover more than 180 degrees in a single shot. This 'rule' means that the camera never shows the half of the circle it occupies. This practice derives from the imperative that the camera deny its own existence as much as possible. Its purpose is to foster the *illusion* that what is shown has an autonomous existence independent of any technological interference, or any coercive gaze.

The shot/reverse shot formation is a calculated way of keeping the cinematic illusion intact: shot 1 shows a scene, shot 2 locates a spectator in the other 180 degrees of the same circular field, thereby implying that the preceding shot was seen through the eyes of a figure in the cinematic narrative. (Of course, sometimes, this procedure is reversed.) A fictional character looking in shot 2 usually proves sufficient to maintain the illusion that shot 1 visually 'belongs' to that character. As a result, the level of enunciation remains veiled from the viewing subject's scrutiny; the gaze which directs our look seems to belong to a fictional character rather than to the camera.[12]

It is important to understand the shot/reverse formation because it demonstrates the way in which cinema operates to reduplicate the history of the subject. According to suture theory, the viewer experiences shot 1 as an imaginary plenitude, unbounded by any gaze, and unmarked by difference. It is thus the site of a *jouissance* akin to that of the mirror phase prior to the child's discovery of its separation from the ideal image which it has discovered in the reflecting glass.

However, almost immediately, the viewing subject becomes aware of the limitations of what it sees – aware, that is, of an absent field. At this point shot 1 becomes a signifier of that absent field, and *jouissance* gives way to unpleasure. In the moment of unpleasure the viewing subject perceives that it is lacking something. The viewer realises that the camera is hiding things and therefore distrusts it. S/he feels s/he is being prevented from seeing. S/he realises that s/he is only authorised to see what happens to be in the axis of the gaze of another spectator, who is ghostly or absent. This spectator, called the 'Absent One' or the 'Other', has all the attributes of the symbolic father: potency, knowledge, self-sufficiency, transcendental vision, and discursive power. It is, of course, *the speaking subject of the cinematic text.*

The speaking subject has everything which the viewing subject feels that s/he lacks. This sense of lack inspires in that subject the desire to see more. On the other hand, it is equally important that the presence of the speaking subject be hidden from the viewer. The classic film must at all costs conceal from the viewing subject the passivity of that subject's position, and this necessitates denying the fact that there is any reality outside of the fiction.

This is where the shot/reverse shot formation is so useful: it alerts the spectator to that other field whose absence is experienced as unpleasurable while at the same time linking it to the gaze of a fictional character. Thus a gaze within the fiction serves to conceal the controlling gaze outside the fiction; as Kaja Silverman puts it, a benign other steps in and obscures the presence of the coercive and castrating Other.[13] Or, to put it in another way, the subject of the speech passes itself off as the speaking subject. In short, the illusionism of the classic film seems to depend on the viewing subject's willingness to permit a fictional character to stand in for it, or by allowing a particular point of view to define what it sees. The operation of suture is successful at the moment that the viewing subject says, 'Yes, that's me!', or 'Yes, that's what I see!'

Two other operations, equally important in the construction of the film, should also be mentioned: cutting and excluding. The camera cannot show us everything; we must be shown only enough to know that there is more, and to want that 'more' to be disclosed. The prime agency of disclosure is the cut, which divides one shot from the next. The cut guarantees that both the preceding and subsequent shots will function as structuring absences to the present shot. These absences make possible a signifying ensemble; they convert one shot into a signifier of the next one, and the signified of the preceding one. Thus each image is defined from those that surround it. To recapitulate, though there are many operations in the making of a film, the values of *absence* and *lack* always play a central role. These values not only serve to deflect attention away from the level of enunciation to that of fiction, but to activate the viewer's desire and transform one shot into a signifier for the next.

I should add that suture is not one theory but a group of overlapping theories. Whereas for some thinkers suture can be isolated in the shot/reverse shot formation, for others it is inherent in all the operations which constitute narrativity. However, the theoreticians of suture agree that it provides the agency whereby the subject emerges within discourse, and takes up a position congruent with the existing cultural order. As suture always implies a sexual differentiation, it is useful to have a full understanding of the symbolic drama of castration.

As I suggested in the last chapter, one of Lacan's achievements has been to transfer some of Freud's hypotheses into the realm of mythic parables to be understood in a symbolic sense. This includes thought about castration, the murder of the father, the Oedipus complex, and the Law. However, the scenario of castration, in its broad lines, does not differ whether one understands it, like Lacan, as an essentially symbolic drama in which castration takes over in a decisive metaphor all the losses, both real and imaginary, that the child has already suffered, or whether on the contrary one tends, like Freud, to take the scenario slightly more literally.

Castration is, first of all, the *mother's* castration. The child who sees the mother's body is constrained to accept that there are human beings deprived of a penis. The young child believes that all human beings originally have a penis and it therefore understands what it has seen as the effect of a mutilation which redoubles its fear that it will be subjected to a similar fate. (The girl fears that she has already been subjected to it.)

The child, in order to avoid too strong an anxiety, holds two contradictory opinions: 'All human beings are endowed with a penis' (primal belief) and 'Some human beings do not have a penis'. In other words, it will retain its former belief beneath the new one, but it will also hold to its new perceptual observation while disavowing it on another level. In disavowal one says 'I know very well, but all the same . . .'

It was mentioned earlier that a similar disavowal takes place in the cinema. On the one hand, the audience is not duped by the illusion; it 'knows' that the screen presents no more than a fiction. Any spectator will tell you that s/he does not believe it – and yet at another level, of course, s/he does.

There is a close link between castration, the fear it inspires and fetishism. Freud pointed out that fetishism involves displacing the sight of woman's imaginary castration on to a variety of reassuring but often surprising objects (shoes, corsets) which serve as signs for the lost penis but have no direct connection with it. For the fetishist the sign itself becomes the source of phantasy and in every case the sign is the sign of the phallus. It is man's narcissistic fear of losing his own phallus, his most precious possession, which causes shock at the sight of the female genitals, and the fetishistic attempt to disguise or divert attention from them.

The fetish, then, is a prop, it is something that disavows a lack and in doing so affirms it without wishing to. It is clear that fetishism, in the cinema as elsewhere, is closely linked to the good object. The function of the fetish is to restore the latter, threatened in its 'goodness' by the terrifying discovery of the lack. Thanks to the fetish, which covers the wound and becomes erotogenic, the object as a whole can become desirable again without excessive fear.

In short, women symbolise the castration which men fear. The spectre of the castrated female, using a phallic substitute to conceal or distract attention from her wound, haunts the male unconscious. (For Freud's analysis of the male unconscious see 'The Medusa's head'.) Difference produces great anxiety. One way of coping with anxiety is polarisation, the representation of difference, which tames and binds anxiety. The classic example is sexual difference, which is represented as polar opposition: passivity – activity, masochism – sadism, exhibitionism – voyeurism. When there are anxieties people require boundaries to demarcate unacceptable difference and otherness.

Voyeurism and fetishism

In an influential essay, Laura Mulvey argues that the classic Hollywood film (text) distinguishes sharply between the male and female subjects, and it does so on the basis of vision.[14] The male subject is defined in his capacity to look (i.e. as a voyeur) and the female subject in terms of her capacity to attract the male gaze (i.e. as an exhibitionist). The male subject is the imagined source of the gaze and the female subject is the imagined recipient of the gaze. Indeed, in our culture, voyeurism is the active or 'masculine' form of the scopophilic drive (pleasure in looking at another person as an erotic object), while exhibitionism is the passive or 'feminine' form of the same drive.

Mulvey writes:

> In a world ordered by sexual imbalance, pleasure in looking has been split between active/male and passive/female. The determining male gaze projects its phantasy onto the female figure, which is styled accordingly. In their traditional exhibitionist role women are simultaneously looked at and displayed, with their appearance coded for strong visual and erotic impact so that they can be said to connote to-be-looked-at-ness.[15]

Drawing on Freud's twin mechanisms of voyeurism and fetishism, Laura Mulvey writes that the dominant Hollywood cinema is built on a series of three basic 'looks', all of which satisfy desire in the male unconscious.

There is, first, the look of the camera in the filming situation; although technically neutral, this look is inherently voyeuristic and usually 'male' in the sense that a man is generally doing the filming. Second, there is the look of the male characters within the film narrative, and these are organised through shot/counter shot formation so as to make the woman the object of their gaze.[16] Finally, there is the look of the spectator which imitates the first two looks; the spectator is forced to identify with the look of the camera, to see as it sees.

Voyeurism and fetishism, then, are mechanisms Hollywood uses to construct the spectator. Voyeurism is a look that is male and phallic; it refers to the keyhole aspect and usually involves a violation of space. Voyeurism is linked to the scopophilic drive. Mulvey suggests that cinema relies on this drive making the spectator essentially a voyeur. Fetishism also comes into play in the cinema, where the female body may be 'fetishised' in order to counteract the male fear of sexual difference, that is of castration. She originally argued that if the spectator is a woman, she has to assume the male position and participate in both mechanisms.

Mulvey suggests that just as a shot of a character within the fiction engaged in the activity of seeing functions to cover over the camera's coercive gaze, so the representation of the male subject in terms of vision has the effect of attributing to him qualities which in fact belong to that same apparatus – the qualities of authority and potency.

The female subject in the film/fiction (usually) signifies the lack which properly belongs to the male and female viewers, who are spoken, not speaking, and whose gazes are controlled, not controlling.[17] The female subject also signifies lack within the fiction of the film, a fiction which inevitably duplicates cultural values. She signifies, that is, the absence of the phallus (of control, privilege, power). As usual, her body provides the means for representing this deprivation. She simultaneously attracts the gaze – appeals to the senses – and represents castration.

The emphasis on the female subject's lack helps to define the male subject as adequate, facilitates his identification with attributes which in fact belong to the apparatuses of enunciation. However, the revelation of female lack can also have a different effect upon the male subject; it can induce in him the fear of a similar deprivation. There are two recurrent solutions to the problem of castration anxiety. The first involves a demonstration that the woman's castrated condition is the result either of wrongdoing or of sickness.

The second strategy for neutralising the anxiety aroused by

female lack involves the transformation of the female body into a fetish, substituting one of its parts or the whole for the missing phallus. Certain parts of the body are subjected to an overvaluation, and in this way compensate for the deficiency which is associated with the female genital region. The mechanisms of fetishism function to reassure the male subject that the woman to whom his identity is keyed lacks nothing, that she has not been castrated after all. The Hollywood song-and-dance number is an example, and, perhaps, the star system itself. To reiterate, there are two strategies for neutralising the anxiety aroused by female lack. The first of these involves establishing either the female subject's guilt or her illness, while the second fetishises her, giving her an erotic over-investment.

Following Mulvey, feminist film critics became interested in what she had theorised as an exclusively 'male' gaze and in discussing what a possible 'female' gaze might be. It was soon realised that the theory applied mainly to the central 'male' genres – the western, gangster, adventure and war films. Recently, women scholars have turned to the one film genre that specifically addresses the female spectator – the melodrama – and issues relating to this genre and women viewers are still being actively debated.

To summarise – it has been stated that Lacanian theory has been extensively used in writings about the cinema. We looked at the work of Christian Metz, who has tried to account for the peculiar fascination that the film has for the spectator. It was stated that the cinema, a field for the scopic drive, situates the spectator in a relation which corresponds to Lacan's Imaginary. The film industry tries to induce 'filmic pleasure' rather than 'filmic unpleasure' by presenting its object as a 'good object', granting what is desired.[18] The screen is a Lacanian mirror, but there is no recognition of the screen as mirror image, because the spectator is deluded into identifying with the camera. Finally, the importance of the look, voyeurism and fetishism, perversions of the sexual drive that underlie 'the scopic regime' of the cinema, were stressed because probably in these lie its unconscious roots.[19] Laura Mulvey's argument – that visual pleasure in narrative cinema is a structure of voyeurism which is oppressive to women and which must be challenged – raises some important questions: is it possible to have visual pleasure other than in terms of voyeurism? Is it possible to create a non-voyeuristic cinema?

Lacan and literature

Introduction

Both dreams and literature have the function of fulfilling a wish. Dreams and literature are not merely linked because they fulfil wishes, but because both have to make use of strategies in order to overcome the resistance of consciousness. 'Work' is done by the dreamer and the artist to transform their primitive desires into culturally acceptable meanings. Freud himself drew attention to the effects of desire in language and, indeed, in all forms of symbolic interaction.

Both psychoanalysis and literature are concerned with narrative, with telling stories. Psychoanalysis reads the past in order to make sense of the present. Like a detective story it starts with effects and traces these effects back to origins. The reader, too, has to find causes and connections and, like the analyst, has to work back through time in order to recover meaning.

Traditional applied psychoanalysis assumed that the work of literature was like a phantasy or dream, and it was treated as a *symptom* of a particular writer. The characters were treated as if they were living beings within the phantasy, and symbols were always interpreted according to a fixed, predictable code. It was assumed that the purpose of the work of art was the same as that which psychoanalysis had taken to be the purpose of the dream: the secret gratification of an infantile and forbidden wish. The psychoanalytic critic believed that by detailed examination of a literary text s/he could make it yield up the psychology of its creator.

The assumption of classical criticism, that the text is the 'patient' and the reader the analyst, no longer holds. The text is not a stable object, immutably fixed for all time by the 'intentions' of its creator, whether these can be seen as conscious or unconscious. In recent years the focus has shifted, as Elizabeth Wright and others have pointed out, from the psychology of the author, or the characters, to that of the reader. Or, more accurately, the emphasis is now on the relations between author, reader, text and language.[1]

Why is Lacan important to students of literature and literary critics? (It is interesting to note that literary critics welcomed Lacan long before the psychologists.) Lacan always reminded people that Freud maintained literary training was the prime requisite for the formation of analysts. Lacan, too, emphasised the need for a broad curriculum in the psychoanalytic institute; and he refused to allow psychoanalysis to be or become a purely medical speciality. He stressed the need for interdisciplinary studies and for the incorporation of the humanities into the training programme. A young science, he said, needs to borrow from other disciplines in order to further its own elaboration.

Lacan believed that students of the human mind wishing to grapple with the problem of meaning could not do better than serve an apprenticeship as students of literature. But notice a difference between the views of Freud and Lacan. Whereas for Freud the supreme extra-scientific model for a dynamic psychology was to be found in the tragic drama of Europe, for Lacan the model most often used is that of the literary text itself, considered as inexhaustibly ambiguous and plural.[2]

Literary critics have been alerted once again by Lacan's work to the implicitness, mobility and ambiguity of much literary meaning. They have been given new ways of looking at plot and figurality. They have been given tools with which to think about literary works as productions of desire. For a Lacanian reading of literature it is important to understand the 'mirror phase', the mother's desire and the desire for the mother; the intervention of the Father's law, and how the 'name-of-the-father' replaces the 'desire of the mother', the interaction between the Imaginary, Symbolic and Real; and the many other concepts that I have discussed in earlier chapters.

I want to argue that the effect of Lacan's theory has been to revitalise literary criticism. His approach focuses on Freud the semiotician as distinct from Freud the humanist, or Freud the biologist. While the older, traditional psychoanalysis set itself the task of using texts as clues to the author's psychology, or the psychology of his characters, Lacan's work calls in question both this theory and its practice by undertaking a thoroughgoing re-assessment of the role of language. As I mentioned in Chapter 4 on language, Lacan sees the unconscious as coming into being simultaneously with language. He maintains not only that the unconscious is structured like a language, but that it is a product of language. Furthermore, he believes that every single utterance, spoken or written, is invaded by the unconscious.

Lacan's influence can be seen in many areas of literary criticism. Many critics use Lacanian concepts.[3] It is not only formalist critics, like Shoshana Felman, who have found in Lacan useful concepts for textual analyses; Marxist critics, like Fredric Jameson, have also found Lacanian concepts, such as the Imaginary and the Symbolic, helpful in their studies. Jameson has suggested that Lacan's theory holds out promise of a new style of materialist social criticism – one that is able to make coherent connections between the structure of the unconscious and the interactive sig-nifying practices that constitute a given culture.

Let us now look, in the sections that follow, at some studies by Lacan. The first one is on Shakespeare's *Hamlet*. But before I present Lacan's interpretation of *Hamlet*, it may be useful to have an outline of Freud's view of the play.

Freud's view of Hamlet

In Freud's view, suffering of every kind was the subject matter of drama and from this suffering it promised to give the audience pleasure. Drama should not cause suffering to the audience, but it should compensate. Of 'psychological drama' Freud wrote:

> The source of the suffering in which we take part and from which we are meant to derive pleasure is no longer a conflict between two almost equally conscious impulses but between a conscious impulse and a repressed one. Here the precondition of enjoyment is that the spec-tator should himself be a neurotic, for it is only such people who can derive pleasure instead of simple aversion from the revelation and the more or less conscious recognition of a repressed impulse.[4]

It is only in neurotics that a struggle can occur of a kind which can be made the subject of a drama; but even in them the dramatist will provoke not merely an *enjoyment* of the liberation but a *resistance* to it as well.

Freud remarks that it can scarcely be owing to chance that three of the masterpieces of literature of all time – *The Oedipus Rex* of Sophocles, Shakespeare's *Hamlet* and Dostoevsky's *The Brothers Karamazov* – should all deal with the same subject, parricide. In all three, moreover, the motive for the deed, sexual rivalry for a woman, is laid bare.

According to Freud, *Hamlet* has as its subject the ways in which a man who has so far been normal becomes neurotic owing to the peculiar nature of the task by which he is faced, a man, that is, in whom an impulse that has hitherto been successfully repressed endeavours to make its way into action. The play has three characteristics. First, the hero is not psychopathic in the course of the action of the play. Second, the repressed impulse is one of those which are similarly repressed in all of us. And third, a necessary precondition of this form of art is that the impulse that is struggling into consciousness, however clearly it is recognisable, is never given a definite name.[5]

In *Hamlet* the wishful phantasy that underlies it remains repressed; and – just as in the case of a neurosis – we learn of its existence only from its inhibiting consequences. The play is built up on Hamlet's hesitations over fulfilling the task of revenge assigned to him; but its text offers no reasons or motives for these hesitations. Does Hamlet represent the type of man whose power of direct action is paralysed by an excessive development of intellect, or is he a pathologically irresolute character who might be classed as neurasthenic? What is it that really inhibits him in fulfilling the task set him by his father's ghost?

The answer, once again, is that it is the peculiar nature of the task. Hamlet is able to do anything – except take vengeance on the man who did away with his father and took that father's place with his mother, the man who shows him the repressed wishes of his own childhood realised. Thus the loathing which should drive him on to revenge is replaced in him by self-reproaches, by scruples of conscience, which remind him that he himself is literally no better than the sinner whom he is to punish.[6]

Freud comments that in *Hamlet* the hero does not commit the crime himself; it is carried out by someone else, for whom it is not parricide. The forbidden motive of sexual rivalry for the woman does not need, therefore, to be disguised. Moreover, we see the hero's Oedipus complex, as it were, in a reflected light, by learning the effect on him of the other's crime. He ought to avenge the crime but finds himself, strangely enough, incapable of doing so. We know that it is his sense of guilt that is paralysing him; but, in a manner entirely in keeping with neurotic processes, the sense of guilt is displaced on to the perception of his inadequacy for fulfilling his task.[7]

Desire in Hamlet

You will have noticed that Lacan writes repeatedly about desire. He says, for example, in *Ecrits*: 'The unconscious is the discourse of the Other . . . But we must also add that man's desire is desire of the Other . . .' Lacan frequently makes use of the term desire to denote both the lived primal lack or need for union with the mother, and the desire to have which succeeds it after the entry of the subject into language. Desire lies beyond demand.[8] To say that desire is beyond demand means that it transcends it, that it is eternal because it is impossible to satisfy it. In short, every desire is the desire to have oneself recognised by the other, and a desire to impose oneself in some way upon the other. Desire is the desire for desire, the desire of the Other. Desire is forever insatiable since it refers back to the ineffable, to the unconscious desire and the absolute lack it conceals.

Lacan makes some insightful remarks about Hamlet (are not his puns, conceits, word play, and mannered speech rather like Lacan's own writing?), Ophelia, Laertes and relates them to his views on desire, and mourning after death. Lacan believes that *Hamlet* has an exceptional power of captivation. The tragedy of Hamlet is the tragedy of desire.[9] In his view the play is dominated by the Mother as Other (*Autre*). This desire, of the mother, is manifested in the fact that, confronted on one hand with an eminent, idealised, exalted object – his father – and on the other with the degraded, despicable object Claudius, the criminal and adulterous brother, Hamlet does not choose. With respect to the desire of the Other, the desire of his mother, Hamlet's situation is one of dependence. His desire becomes distracted and deflected. Hamlet is led to feign madness, which is one of the strategies of the modern hero.

Hamlet, on the one hand, procrastinates and yet, on the other, when he does act, it is always too soon (for example, the incident when Hamlet rushes at whatever is moving behind the arras and kills Polonius). Lacan calls this the 'phenomenology of the neurotic'. Well then, what does Hamlet lack? He never sets a goal for himself; he just does not know what he wants.

Ophelia is the bait in the trap that Hamlet does not fall into. Most of Hamlet's relations with Ophelia seem to be carried on in a sarcastic style of cruel aggression. In the later scenes we see the destruction and loss of the object. Lacan contends that the object is here the equivalent of, assumes the place of, indeed is – the phallus. Ophelia is *O phallus*. She is the phallus, exteriorised and rejected by the subject as a symbol signifying life.

In the last scene, Hamlet is interested in the tournament for the sake of honour – what Hegel calls the fight for pure prestige – interested for the sake of honour in a contest that pits him against a rival whom he moreover admires. At this point Laertes is for Hamlet his double. On Hamlet's attitude towards Laertes before the duel, Lacan writes:

> The playwright situates the basis of aggressivity in this paroxysm of absorption in the imaginary register, formally expressed as a mirror relationship, a mirrored reaction. The one you fight is the one you admire the most. The ego ideal is also, according to Hegel's formula which says that coexistence is impossible, the one you have to kill.[10]

It was stated earlier that Hamlet constantly treats Ophelia with demeaning aggression; he humiliates her. She is the symbol of the rejection of his desire. But in the burial scene, suddenly, the object (Ophelia) regains its immediacy and its worth for him. He cries out: 'I loved Ophelia. Forty thousand brothers could not with all their quantity of love make up my sum. What wilt thou do for her?' Lacan argues that hysteria is characterised by the function of an unsatisfied desire, and obsession by the function of an impossible desire. He suggests that:

> Only insofar as the object of Hamlet's desire has become an impossible object can it become once more the object of his desire. In the desires

of obsessional neurotics we have already encountered the impossible as object of desire . . . The very structure at the basis of desire always lends a note of impossibility to the object of human desire . . . The obsessional neurotic sets everything up so that the object of his desire becomes the signifier of this impossibility.[11]

Throughout the play all anyone talks about is mourning. What is the connection between desire and mourning? In the burial scene Laertes leaps into the grave and embraces the object whose loss is the cause of his desire, an object that has attained an existence that is all the more absolute because it no longer corresponds to anything in reality. The one unbearable dimension of possible human experience is not the experience of one's own death, which no one has, but the experience of the death of another. In Lacan's view, a gap, a hole results from this loss and it calls forth mourning on the part of the subject. We must consider the function of *ritual* in mourning. The work of mourning is first of all performed to overcome the disorder that is produced by the inadequacy of signifying elements to cope with the hole that has been created in existence. Ritual, in other words, introduces some mediation of the gap opened up by mourning.

In all the instances of mourning in *Hamlet*, one element is always present: the rites have been cut short and performed in secret. For political reasons, Polonius is buried secretly, without ceremony, post-haste. Ophelia's burial is with limited rites because she has committed suicide. And, of course, there is the ghost of Hamlet's father who has an inexpiable grievance. All these are significant 'clues' that point to the relationship of desire to mourning.

At the bottom of this mourning, in *Hamlet* as in *Oedipus*, there is a crime. Up to a certain point the whole rapid succession, one instance of mourning after another, can be seen as consequences of the initial crime. The thing that distinguishes Hamlet from Oedipus is that Hamlet *knows* the crime.[12]

It is interesting to compare *Hamlet* with the play *Oedipus Rex*. Sophocles's play opens with an enigma. Thebes is inflicted with a plague and Oedipus undertakes to find out why. In this process Oedipus takes on the role of investigator. But it only gradually emerges that he is telling his own story, revealing, as detective hero, the hidden meaning behind his actions as the hero of the folk tale. Oedipus goes through the same three adventures as the fairy-tale hero. He kills the old king, he solves the riddle of the Sphinx and rids the city of distress, and he receives the hand of the queen.

As Freud says, the play unfolds 'like the process of psycho-analysis itself'. The story Oedipus investigates is his own; he is the criminal in his detective story. But what is specific about Oedipus, the crucial issue that separates him from the simple detectives of the whodunit, is the theme of internal transformation.

It has been said that there is a parallel development between *Oedipus Rex/Oedipus at Colonus* and *The Interpretation of Dreams/Beyond the Pleasure Principle*.[13] In each case, the first work is about sexuality and Oedipal desire and the second is the compulsion to repeat and the death drive. It is quite likely that Lacan identified with the exiled Oedipus, personally because of his expulsion from the International Psychoanalytic Association, and he identified with *Oedipus at Colonus* theoretically because of its relation to *Beyond the Pleasure Principle* and because it tells, not a mythic story, but the story of the coming into being of a myth.

One important difference between Freud and Lacan is this: while Freud elevated the artist to a sacrificial position, one whose repressed neuroses provide others with cathartic release, Lacan argued the opposite. Artistic productions are not in and of themselves pathological or neurotic. The purpose of art is not to permit repression, but to pose a question that the artist himself or herself has not answered or resolved. This is, in short, what Lacan says about James Joyce.

Lacan, who gave seminars on Joyce in 1975 and 1976, argued that Joyce's deteriorating eye condition, the psychosis of his daughter Lucia (the name means the goddess of seeing, of light, the gaze), and his increasingly arcane prose were all symptoms of a man whose desire was encumbered by an oppression of *jouissance*. *Jouissance* always concerns the relations of desire to the position of the Father's Name (or the phallus). Lacan suggests that the character Stephen Dedalus was Joyce's Imaginary alter ego through whom he fictively and unconsciously sought to decipher his own life enigmas. Joyce's art reveals that writers create or invent in order to live, not the reverse.

Lacan admired Joyce for his ability to live his symptoms through a sheer will of words.[14] It seems that we cling to our symptoms because they are familiar and give us a sense of being unified and consistent.[15] Till the writing of *Ulysses* (1922), the Father's Name signifier was represented by a country, a race, a religion, and a name for Joyce himself: the Artist. Then came *Finnegans Wake* (1939). Lacan thought of *Finnegans Wake* as language rushing in to fill up a hole in Joyce's being. The book is not intended to mystify readers, but is Joyce's desperate effort to keep a link to the Symbolic order intact. *Finnegans Wake* is characterised by something very close to what in psychiatry is called mania. It fascinates by the *jouissance* it attests.

This brings us back to questions about the role and function of the Symbolic order. In the next section I will focus on Lacan's paper on one of Poe's short stories which, Lacan argues, is about how the signifier, which is within the Symbolic order, dominates the human subject.

Poe's 'Letter'

In order to see how in a Lacanian approach analogies from psycho-analysis are used to explain the workings of the text (as distinct from the workings of a particular author's, character's or even reader's mind), let us have a look at Lacan's 'Seminar on "The Purloined Letter"' in which his main concern is to bring out the repetition of a structure. Just as for Freud there was a repetition of patterns of behaviour within the course of a single individual's life, so for Lacan in the plot of Poe's story there is a recurrence of an ambiguous relationship affecting the positions of the actors.

It is significant that the first essay in the French edition of *Ecrits* (1966) is a seminar on Edgar Allan Poe's short story, 'The Purloined Letter'.[16] Briefly, the story is this: while reading a letter the Queen is interrupted by her husband, the King, and forced to leave it on the table. The Minister notices the Queen's distress and sees the letter. He manages to steal the letter by producing from his pocket a second envelope almost identical to the one containing the Queen's letter and substituting the former for the latter.

The Queen therefore knows that the Minister has stolen the letter, and the Minister knows that the Queen knows he is the thief. The Prefect of Police is asked to help. He searches the Minister's house with a fine tooth-comb but without any success. He therefore begs Dupin the detective to help him recover the letter.

Dupin finds the letter in the best of hiding places: visible to all, the very obviousness of the location disguises the purloined letter and actually makes it invisible. The detective then steals the letter. He lets the Minister know that he has stolen the letter by writing on the page that he substitutes for the letter in the envelope. We never know who wrote the letter or what was in it.

Lacan refers to 'The Purloined Letter' as 'an absolutely sensational short story, which could even be considered as essential for a psychoanalyst'.[17] He writes: 'Besides his remarks about the game of even and odd, Dupin makes linguistic, mathematical, observations, he constantly speculates about the symbol . . .' Lacan reads the story as an allegory of the supremacy of the signifier, subjects being at the mercy of the law that made them. In 'The Seminar on Poe's "Purloined Letter"' Lacan traces the effect of a letter as it changes hands. The letter, like a signifier, forms a signifying chain. The subjects are changed at each turning point, as they lose, receive, or search for the letter.

Obviously a letter means a 'written or printed character' as well as an item of correspondence. In the story the letter, as item of correspondence, comes to mean a signifier. The letter is what is not seen (by some) and seen differently (by others). In each case the possessor of the letter is made to stand helplessly by while the theft takes place. Each time the letter is appropriated, the subject is captured by a signifier, for which the real letter stands: a love letter whose content is never revealed. In this Lacanian reading the purloined letter becomes a metaphor for the unconscious, a signifier of unconscious desire.

Lacan was particularly interested in Freud's notion of the repetition compulsion. Freud has noticed that dreams occurring in traumatic neuroses have the characteristic of repeatedly bringing the patient back into the distressing situation of his accident. In ordinary human relations, too, there are often repetitions: the perpetual recurrence of the same thing, such as the lover each of whose love affairs passes through the same phases and reaches the same conclusion. Freud also discussed repetition in the analytic relationship where patients repeat painful emotions in the transference. They might, for example, find objects for their jealousy similar to those of their own childhood.

In 'Beyond the pleasure principle' Freud argued that many phenomena could not be explained in terms of the pleasure/

unpleasure principle whereby mental events are regulated by the avoidance of unpleasure or the production of pleasure.[18] Freud postulated a principle beyond the pleasure/unpleasure principle – the repetition compulsion which was independent of it. The repetition compulsion was a manifestation of the repressed striving for expression and at times overriding the pleasure/unpleasure principle to which the ego clung.

Lacan linked the repetition of the unconscious repressed to the insistence of the signifying chain. Lacan used the word 'insistence' to express the notion of the repetition compulsion, that is to say, the meaning of the unconscious subject is pressing or insisting on being expressed. (We should remember that for Lacan the true subject is the subject of the unconscious and not the ego). What Lacan does in the Poe essay is to stress the importance for the subject of the repetition of a chain of meaning in a symbolic circuit.

Let us now consider the structure of the repetition in the story. For Lacan the story is structured around two scenes which he calls 'primal scene' and 'repetitive scene'. There is a change of locale and a repetition of a pattern involving three protagonists: scene 1 in the royal boudoir, with the King, Queen and the Minister; scene 2 in the Minister's apartment, with the police, the Minister and Dupin. There is a parallel operation: the Minister/Dupin takes the letter that the Queen/Minister leaves unguarded, while the King/police are oblivious. It is this repeated structure, rather than the theft itself, which interests Lacan

There are, then, two basic scenes: the first, in which the letter is stolen, and the second, a repetition of the first, in which the letter is retrieved. The first scene described by the Prefect to Dupin, is played as between a deaf man and the one who hears. The second scene, described by Dupin to the narrator, takes full account of the register of truth. One can see in these two dialogues, Lacan writes, the opposite use they make of the power of speech, and it is the contrast between them that helps to constitute the drama. Lacan compares the first scene to a primal scene, a scene of sexual intercourse between the parents which the child observes, or his phantasy of what he observes. (Freud emphasised that the primal scene is grasped and interpreted by the child retroactively when he can put it into words.) The powerlessness of the Prefect confronted by the drama he describes has something of the quality of a child who has not been able to grasp the meaning of what he sees, and is still lost in the imaginary experience.

Lacan sheds light on the situation by emphasising the similarity of the two basic scenes in terms of what he called the repetition of an 'inter-subjective complex', made up of a triad of three positions and involving three subjects – the loser, the robber and the third person.

- Position one involves the third person – the King, and then the police, both of whom see nothing. The position of the King, blind to the truth, reminds one of the blind ego.
- Position two involves the loser – the Queen, and then the Minister. They both see that the third person sees nothing.
- Position three involves the robber – the Minister and then Dupin, who both see that what should be hidden is exposed to whoever wants to seize it. This triad of positions is repeated in each scene, but with the various characters changing place.

Lacan sees the second scene as the repetitive scene. This takes place in the Minister's flat, and the participants are the police, the Minister and Dupin. Here the police are in the first position, in the place formerly occupied by the King, and like the King, they see nothing. The Minister is in the second position and makes the same mistake that the Queen formerly made: he deludes himself as to the secrecy of what he hides. And Dupin is in the third position: like the Minister in the first scene he sees that what should be hidden is left exposed. The operation is that Dupin takes the letter from the Minister and puts another in its place.

It should be noticed that it is neither the character of the individual subjects, nor the contents of the letter, but *the position of the letter* within the group that decides what each person will do next. The letter does not function as a unit of meaning (a signified) but as *that which produces certain effects* (a signifier). This, of course, illustrates Lacan's point that it is the Symbolic order that constitutes the human subject. The letter acts like a signifier precisely to the extent that its function in the story does not require that its meaning be revealed.[19]

This story obviously appeals to Lacan because the letter is a signifier. As it moves it attracts different meanings to itself, it mediates different kinds of power relationships and determines subjects in what they do and are. 'The Purloined Letter' is a fable of the analytic process and of the constitutive function of the signifier. To recapitulate: the subjects of the story are modified by the path of the letter; each subject is transformed by the effects of the signifier. The letter, a mobile signifier, passes around in a signifying chain, each person unconsciously aware of what is happening. Lacan emphasises how the letter determines the acts and destiny of the subjects. The signifier, which is within the Symbolic order, dominates the subject. The Symbolic order can no longer be conceived as constituted by, but as constituting.

It could be said that this story is a model of all communication: the transmitter receives his own message back in inverted form from the receiver. One important point to remember about this story is that it concerns an act of *theft*. Lacan stated that anyone, in this case the unscrupulous Minister, who retains a signifier that belongs to someone else will come to be identified with the person who is the rightful possessor of the signifier (here the Queen).[20]

In his seminar on the story Lacan distinguishes between two registers. The first register is that of exactitude, measurement and accuracy. This register is expressed in the account given by the Prefect of Police. His narrative depends on its exactitude being guaranteed by his neutrality: he is merely a messenger, a means of 'linguistic transmission'. The other register is of 'truth', the narrative register which introduces Dupin with all manner of ambiguities, aporias (paradoxes beyond which thought cannot press) and enigmas. Lacan makes a distinction between *la parole* and *le mot*. *La parole* refers to the register of accuracy, exactitude and correctness. *Le mot* (*d'esprit*), though apparently 'freer', is the register which has overtones of wit, the pun and the joke.

Lacan's text raises some interesting questions. Is 'The Purloined Letter' a parable about psychoanalysis? But who is the analyst? Is it Dupin? (Dupin certainly fits the popular image of the psychoanalyst. He is clever at guessing what goes on in other people's minds.) Or is it the neutral American narrator who functions as an analyst?

There is a similarity between the structural positioning of those in the story who pass the purloined letter on and those in life who are determined by a single signifier in inter-subjective discourse, a signifier invested with their desire without being aware of it. This same structure recurs in psychoanalysis itself, where a symptom is repeated in a variety of displacements, unrecognised by the analysand. What often happens is that the analysand, instead of remembering, that is, instead of representing the past as past, and hence as representation, repeats the past as though it were present. The past, instead of being remembered, is re-enacted.

Dupin, in returning the letter to the Queen, is like an analyst, who rids the patient of a symptom. As analyst, Dupin is in a position to understand in what way the second scene is a repetition of the first. It should be remembered, however, that for Lacan, the analyst is *not* to be regarded as the 'the subject who is supposed to know' (unlike American ego-psychologists who know it all). In Lacan's theory the analyst is absent in order that the analysand may do the analysing, refusing the place assigned to him or her as 'subject presumed to know', playing (what in bridge is called) the dummy instead.[21]

Lacan reads Poe's story as an allegory of psychoanalysis, but it is also an allegory of reading, because it shows that both literary and psychoanalytic narrative depend on structures of repetition in order to make sense of experience retrospectively. It is the second scene in the story which allows for an understanding and re-interpretation of the first, because it illustrates how we understand and evaluate the events of the past only when we find ourselves in a position of repeating certain scenarios. Lacan certainly uncovered similarities between Poe's story and the psychoanalytical situation. In analysis, too, a 'letter' can be found, put aside, diverted or hidden by the patient. The basic analytic task is to find this letter.

Jacques Derrida, a French philosopher, has made an interesting critique of Lacan's reading of Poe's story.[22] Derrida accuses Lacan of everything his psychoanalytic adversaries have criticised him for: the failure to give sufficient weight to the imaginary and to narcissism. Lacan has been criticised by Derrida for the overvaluation of the Oedipus complex, the overestimation of the phallus, failing to take into account the pre-Oedipal fears and anxieties of corporal fragmentation, failure to give importance to the ego, for an insufficient stress on feelings and emotions, for being too interested in philosophy and for overintellectualising everything.[23] While asserting that the letter's meaning is lacking, Lacan, according to Derrida, makes this lack into *the* meaning of the letter. Derrida deduces from Lacan's text the fact that, for Lacan, the letter belongs to the Queen as a substitute for the phallus she does not have. Derrida challenges Lacan's 'closure' of Poe's text which he claims results from the drive to analytical mastery. He also attacks Lacan's 'phallogocentrism', his privileging of the phallus as the transcendental signifier. And Lacan's 'style' is dismissed as mere ornament.

In spite of these abrasive remarks, there can be no doubt that Lacan's work was highly suggestive for Derrida, who has continued to think about the terms Lacan seemed most fascinated by: reading, the word, the voice, the ear, the centre and the sun. Indeed, Lacan mentioned on several occasions that he had 'shown Derrida the way'.[24]

What are the main *similarities* between Lacanian psychoanalysis and Derridian philosophy? Both discourses are the product of a similar overlap between the phenomenological currents of the immediate post-war period, and the theoretical innovations of structuralism. Common themes include the relation between language and meaning to subjectivity and consciousness. Their work is united in its emphasis on the priority of the text, or what Lacan calls the 'primacy of the symbolic' (that is to say, the primacy of the symbolic order over the individual being who enters into it). In Lacan's view the Symbolic order cannot be seen as representing the real. He always emphasises that there is no point at which language abuts directly on to the real, since the reference of a term always requires interpretation.

Recently, post-structuralist thinkers such as Derrida, Foucault, Lyotard and Baudrillard have challenged the absolutist or universalist status of the foundational narratives in the West, especially those upon which the Enlightenment, with its social project for global, human emancipation, is based. It has been contentiously suggested by Henry Sussman that one effect of Lacan's work has been to bring the discourse of psychoanalysis out of its modernist and into its postmodernist phase.[25]

Post-structuralists, like Derrida, have made us aware of the value of reading theoretical texts as 'literature'. They also believe that it is important to search in purely literary texts for propositions containing a theory about their own functioning. To put it concisely, post-structuralists put in parentheses their claim to truth in order to expose the textual mechanisms and devices that produce the 'truth effect'.

In post-structuralism the classic opposition between the object-text and its external interpretive reading is replaced by a continuity of an infinite literary-text (which includes a distance towards itself). They are, therefore, against the Lacanian idea of the *point de capiton*, which they see as an attempt to master and restrain the 'dissemination' of the textual process. Post-structuralists insist that every text, their own included, is caught in a decentred network of plural processes, and that the textual process always subverts what its 'author' intended to say.

As Slavoj Zizek correctly points out, it was Lévi-Strauss who, in spite of his criticisms of post-structuralism, opened the way to deconstruction by suggesting that theoretical interpretations of myths were new versions of the same myth.[26] He conceived Freud's theory of the Oedipus complex, for example, as just a new variation of the Oedipus myth.

The new postmodern universe, with its celebration of the look, surfaces, textures, the self-as-commodity, threatens to reduce everything to the image/representation/ simulacrum. There is no longer a realm of the real versus that of imitation or mimicry, but rather a level in which there is only simulation.[27] This involves the obliteration of any distinction between an 'inside' and an 'outside'. We live in a world in which all we have are simulations, there being no 'real' external to them, no 'original' that is being copied. The concept of the postmodern involves the blurring of hitherto sacrosanct boundaries and polarities, the elimination of any position from which to speak or judge.[28] The main point is this: post-structuralism is a theory which excludes the truth-dimension; it reduces the truth-dimension to a textual 'truth-effect'. This is in contrast with Lacan, who always insists on psychoanalysis as a truth-experience.

Notes

The historical and social context: The emergence of French psychoanalytic culture

1. In this section I have drawn on Sherry Turkle, *Psychoanalytic Politics: Freud's French Revolution* (London: Burnett Books, 1979).
2. Louis Althusser, 'Freud and Lacan', in *Lenin and Philosophy and Other Essays* (London: New Left Books, 1971). Althusser argued that one must learn to read correctly. A word or concept cannot be considered in isolation; it exists only in the theoretical or ideological framework in which it is used: its problematic. It is *not* a world-view, it is not the essence of the thought of an individual or epoch, it is centred on the *absence* of problems and concepts within the problematic as much as their presence; it can therefore be reached only by a symptomatic reading on the model of the Freudian analyst's reading of his or her patient's utterances. Louis Althusser, the greatest and the most controversial Marxist philosopher of modern times, a writer whose work influenced many disciplines, died in 1990.
3. In my personal experience this is what happened in Britain also. Many of the people that I first met in 'Capital' reading groups some years ago, I see now in Lacanian study groups.
4. Turkle, op. cit., p. 230.

Chapter 1: The Freudian terrain

1. If we consider Freud's work in 'phases' the 'first phase' represents Freud's views from the time he returned from working with Charcot in Paris in 1886 till 1887 when he abandoned his seduction theory. In this period he believed that his patients were the victims of 'forgotten' childhood seductions (actually not consciously forgotten but repressed). The abandonment of the seduction theory marked the beginning of the second phase in psychoanalysis, which ran from 1897 until 1923. The key theoretical idea of this phase was the Oedipus complex, the theory which suggests that young children have phantasies of sexual desire for their parents.

2. Richard Wollheim, *Freud* (London: Fontana/Collins, 1971), p. 9.

3. Useful books on Freud include: Ronald Clark, *Freud: The man and the cause* (London: Paladin/Granada, 1982); Frank Sulloway, *Freud, Biologist of the Mind* (London: Fontana/Collins, 1980); J.N. Isbister, *Freud: An introduction to his life and work* (Cambridge: Polity Press, 1985).

4. Sigmund Freud, see the volumes in the Pelican Freud Library (London: Penguin, 1973).

5. Sigmund Freud, *New Introductory Lectures on Psycho-Analysis*, S.E. XXII, p. 77.

6. Ibid., p. 80.

7. Sigmund Freud, vol. 14: *Art and Literature* (London: Penguin, 1985), p. 65.

8. A striking independent confirmation of Freud's doctrine may be D.H. Lawrence's *Sons and Lovers*. Without appearing to be at all aware of it, it is a profoundly Oedipal novel. For a Freudian analysis see Terry Eagleton, *Literary Theory: An introduction* (Oxford: Basil Blackwell, 1983), pp. 174–8.

9. Prior to his work on dreams Freud's work had been concerned only with the abnormal and pathological; with his work on dreams he could enter the world of the normal. Sigmund Freud, vol. 4: *The Interpretation of Dreams* (London: Penguin, 1976).

10. Dreams and art are not merely linked because they fulfil wishes, but because both have to make use of strategies in order to overcome the resistance of consciousness: 'work' is done by the dreamer and the artist to transform their primitive desires into culturally acceptable meanings. See Elizabeth Wright, *Psychoanalytic Criticism: Theory in practice* (London: Methuen, 1984), p. 28.

11. Freud was later to exclude secondary revision from the dream-work. For a detailed exposition of the mechanisms see Freud, *The Interpretation of Dreams*, Chapter 6.
12. A most useful reference work to have available is Laplanche and J.-B. Pontalis, *The Language of Psycho-Analysis* (London: Hogarth Press, 1973).
13. Ibid., p. 458.
14. Ibid., p. 92.
15. See John Forrester, *Language and the Origins of Psychoanalysis* (London: Macmillan, 1980).
16. Anika Lemaire, *Jacques Lacan* (London: Routledge & Kegan Paul, 1977).
17. Catherine Clément, *The Lives and Legends of Jacques Lacan* (New York: Columbia University Press, 1983), p. 2.

Chapter 2: The legacy of surrealism

1. Bice Benvenuto and Roger Kennedy, *The Works of Jacques Lacan: An introduction* (London: Free Association Books, 1986), p. 33.
2. David Macey, *Lacan in Contexts* (London: Verso, 1988), p. 48.
3. Anna Balakian, *Surrealism: The road to the absolute* (New York: a Ditton paperback, 1970), p. 128.
4. A collection of key documents, including Breton's manifestoes, is in Patrick Waldberg, *Surrealism* (London: Thames & Hudson, 1965).
5. The surrealists exalted certain values. The first among these was 'convulsive beauty', the beauty which results from a sharp conflict between movement and immobility. The second value was 'objective chance', that is the sum total of the coincidences which control a destiny. The third was 'black humour', which has in it tragic undertones, and the fourth value was *amour fou*, extravagant love. For an account of the movement see Sarane Alexandrian, *Surrealist Art* (London: Thames & Hudson, 1970), p. 118.
6. Sigmund Freud, 'Delusions and dreams in Jensen's "Gradiva"' (1907), in vol. 14: *Art and Literature* (London: Penguin, 1985).
7. Whitney Chadwick, *Myth in Surrealist Painting 1929–1939* (Michigan: UMI Research Press, 1980), p. 9.
8. Sigmund Freud, 'Totem and taboo' (1913), in vol. 13: *The Origins of Religion* (London: Penguin, 1985).
9. Quoted in Whitney Chadwick, op. cit., p. 62.
10. Ibid., pp. 62–4.
11. Magritte thus calls into question the whole process of representation. These ideas are discussed in Suzi Gablik, *Magritte* (London: Thames & Hudson, 1970), p. 128. The signifier is the physical object, for

example, a sound, a printed word, or image. The signified is a mental concept. The sign is the associated total which relates the two together. The referent is the real object.

12. Jacques Lacan, *Ecrits: A selection* (London: Tavistock, 1977).

13. Magritte continually formulated and explored in his work the tension between reality and illusion. In *The Human Condition*, I (1933) he tried to define the ambiguity which exists between a real object, one's mental image of it, and the painted representation. Looking at these pictures we ask: is the landscape we see one which is painted on the canvas inside the room, or is it one which is outside the window? See Gablik, op. cit., p. 85.

14. The skull is painted in a literally quite different optic from everything else in the picture. If the skull had been painted like the rest, its metaphysical implication – its continual reminder of the presence of death – would have disappeared; it would have become an object like everything else. For a political reading of 'The Ambassadors', see John Berger, *Ways of Seeing* (London: Penguin, 1972), pp. 89–97.

15. Jacques Lacan, *The Four Fundamental Concepts of Psychoanalysis* (London: Penguin, 1979), pp. 88–9.

16. Salvador Dali often exploits the device of the double image. He contrives that the two images should be interchangeable, in such a way that the second image will completely replace the first in a given moment of perception. The image of a horse, for example, is at the same time the image of a woman. With this method he hoped to induce a paranoid state in the spectator, who is confused and uncertain as to what s/he has just seen. As a result, Dali's world is one in which nothing is what it seems to be because everything is really something else.

17. Rosalind Krauss and Jane Livingstone, *L'Amour Fou: Photography and surrealism* (London: Arts Council of Great Britain, 1986), p. 70.

18. Roger Caillois, 'La Mante religieuse', *Minotaure*, no. 5, 1934.

19. Roger Caillois, 'Mimétisme et psychasthénie légendaire', *Minotaure*, no. 7, 1935.

20. See Jacques Lacan, *Ecrits*, p. 3.

21. A fascinating story: see Sigmund Freud and Joseph Breuer, vol. 3, *Studies on Hysteria* (London: Penguin, 1974), p. 83. For the theory of the talking cure, see John Forrester, *Language and the Origins of Psychoanalysis* (London: Macmillan, 1980), Chapter 1. This book demonstrates the fundamental nature of the theory and practice of language and speech in psychoanalysis. Though there is nothing in the book about Lacan, it can be seen as a prolegomena to the Lacanian school of analysis.

22. Lacan's thesis was published in France in 1975.

23. Jacques-Alain Miller claims that Lacan, having read Freud's theories on the superego and masochism, and through examining a clinical history, produced a new clinical category: self-punitive psychosis. See Jacques-Alain Miller, 'How psychoanalysis cures according to Lacan', in *Newsletter of the Freudian Field*, vol. 1, no. 2, Fall 1987, p. 7.

Chapter 3: The uses of philosophy

1. Spinoza spent most of his short life (1632–77) in poverty. Excommunicated from the Jewish community and feared by Christians – who regarded him as an atheist – Spinoza's masterpiece, *The Ethics*, did not appear till 1677, after his death. It should be noted that Lacan's contemporary, Louis Althusser, was also greatly influenced by Spinoza's *Ethics*. As Anderson remarks: 'Nearly all the novel concepts and accents of Althusser's Marxism . . . were in fact drawn from Spinoza.' See Perry Anderson, *Considerations on Western Marxism* (London: Verso, 1976), pp. 64–5.
2. Alexandre Kojève, *Introduction to the Reading of Hegel: Lectures on 'The Phenomenology of Spirit'* assembled by Raymond Queneau (Ithaca/London: Cornell University Press, 1980), p. 3.
3. In Hegel 'I' refers to the self – there is no distinction, as there is in Lacan, between the I that speaks and the I that is spoken (the true speech that arises from the unconscious). Second, Lacan distinguishes, unlike Hegel, between need, demand and desire.
4. Studies by contemporary psychoanalysts show how a person may be denied recognition. Actions and utterances which express one's own individuality may be persistently ignored, or dismissed. Within a closed institution such as the family this denial of recognition may, quite literally, lead to the disintegration of a person's sense of identity and to schizophrenia. See, for example, R.D. Laing, *Self and Others* (London: Penguin, 1971).
5. Peter Dews, *Logics of Disintegration* (London: Verso, 1987), p. 54.
6. There is an astonishing one-act play, *The Maids* (1947), about the Master–Slave relationship, by Jean Genet. Two maids, Claire and Solange, both love and hate their wealthy employer. They dream of murder. Claire plays at being Madame, and Solange at being Claire. And we await the return of Madame which will restore them to their true situation as servants. Each of the two maids has no other function than to be the other, to be – for the other – herself as other. The dyad of the maids is haunted by a phantom of unity. Each sees in the other only herself at a distance from herself. Each bears witness to the other of the impossibility of being herself. Claire remarks, 'And

me, I'm sick of seeing my image thrown back at me by a mirror, like a bad smell. You're my bad smell.' Jean Genet, *The Maids* (1947) and *Deathwatch*, two plays with an introduction by Jean-Paul Sartre (London: Faber & Faber, 1989).

7. Jacques-Alain Miller (ed.), *The Seminar of Jacques Lacan*, Book I, *Freud's Papers on Technique, 1953–1954* (Cambridge: Cambridge University Press, 1988), p. 215. For Lacan's comments on the Master–Slave dialectic, see p. 223.

8. Jacques Lacan, *The Four Fundamental Concepts of Psychoanalysis* (London: Penguin, 1979), p. 96.

9. Sartre discusses Hegel and the Master–Slave relation in *Being and Nothingness* (London: Routledge & Kegan Paul, 1969).

10. Lacan makes these criticisms in his paper on the mirror phase. See *Ecrits: A selection* (London: Tavistock, 1977), p. 6.

11. Ibid., pp. 47–8.

12. Martin Heidegger, *Being and Time* (Oxford: Basil Blackwell, 1962).

13. Martin Heidegger, 'Building, Dwelling, Thinking' (1951) in *Poetry, Language, Thought* (New York: Harper & Row, 1971), p. 146.

14. For a useful discussion of these concepts see George Steiner, *Heidegger* (London: Fontana, 1978), pp. 92–3.

15. Sigmund Freud, 'On narcissism: An introduction' (1914), in vol. 11: *On Metapsychology, the Theory of Psychoanalysis* (London: Penguin, 1984).

16. See, for example, the reference to La Rochefoucauld in Lacan, op. cit. p. 24.

17. See the discussion in ibid., pp. 128–9 and 299–300.

18. Jacques Lacan, 'Television', in *October 40*, MIT Press, Spring 1987, p. 7.

19. Sigmund Freud and Joseph Breuer, vol. 3, *Studies in Hysteria* (London: Penguin, 1974).

20. William J. Richardson, 'Lacan and non-philosophy', in Hugh J. Silverman (ed.), *Philosophy and Non-Philosophy since Merleau-Ponty* (London: Routledge, 1988), p. 133.

Chapter 4: The functions of language

1. This example is from Jacques-Alain Miller, 'How psychoanalysis cures according to Lacan', in *Newsletter of the Freudian Field*, vol. 1, no. 2, Fall 1987, p. 17.

2. This is quoted by Jean-Jacques Lecercle, *Philosophy through the Looking-Glass: Language, nonsense, desire* (London: Hutchinson, 1985), p. 133.

3. Jacques Lacan, *Ecrits: A selection* (London: Tavistock, 1977), p. 61.

4. It should be remembered that Lévi-Strauss had begun to apply a linguistic model to the analysis of kinship systems in 1945. The application to psychoanalysis of Saussure's linguistics by Lacan received its full expression in the papers: 'The function and field of speech and language' (1953), 'The Freudian thing' (1955) and 'The agency of the letter' (1957).

5. Lacan, op. cit., p. 149.

6. Claude Lévi-Strauss, *The Elementary Structures of Kinship* (London: Tavistock, 1970), and see Lacan, op. cit., p. 66.

7. For a detailed discussion of metaphor and metonymy see part IV of Christian Metz, *Psychoanalysis and the Cinema* (London: Macmillan, 1982); and Lacan op. cit., pp. 156–8.

8. The privileging of metaphor over metonymy has been related to the phallocentric neglect of femininity. Luce Irigaray, in a critique of Lacan, accuses the privilege of metaphor (quasi solid) over metonymy (which has more to do with fluids). She believes that science has studied solids and neglected fluids. She then links this to the neglect of feminine sexuality in psychoanalysis, by asserting that the feminine is fluid. For the argument that Lacan neglects fluids, and thus women, in favour of the solidity of the phallus, see Luce Irigaray, *This Sex which is not One* (Ithaca: Cornell University Press, 1985).

9. Lacan, op. cit., p. 155.

10. According to Freud the cotton reel was the child's symbol for his mother, and the 'fort-da' game gave him the illusion of control over her (desirable) presence and (undesirable) absence. Lacan accepts this symbolism but makes it depend rather less upon the object and rather more upon the words which polarise a 'here' and a 'there' location for both the mother and the cotton reel. For Lacan, the child's assimilation under the control of language is far more important than the illusion of control over his mother. He remarks: 'This is the point of insertion of a symbolic order that pre-exists the infantile subject and in accordance with which he will have to structure himself.' See Lacan, op. cit., p. 254.

11. Sigmund Freud, vol.6, *Jokes and Their relation to the Unconscious* (London: Penguin, 1977). See Lacan, op. cit., p. 173.

Chapter 5: The development of the theory

1. Catherine Clément, *The Lives and Legends of Jacques Lacan* (New York: Columbia University Press, 1983), p. 58.

2. The two articles by Lacan published in *Minotaure* have been published, together with his thesis on medicine, under the title *Premiers Ecrits sur la paranoia* (Paris: Seuil, 1975).
3. Clément, op. cit., p. 71.
4. See Sigmund Freud and Jose Breuer, vol.3 *Studies on Hysteria* (London: Penguin, 1974), p. 124.
5. Jacques Lacan, *Ecrits: A selection* (London: Tavistock, 1977), p. 4.
6. See Juliet Mitchell (ed.), *The Selected Melanie Klein* (London: Penguin, 1986), p. 41.
7. The fort-da game is, perhaps, the shortest story we can imagine: an object is lost, and then recovered. But even the most complex narratives can be read as variants on this model: an original settlement is disrupted and ultimately restored. From this viewpoint, narrative is a source of consolation: lost objects are a cause of anxiety to us, symbolising certain deeper unconscious losses. The fort-da game is described in Sigmund Freud, 'Beyond the Pleasure Principle', in *On Metapsychology* (London: Penguin, 1984), p. 284.
8. Juliet Mitchell and Jacqueline Rose, *Feminine Sexuality: Jacques Lacan and the école Freudienne* (London: Macmillan Press, 1982), p. 32.
9. One might believe that it is the other, one's sexual other half, that the living being seeks to love, but Lacan stresses the search by the subject, not of the sexual complement, but of the part of him- or herself, lost for ever. See Jacques Lacan, *The Four Fundamental Concepts of Psychoanalysis* (London: Penguin, 1979), p. 205.
10. Marguerite Duras, *Le Ravissement de Lol. V. Stein* (Paris: Gallimard, 1964).
11. See Sherry Turkle, *Psychoanalytic Politics: Freud's French revolution* (London: Burnett Books, 1979), especially Chapters 4 and 5. Some of the documents about the split of 1953, and subsequent events, are included in an American journal; see Joan Copjec, 'Dossier on the institutional debate', in *October* 40, MIT Press, Spring, 1987.
12. Lacan, op cit., pp. 128–9.
13. Ibid., p. 98.
14. Stuart Schneiderman, *Jacques Lacan: The death of an intellectual hero* (Cambridge, MA/London: Harvard University Press, 1983), p. 135.
15. Ibid., p. 138.
16. Ibid., p. 97. The reference here is to Freud's case study of the 'Wolf-Man'. Letters of the alphabet are important in particular unconscious processes; consider the role of the Roman number V in the Wolf-Man's unconscious. The figure is first isolated in the dream image of a butterfly flapping its wings; the patient associates this with a woman standing with her legs apart, and Freud reminds us that the fifth hour of the day was for the Wolf-Man the time for depression.

Of course, sometimes, a word may function as a letter. See Sigmund Freud, vol. 9: *Case Histories II, 'Rat Man', Schreber, The 'Wolf-Man', A Case of Female Homosexuality* (London: Penguin, 1979).

17. What is the meaning of the term Other? There are several meanings: sometimes, the unconscious is 'the discourse of the Other'. At other times it can refer to one term in the dialectical couple Subject–Other; it can also refer to 'otherness' in the sense of heterogeneity. For Lacan as for Freud the primal Other is the father within the Oedipal triangle, who forbids incest, threatens castration and by placing an absolute prohibition upon the child's desire for its mother becomes the inaugurating agent of Law. Lacan is not concerned with the real or imaginary fathers of a given individual but with the symbolic father. Other, then, can be variously defined as the Father, the Law, a place, any dialectical partner, the signifier, or the repository of language and culture.

18. Jacques Lacan, *The Four Fundamental Concepts of Psychoanalysis,* (London: Penguin, 1979), p. 25.

19. It may be useful to know, at this stage, some of the differences between the Kleinian and Lacanian approaches: in Kleinian theory there is an emphasis on the mother rather than the father. There is an emphasis on the breast rather than the phallus. There is also an emphasis on the ego and its development. Klein is close to ego-psychology. Like Kris, Hartmann and Loewenstein, she wants to increase the strength of the ego. Klein argues that the child is born with a rudimentary ego. In Lacanian theory, when the child is born the unconscious does not exist. It comes into being when the child enters language (the symbolic). Moreover, the ego develops at the mirror phase, it is not there from the beginning. While Klein emphasises the incapacity of the ego to tolerate anxiety, Lacan stresses loss, lack. For Klein, language is fixed, there is a direct link between signifier and signified. In Lacan signifier and signified are separated. Signifiers refer not to signified but other signifiers. Kleinian analysts believe that they can give complete explanations to their patients. The Lacanian view of an analyst is that s/he acts as a (neutral) screen. The aim is not to get the analysand to identify with the ego of the analyst, but for the analysand to attain some sort of self-understanding, to say at the end of analysis: 'That's me!'

Chapter 6: Lacan's Ecrits*: A review*

1. Jacques Lacan, *Ecrits: A selection* (London: Tavistock, 1977).
2. See Jacques-Alain Miller (ed.), *The Seminar of Jacques Lacan,* Book I, *Freud's Papers on Technique 1953–1954*; Book II, *The Ego in*

186   *Notes*

Freud's Theory and in the Technique of Psychoanalysis 1954–1955. Both books were published by Cambridge University Press, 1988. See also Book XI, *The Four Fundamental Concepts of Psychoanalysis* (London: Penguin, 1979).

3. Roland Barthes, *Critical Essays* (Evanston: Northwestern University Press, 1972).
4. David Macey, *Lacan in Contexts* (London: Verso, 1988), p. 13.
5. Lacan, op. cit., p. 22.
6. Bice Benvenuto and Roger Kennedy, *The Works of Jacques Lacan: An introduction* (London: Free Association Books, 1986), p. 61.
7. Lacan's paper has also been translated with notes and commentary by Anthony Wilden, *Speech and Language in Psychoanalysis* (Baltimore: The Johns Hopkins University Press, 1984). It was originally published in 1968 as *The Language of the Self*.
8. Lacan, op. cit., pp. 103–4, 113. Sigmund Freud, 'Beyond the pleasure principle', in vol. 11: *On Metapsychology: The theory of psychoanalysis*, p. 284.
9. Lacan, op. cit., p. 149.
10. Slavoj Zizek, *The Sublime Object of Ideology* (London: Verso, 1989), p. 87.
11. Students will find the following book very helpful: Kaja Silverman, *The Subject of Semiotics* (London: Oxford University Press, 1983). For more advanced students: Jean-François Lyotard, 'The dream work does not think', in Andrew Benjamin (ed.), *The Lyotard Reader* (Oxford: Basil Blackwell, 1989).
12. Joan Rivière, 'Womanliness as a masquerade', *IJPA* 10, 1982, reprinted in *Formations of Fantasy* (London: Routledge, 1986).
13. Ibid., p. 36.
14. Ibid., p. 37.
15. Stephen Heath, 'Joan Rivière and the masquerade', in *Formations of Fantasy*, p. 50.
16. Jacques Lacan, 'The signification of the phallus', in op. cit., p. 290. This paper is also in Juliet Mitchell and Jacqueline Rose (eds), *Feminine Sexuality: Jacques Lacan and the école Freudienne* (London: Macmillan, 1982), p. 84.
17. Lacan, op. cit., p. 322.
18. Ibid., p. 283.
19. Sigmund Freud, vol.4, *The Interpretation of Dreams* (London: Penguin, 1976) p. 559. Besides the dead father dream, read the burning child dream, p. 652. In both dreams, regardless of who is dead, it is the father who does not know.
20. Lacan, op. cit., p. 300.
21. Ibid., pp. 301-2.

22. Ibid., pp. 314-15.
23. Ibid., p. 315.

Chapter 7: The Imaginary, the Symbolic and the Real

1. The Imaginary is the order of mirror images, identifications. The imaginary is *not* the same as the illusory in that the phantasmatic constructions comprising the Imaginary order are highly durable and can have effects in the Real.
2. Sigmund Freud, vol. 11: *On Metapsychology: The theory of psycho-analysis* (London: Penguin Books, 1984), p. 84.
3. Lacan took the notion of the impossible from Alexandre Koyré, *Galileo Studies* (Brighton: Harvester, 1977). It should be added that the Imaginary, the Symbolic and the Real are not mental forces but orders, each of which serves to position the individual within a force-field that traverses him or her. The three orders pressurise each other continuously.
4. Each of the Lacan's orders harks back to Freud: the Symbolic to the superego, the Real to the Id, and the Imaginary to the ego. See Catherine Clément, *The Lives and Legends of Jacques Lacan* (New York: Columbia University Press, 1983), p. 169.
5. Stuart Schneiderman, *Jacques Lacan: The Death of an Intellectual Hero*, (London: Harvard University Press, 1983), p. 119.
6. Freud's analysis of Schreber's case is in the Pelican Freud Library, vol. 9: *Case Studies* II (London: Penguin, 1979), pp. 131–223. Lacan's analysis of Schreber, as yet untranslated, is in *Seminaire III: Les psychoses* (Paris: Seuil, 1981). For a useful discussion of Schreber see Jean-Jacques Lecercle, *Philosophy through the Looking Glass* (London: Hutchinson, 1985), pp. 120–38. A full account can be found in *Memoirs of My Nervous Illness*, edited by Ida Macalpine and Richard A. Hunter (London: Dawson & Sons, 1955).
7. Bankruptcy of the paternal metaphor also lies behind a celebrated case described by Michel Foucault (ed.), *I, Pierre Rivière . . . A Case of Parricide in the 19th Century* (London: Penguin, 1978).
8. For a full discussion of foreclosure see J. Laplanche and J.B. Pontalis, *The Language of Psychoanalysis* (London: Hogarth Press, 1973), pp. 166–8.
9. Bice Benvenuto and Roger Kennedy, *The Works of Jacques Lacan: An introduction* (London: Free Association Books, London, 1986), p. 144.
10. Leclaire, quoted in ibid., p. 153.
11. Jacques Lacan, *Ecrits: A selection* (London: Tavistock, 1977), p. 215.

12. Benvenuto and Kennedy, op. cit., p. 160.
13. Fredric Jameson, 'Imaginary and symbolic in Lacan: Marxism, psychoanalytic criticism, and the problem of the subject', in Shoshana Felman (ed.), *Literature and Psychoanalysis* (Baltimore: Johns Hopkins University Press, 1977), p. 349.
14. Juliet Mitchell (ed.), *The Selected Melanie Klein* (London: Penguin, 1986).
15. Lacan, op. cit., p. 312.
16. Jameson, op. cit., p. 349.
17. See Jacques Lacan, *The Four Fundamental Concepts of Psychoanalysis* (London: Penguin, 1979), pp. 85 and 131. Anamorphosis is a distorted drawing or painting which appears regular from one point; see, for example, the depiction of the skull in Hans Holbein's 'The Ambassadors' in the National Gallery, London.
18. The German mathematician and astronomer Augustus Möbius (1790–1868) introduced the one-sided strip which has all kinds of unexpected properties. Another German mathematician, Felix Klein (1849–1925), following Möbius's lead, devised a bottle with but one surface; that is to say, it has an outside but no inside. Such a bottle, if it could be cut in half lengthwise, would fall into two Möbius strips. For a clear introduction see H. Steinhaus, *Mathematical Snapshots* (Oxford: Oxford University Press), 1983. For knots see p. 266, and for the Möbius band, pp. 269–73.
19. The imbrication of real, symbolic and the imaginary in terms of the topology of knots was discussed by Lacan in 1975. For a diagram of the Borromean knot see Schneiderman, op. cit., p. 33. They are also illustrated in Sherry Turkle, *Psychoanalytical Politics: Freud's French revolution* (London: Burnett Books, 1979), p. 235.
20. Ibid., p. 182.
21. Clément, op. cit., p. 28.
22. Turkle, op. cit., p. 245.
23. Malcolm Bowie, *Freud, Poust and Lacan: Theory as fiction* (Cambridge: Cambridge University Press, 1987), p. 130.
24. Peter Dews, *Logics of Disintegration: Post-structuralist thought and the claims of critical theory* (London: Verso, 1987), p. 106.
25. J.G. Merquior, *From Prague to Paris: A critique of structuralist and post-structuralist thought* (London: Verso, 1986), p. 153.
26. Emile Benveniste, *Problems in General Linguistics* (Miami: Miami University Press, 1971), Chapter 7.
27. Merquior, op. cit., p. 150.
28. Luce Irigaray, *This Sex which is not One* (Ithaca: Cornell University Press, 1985).

29. Stephen Frosh, *The Politics of Psychoanalysis* (London: Macmillan, 1987), p. 194.
30. Dews, op. cit., p. 105.
31. Ibid., p. 108.

Chapter 8: Sexuality, love and feminism

1. Juliet Mitchell and Jacqueline Rose (eds.) *Feminine Sexuality: Jacques Lacan and the école Freudienne*, London, Macmillan, 1982, p. 7. Juliet Mitchell claims that feminists have not adequately understood Lacan's position. She argues that Lacan provides an accurate *description* (it is not a prescription) of patriarchal power relations; the psychoanalytic explanation of patriarchy is not simply about the relations between men and women, but the relations both have to the phallus. Mitchell's influential *Psychoanalysis and Feminism* (London: Penguin, 1975) alerted feminists to the ways in which Freud's insights have been misrepresented. The text is clearly indebted to Lacan's reading of Freud, with its emphasis on social and significatory rather than instinctual and hereditory forms of explanation.
2. Sigmund Freud, vol. 7, *on Sexuality* (London: Penguin, 1977).
3. Bice Benvenuto and Roger Kennedy, *The Works of Jacques Lacan: An introduction* (London: Free Associations Books, London, 1986), p. 131. Lacan's argument is that the symbolic is the condition of sanity; outside the symbolic law there is psychosis. Generally, Lacanians insist that the symbolic is patriarchal because the woman is the primary care-giver, the man the intervening third party, occupying the position coincident with language. One problem with this view is that it makes patriarchy seem inevitable.
4. Lacan, 'A Love Letter', in Mitchell and Rose, op. cit., p. 157.
5. Lacan, 'Seminar of 21 January, 1975' in ibid ., p. 168.
6. Lacan, 'God and the Jouissance of Woman' in ibid., p. 144.
7. Lacan, quoted ibid., p. 46.
8. Lacan, 'Seminar on 21 January 1975' in ibid., p. 142.
9. Ibid., p. 141. The aim of courtly love is to generate pleasure, but this goal is suspended. In any sort of love the structure of the super ego is modified, changed. Now, one of the functions of the super ego is to punish – it systematically denies the working of desire. Lacan believed that the authority of the super ego must be replaced by the law of desire.
10. Quoted in Georges Bataille, *Eroticism* (London: Marion Boyars, 1987), p. 224. This book contains a useful discussion of mysticism and sensuality. It has been argued by David Macey that the imagery Lacan selects to illustrate *Encore* belongs to the surrealist movement

which focuses on convulsive beauty and erotic ecstasy. He contends that the iconography of female sexuality, elaborated by the surrealists in the 1920s, influenced Lacan's later explorations of 'the dark continent' of feminine sexuality. See David Macey, *Lacan in Contexts* (London: Verso, 1988), p. 72.

11. Lacan, 'God and the Jouissance of Woman', in Mitchell and Rose, op cit., p. 142.
12. Ibid., p. 147.
13. Ibid., p. 146.
14. Benvenuto and Kennedy, op. cit., p. 192.
15. Jerry Aline Flieger, 'The Female Subject: (What) Does Woman Want?' in Richard Feldstein and Henry Sussman (eds), *Psychoanalysis and . . .* (London: Routledge, 1990), p. 72.
16. Toril Moi, *Sexual/Textual Politics: Feminist literary theory* (London: Methuen, 1985), p. 96.
17. Hélène Cixous and Catherine Clément, *The Newly Born Woman* (Manchester: Manchester University Press, 1986), p. 63.
18. Ibid., p. 92.
19. Morag Shiach, 'Their 'symbolic' exists, it holds power - we, the sowers of disorder, know it only too well', in Teresa Brennan (ed.) *Between feminism and psychoanalysis* (Routledge: London, 1989), p. 165. See also Morag Shiach, *Hélène Cixous: A politics of writing* (London: Routledge, 1991).
20. Logocentric thinking is that which privileges the Logos, the Word as a metaphysical presence. Phallocentrism is a system that privileges the phallus as the symbol or source of power. The fusion of logocentrism and phallocentrism is often called, after Derrida, phallogocentrism. Perhaps it is *because* of Lacan's logocentric and phallocentric commitments that his work is so useful in the projects of many feminists. See Elizabeth Grosz's excellent book, *Jacques Lacan: A feminist introduction* (London: Routledge, 1990), p. 189.
21. Luce Irigaray's best-known works include: *Speculum of the Other Woman* (Ithaca and New York: Cornell University Press, 1985); *This Sex which is not One* (Ithaca and New York: Cornell University Press, 1985).
22. The difficulty of women effecting separation is discussed in, for example, Nancy Chodorow, *The Reproduction of Mothering: Psychoanalysis and the sociology of gender* (Berkeley: University of California Press, 1978).
23. Irigary, *Speculum*, p. 48.
24. Sigmund Freud, 'The "Uncanny"' in vol. 14: *Art and Literature* (London: Penguin, 1985). I discuss the gaze and voyeurism in Chapter 9 on film.

25. See Margaret Whitford, 'Rereading Irigaray' in Teresa Brennan (ed.), op. cit., p. 120. On Irigaray's claim that Western reason is premised on the suppression of sexual difference, and her engagement with Lacanian and Derridean theory see Margaret Whitford, *Luce Irigaray: Philosophy in the feminine* (London: Routledge, 1991).
26. Julia Kristeva, 'Women's time' in Toril Moi (ed.), *The Kristeva Reader* (Oxford: Blackwell, 1986), p. 194.
27. Toril Moi, *Sexual/Textual Politics: Feminist literary theory* (London: Methuen, 1985), p. 152.
28. Ibid., p. 169.
29. Julia Kristeva, *About Chinese Women* (London: Marion Boyars, 1977), pp. 28–9.
30. See the essays 'Giotto's joy' and 'Motherhood according to Giovanni Bellini' in Julia Kristeva, *Desire in Language: A semiotic approach to literature and art* (Oxford: Basil Blackwell, 1981).
31. Stephen Frosh, *The Politics of Psychoanalysis: An introduction to Freudian and post-Freudian theory* (London: Macmillan, 1987), p. 205.
32. Jane Gallop, *Feminism and Psychoanalysis: The daughter's seduction* (London: Macmillan, 1982), p. 155.

Chapter 9: Lacan and film

1. Christian Metz, *Psychoanalysis and the Cinema: The imaginary signifier* (London: Macmillan, 1982), p. 31.
2. Jacques Lacan, *Ecrits: A selection* (London: Tavistock, 1977), pp. 1–7.
3. Metz, op. cit., p. 97.
4. Ibid. pp. 101–42.
5. Lyotard is critical of Lacan because he thinks that Lacan underestimates the dream-work's considerations of figurability, the role of images. He believes that Lacan is motivated to find in the dream-work the operations of speech. Lyotard's argument is that the dream is *not* a discourse because it is intrinsically different from the operations of speech. This is not only against Lacan's view, it is also counter to the current tendency to stuff all of semiology into linguistics. For Lyotard reverie, dream, phantasm are mixtures containing both viewing and reading matter. The dream is not a language; it is the effect on language of the force exerted by the figural (as image or as form). See Jean-François Lyotard, 'The dream work does not think', in Andrew Benjamin (ed.), *The Lyotard Reader* (Oxford: Blackwell, 1989), p. 51

6. To understand fully why Lacan identifies condensation with metaphor and displacement with metonymy, one has to return to Roman Jakobson's work. Jakobson argued that in every speech act there is an act of selection which corresponds to the paradigm, and an act of combination to the syntagm. He linked this with his study of aphasia. He believes that two forms of aphasia may be distinguished according to whether the illness attacks the selective activity (disruption of similarity), or whether, on the other hand, it affects the combinatory activity (the relations of contiguity). As is well known, Jakobson also applied his criterion of similarity/contiguity to literary discourse. Similarity is associated with metaphor, contiguity with metonymy. See R. Jakobson and M. Halle, *Fundamentals of Language* (The Hague: Mouton, 1956).

   Lyotard believes that Jakobson starts off from a notion of substitution based on a strictly structuralist concept of language. In Lyotard's view, the creative spark of the metaphor does not spring from the presentation of two images, that is of two signifiers equally actualised, but rather, from the eclipse of one term for which another is substituted. The true metaphor, the trope, begins with the too-wide gap, the transgression of the range of acceptable substitutes sanctioned by usage. The true metaphor defies usage.

7. Metz, op. cit., pp. 69–74.
8. Ibid., p. 48.
9. The French terms *énonciation* and *énoncé* refer respectively to the act of speaking (or writing, or constructing a sequence of images, etc.) and to what is said (written, etc). In Metz these terms are translated as 'enunciation' and 'statement'.
10. Ibid., p. 89.
11. See Sandy Flitterman-Lewis, 'Psychoanalysis, film, and television', in Robert Allen (ed.), *Channels of Discourse* (London: Methuen, 1987), p. 186.
12. This section draws on Kaja Silverman's useful summary of suture in *The Subject of Semiotics* (Oxford: Oxford University Press, 1983), Chapter 5.
13. Ibid., p. 204.
14. Laura Mulvey, 'Visual pleasure and narrative cinema', *Screen*, vol. 16, no. 3, Autumn 1975, p. 11. This essay is now in her book *Visual and Other Pleasures* (London: Macmillan, 1989).
15. Ibid., p. 19. For her self-criticisms of the article see p. 62.
16. In some films the look is central to the plot and oscillates between voyeurism and fetishistic fascination. See, for example, Alfred Hitchcock's *Rear Window*, Michael Powell's *Peeping Tom*, and Krzystzof Kieslowski's *A Short Film about Love*.

17. Most Lacanian readings focus on the problem of desire and, specifically, sexuality in a text. (I do not have to repeat that sexuality consists of a multiplicity of conflicting forces; its meaning can by no means be univocal or unified, but must necessarily be ambiguous. Lacanian criticism opposes the notion of 'a self-present literal meaning' but focuses on 'meaning as a loss and as a flight'.

18. At the beginning of this chapter I said that the viewer in the cinema, in some sense, 'hallucinates' the film. I would like to make it clear that television viewing is very different. Instead of a more or less monolithic gaze, as was found in the Hollywood film, there is a wide range of 'gazes' on TV. In Ann Kaplan's view the televisual Imaginary is more complex than the cinematic one and does not involve the same regression to the Lacanian mirror phase that theorists discovered in the cinematic apparatus. In television, because there is no artificial regression, primary voyeuristic identification is not engaged. Television substitutes liveness and directness for the dream state, immediacy and presentness for regression. Its 'immediate presence' invokes the illusion of a reality presented directly and expressly for the viewer. It follows that methodologies worked out for the Hollywood film do not automatically apply to the different televisual apparatus. See E. Ann Kaplan, 'Feminist criticism and television', in Robert Allen (ed.), op. cit., p. 235.

19. Some of the most vital Lacanian research can be found in film journals such as *Screen, Ciné-tracts, camera obscura, Film Form, Filmwork*.

Chapter 10: Lacan and literature

1. See Elizabeth Wright, *Psychoanalytic Criticism: Theory in practice* (London: Methuen, 1984). She stresses the point that there are many psychoanalytical approaches to literature. Some of the well-known ones include: classical Freudian criticism (id psychology), Post-Freudian criticism (ego psychology), archetypal criticism (Jung), object-relations theory (Klein), and structural analysis (Lacan). For a clear introduction to the relationship of literature and psychoanalysis see Terry Eagleton, *Literary Theory: An introduction* (Oxford: Basil Blackwell, 1983), Chapter 5.

2. Malcolm Bowie, *Freud, Proust and Lacan: Theory as fiction* (Cambridge: Cambridge University Press, 1987), p. 136. Some critics believe that in artists Freud saw his precursors, and that in literary texts he saw an opportunity to verify the analytic method. From Sophocles to Goethe via Jansen and Dostoyevsky, he found in literary fiction an anticipation of the unconscious. Colette Soler has

argued that Freud lapsed into applied psychoanalysis; treating the artist's know-how as equivalent to what he himself called the work of the unconscious, putting artistic and literary works on the same level as dreams, slips of the tongue, bungled actions and symptoms, all of which are interpretable. In her view Lacan reverses Freud's position: it is not that the written text 'must be psychoanalysed; rather, it is that the psychoanalyst must be well read'. See Colette Soler, 'Literature as symptom', in Ellie Ragland-Sullivan and Mark Bracher (eds), *Lacan and the Subject of Language* (London: Routledge, 1991), p. 213.

3. Use of Lacan's concepts is widespread: the phallicised signifier in both semiotic and feminist criticism (Kristeva, Culler, Gallop, Mitchell), the gaze and suture in film studies (Mulvey, Berger), the figure and the body in deconstructive criticism (Derrida, de Man, Hartman, Spivak), transference in formalist criticism (Felman).

4. Sigmund Freud, 'Psychopathic characters on the stage' in vol. 14: *Art and Literature* (London: Penguin, 1985), p. 125.

5. Ibid., p. 126.

6. Sigmund Freud, vol. 4: *The Interpretation of Dreams* (London: Penguin, 1976).

7. Freud, vol. 14: *Art and Literature*, p. 454.

8. Jacques Lacan, *Ecrits: A selection* (London: Tavistock, 1977), p. 265.

9. Lacan held seminar sessions devoted to *Hamlet* and *Antigone* in 1959. See Jacques Lacan, 'Desire and the interpretation of desire in *Hamlet*', in Shoshana Felman (ed.), *Literature and Psychoanalysis* (Baltimore: Johns Hopkins University Press, 1982), p. 11.

10. Ibid., p. 31.

11. Ibid., p. 36.

12. For a useful psychoanalytic overview of Shakespeare's play see 'Hamlet – the Mona Lisa of literature', Chapter 5 of Jacqueline Rose, *Sexuality in the Field of Vision* (London: Verso, 1986), pp. 123–40. This essay discusses T.S. Eliot's critique of *Hamlet*, Ernest Jones and Sigmund Freud's interpretations, and André Green's and Jacques Lacan's essays on the play. While Green focuses on the body of the mother, Lacan emphasises the law of the father (the Symbolic).

13. Using Barthes and Propp, an interesting analysis has been made by Laura Mulvey, 'The Oedipus myth: Beyond the riddles of the Sphinx', in *Visual and Other Pleasures* (London: Macmillan, 1989).

14. See Ellie Ragland-Sullivan, 'Lacan's seminars on James Joyce; Writing as symptom and singular – solution', in Richard Feldstein and Henry Sussman (eds), *Psychoanalysis and . . .* (London: Routledge, 1990), p. 72. This book also contains studies on Faulkner, James, Shakespeare and Woolf.

15. The meaning of symptoms is not discovered but constructed retro-actively. It is generally assumed that when the patient can verbalise his or her symptom that it dissolves. But, sometimes, in spite of its interpretation the symptom does not dissolve. Why does it persist? The answer is that the symptom is not only a coded message, it is at the same time a way for the subject to organise his or her enjoyment. Lacan created the neologism *sinthome*, a synthesis of symptom and phantasy to refer to a signifier permeated with enjoyment. Renuncia-tion, the giving up of enjoyment, itself often produces a certain 'surplus enjoyment'. A symptom, in short, is a way human subjects avoid madness through the binding of enjoyment to a certain signify-ing symbolic formation which assures a minimum of consistency to our being-in-the-world. See Slavoj Zizek, *The Sublime Object of Ideology* (London: Verso, 1989), p. 56. Zizek attempts to give Hegelian dialectics a new reading on the basis of Lacanian analysis which he claims opens up a new approach to ideology.

16. Edgar Allan Poe, 'The Purloined Letter', in *The Fall of the House of Usher and Other Writings* (London: Penguin, 1986). For a com-prehensive discussion of the story see John Muller and Wiliam Richardson (eds), *The Purloined Poe: Lacan, Derrida, and psychoana-lytic reading* (Baltimore: The Johns Hopkins University Press, 1988).

17. For Lacan's discussion of 'The Purloined Letter' see Jacques-Alain Miller (ed.), *The Seminar of Jacques Lacan*, Book II: *The Ego in Freud's Theory and in the Technique of Psychoanalysis 1954–1955* (Cambridge: Cambridge University Press, 1988), pp. 179–202. The seminar is also in *Yale French Studies*, no. 48, 1973, pp. 38–72.

18. Sigmund Freud, 'Beyond the pleasure principle', vol. 11: *On Meta-psychology: The theory of psychoanalysis* (London: Penguin, 1984), p. 275.

19. Barbara Johnson, 'The frame of reference: Poe, Lacan, Derrida', in Robert Young (ed.), *Untying the Text: A post-structuralist reader* (London: Routledge, 1981).

20. Stuart Schneiderman, *Jacques Lacan: The death of an intellectual hero* (Cambridge MA/London: Harvard University Press, 1983), p. 61.

21. Jacques Lacan, *Ecrits: A selection* (London: Tavistock, 1977), p. 229.

22. Jacques Derrida, 'The purveyor of truth', in *Yale French Studies*, no. 52, 1975, pp. 31–113.

23. Stuart Schneiderman, 'Fictions', in Ellie Ragland-Sullivan and Mark Bracher (eds), *Lacan and the Subject of Language* (London: Routledge, 1991), p. 154.

24. *Ornicar?* 11, 1977, 3.

25. Feldstein and Sussman (eds), op. cit., p. 142.

26. Slavoj Zizek, 'Why Lacan is not a "post-structuralist" ', *Newsletter of the Freudian Field*, vol. 1, number 2, Fall 1987, p. 31.
27. See Jean Baudrillard, *Selected Writings*, edited, with an introduction by Mark Poster (Stanford: Stanford University Press, 1988), pp. 166–84; and Douglas Kellner, *Jean Baudrillard from Marxism to Postmodernism and Beyond* (Cambridge: Polity Press, 1989), p. 79.
28. Recent books on this topic include Hal. Foster (ed.), *Postmodern Culture* (London: Pluto, 1985); Jean François Lyotard, *The Postmodern Condition* (Manchester: Manchester University Press, 1984); Madan Sarup, *An Introductory Guide to Post-structuralism and Postmodernism* (London: Harvester Press, 1988); *Theory, Culture and Society*, vol. 5, nos 2–3, special issue on 'Postmodernism' (London: Sage, 1988).

Bibliography

Works by Jacques Lacan

Lacan, Jacques, *Speech and Language in Psychoanalysis*, ed. and transl. by Anthony Wilden (Baltimore: Johns Hopkins University Press, 1968).

Lacan, Jacques, *Premiers Ecrits sur la paranoia* (Paris: Seuil, 1975).

Lacan, Jacques, *Le séminaire 20: Encore (1972–3)* (Paris: Seuil, 1975).

Lacan, Jacques, *Ecrits: A selection*, translated by Alan Sheridan (London: Tavistock, 1977).

Lacan, Jacques, *The Four Fundamental Concepts of Psychoanalysis* (London: Penguin, 1979).

Lacan, Jacques, *Seminaire III: Les psychoses* (Paris: Seuil, 1981).

Lacan, Jacques, 'Television', in *October* 40, MIT Press, Spring, 1987.

Lacan, Jacques, *The Seminar of Jacques Lacan*, edited by Jacques-Alain Miller, Book I: *Freud's Papers on Technique 1953–1954* (Cambridge: Cambridge University Press, 1988).

Lacan, Jacques, *The Seminar of Jacques Lacan*, edited by Jacques-Alain Miller, Book II: *The Ego in Freud's Theory* (Cambridge: Cambridge University Press, 1988).

Secondary Criticism

Alexandrian, Sarane, *Surrealist Art* (London: Thames & Hudson, 1970).

Allen, Robert (ed.), *Channels of Discourse* (London: Methuen, 1987).

Althusser, Louis, 'Freud and Lacan', in *Lenin and Philosophy and Other Essays* (London: New Left Books, 1971).

Barthes, Roland, *Critical Essays* (Evanston: Northwestern University Press, 1972).

Bataille, Georges, *Eroticism* (London: Marion Boyars, 1987).

Benjamin, Andrew, *The Lyotard Reader* (Oxford: Blackwell, 1989).

Benvenuto, Bice, and Kennedy, Roger, *The Works of Jacques Lacan: An introduction* (London: Free Association Books, 1986).

Berger, John, *Ways of Seeing* (London: Penguin, 1972).

Bowie, Malcolm, 'Jacques Lacan', in Sturrock, John (ed.), *Structuralism and Since* (Oxford: Oxford University Press, 1979), pp. 116–53.

Bowie, Malcolm, *Freud, Proust and Lacan: Theory as fiction* (Cambridge: Cambridge University Press, 1987).

Bowie, Malcolm, *Lacan* (London: Fontana Press, 1991).

Brennan, Teresa (ed.), *Between Feminism and Psychoanalysis* (London: Routledge, 1989).

Caillois, Roger, 'La Mante religieuse', *Minotaure*, no. 5, 1934.

Caillois, Roger, 'Mimétisme et psychasthénie legendaire', *Minotaure*, no. 7, 1935; this article, 'Mimicry and legendary psychaesthenia', is reprinted in *October* 31, Winter 1984, pp. 17–32.

Cixous, Hélène, and Clément, Catherine, *The Newly Born Woman* (Manchester: Manchester University Press, 1986).

Clément, Catherine, *The Lives and Legends of Jacques Lacan* (New York: Columbia University Press, 1983).

Derrida, Jacques, 'The purveyor of truth', *Yale French Studies*, 52, 1975.

Derrida, Jacques, 'Freud and the scene of writing', in *Writing and Difference* (London: Routledge & Kegan Paul, 1978).

Dews, Peter, *Logics of Disintegration: Post-structuralist thought and the claims of critical theory* (London: Verso, 1987).

Duras, Marguerite, *Le Ravissement de Lol. V. Stein* (Paris: Gallimard, 1964).

Eagleton, Terry, *Literary Theory: an Introduction* (Oxford: Basil Blackwell, 1983).

Feldstein, Richard and Sussman, Henry (eds), *Psychoanalysis and . . .* (London: Routledge, 1990).

Felman, Shoshana (ed.), *Literature and Psychoanalysis* (Baltimore: Johns Hopkins University Press, 1977).

Forrester, John, *Language and the Origins of Psychoanalysis* (London: Macmillan, 1980).

Foucault, Michel (ed.), *I, Pierre Rivière . . . A case of parricide in the 19th century* (London: Penguin, 1978).

Freud, Sigmund, and Breuer, Joseph, vol. 3: *Studies in Hysteria* (London: Penguin, 1974).

Freud, Sigmund, vol. 4: *The Interpretation of Dreams* (London: Penguin, 1976).

Freud, Sigmund, vol. 5: *The Psychopathology of Everyday Life* (London: Penguin, 1976).

Freud, Sigmund, vol. 6: *Jokes and Their Relation to the Unconscious* (London: Penguin, 1977).

Freud, Sigmund, vol. 7: *On Sexuality* (London: Penguin, 1977).

Freud, Sigmund, vol. 9: *Case Histories II: The 'Rat Man', Schreber, The 'Wolf Man', a case of female homosexuality* (London: Penguin, 1984).

Freud, Sigmund, vol. 14: *Art and Literature* (London: Penguin, 1985).

Frosh, Stephen, *The Politics of Psychoanalysis: An introduction to Freudian and post-Freudian theory* (London: Macmillan, 1987).

Gablik, Suzi, *Magritte* (London: Thames & Hudson, 1970).

Gallop, Jane, *Reading Lacan* (Ithaca: Cornell University Press, 1985).

Genet, Jean, *The Maids and Deathwatch: Two plays* (London: Faber & Faber, 1989).

Grosz, Elizabeth, *Jacques Lacan: A feminist introduction* (London: Routledge, 1990).

Heath, Stephen, 'Difference', in *Screen*, London, vol. 19, no. 3, Autumn 1978.

Hegel, Georg, *The Phenomenonology of Mind* (London: Allen & Unwin, 1931).

Hegel, Georg, *Phenomenology of Spirit* (Oxford: Clarendon Press, 1977).

Heidegger, Martin, *Being and Time* (Oxford: Basil Blackwell, 1962).

Heidegger, Martin, *Poetry, Language, Thought* (New York: Harper & Row, 1971).

Irigaray, Luce, *Speculum of the Other Woman* (Ithaca: Cornell University Press, 1985).

Irigaray, Luce, *This Sex which is not One* (Ithaca: Cornell University Press, 1985).

Jakobson, R. and Halle, M., *Fundamentals of Language* (The Hague: Mouton, 1956).

Johnson, Barbara, 'The frame of reference: Poe, Lacan, Derrida', in Robert Young (ed.), *Untying the Text: A post-structuralist reader* (London: Routledge, 1981).

Kojève, Alexandre, *Introduction to the Reading of Hegel: Lectures on the 'Phenomenology of Spirit'*, assembled by Raymond Queneau, (Ithaca/London: Cornell University Press, 1980).

Krauss, Rosalind and Livingstone, Jane, *L'Amour Fou: Photography and surrealism* (London: Arts Council of Great Britain, 1986).

Kristeva, Julia, *About Chinese Women* (London: Marion Boyars, 1977).

Kristeva, Julia, *Desire in Language: A semiotic approach to literature and art* (Oxford: Basil Blackwell, 1981).

Laing, R.D., *Self and Others* (London: Penguin, 1971).

Laplanche, J. and Pontalis, J.-B., *The Language of Psychoanalysis* (London: Hogarth Press, 1973).

Lecercle, Jean-Jacques, *Philosophy through the Looking-Glass: Language, nonsense, desire* (London: Hutchinson, 1985).

Lemaire, Anika, *Jacques Lacan* (London: Routledge & Kegan Paul, 1977).

Lévi-Strauss, Claude, *The Elementary Structures of Kinship* (London: Tavistock, 1970).

Macalpine, Ida and Hunter, Richard A. (eds), *Memoirs of My Nervous Illness* (London: Dawson & Sons, 1955).

Macey, David, *Lacan in Contexts* (London: Verso, 1988).

Metz, Christian, *Psychoanalysis and the Cinema: The imaginary signifier* (London: Macmillan, 1982).

Mitchell, Juliet (ed.), *The Selected Melanie Klein* (London: Penguin, 1986).

Mitchell, Juliet, and Rose, Jacqueline, *Feminine Sexuality: Jacques Lacan and the école Freudienne* (London: Macmillan, 1982).

Moi, Toril, *Sexual/Textual Politics: Feminist literary theory* (London: Methuen, 1985).

Moi, Toril (ed.), *The Kristeva Reader* (Oxford: Blackwell, 1986).

Mulvey, Laura, *Visual and Other Pleasures* (London: Macmillan, 1989).

Nietzsche, Friedrich, *On the Genealogy of Morals* (New York: Vintage Books, 1973).

Poe, Edgar Allan, *The Fall of the House of Usher and Other Writings* (London: Penguin, 1986).

Ragland-Sullivan, Ellie and Bracher, Mark (eds), *Lacan and the Subject of Language* (London: Routledge, 1991).

Rivière, Joan, 'Womanliness as masquerade', in *Formations of Fantasy* (London: Routledge, 1986).

Rose, Jacqueline, *Sexuality in the Field of Vision* (London: Verso, 1986).

Roudinesco, Elizabeth, *Jacques Lacan & Co. A history of psychoanalysis in France, 1925–1985* (London: Free Association Books, 1990).

Sartre, Jean-Paul, *Being and Nothingness* (London: Routledge & Kegan Paul, 1969).

Saussure, Ferdinand de, *Course in General Linguistics*, with an introduction by Jonathan Culler (London: Fontana/Collins, 1974).

Schneiderman, Stuart, *Jacques Lacan: The death of an intellectual hero* (Cambridge MA/London: Harvard University Press, 1983).

Silverman, Hugh J. (ed.), *Philosophy and Non-Philosophy since Merleau-Ponty* (London: Routledge, 1988).

Silverman, Kaja, *The Subject of Semiotics* (London: Oxford University Press, 1983).

Steiner, George, *Heidegger* (London: Fontana, 1978).

Turkle, Sherry, *Psychoanalytic Politics: Freud's French revolution* (London: Burnett Books, 1979).

Waldberg, Patrick, *Surrealism* (London: Thames & Hudson, 1965).

Wright, Elizabeth, *Psychoanalytic Criticism: Theory in practice* (London: Methuen, 1984).

Young, Robert (ed.), *Untying the Text: A post-structuralist reader* (London: Routledge & Kegan Paul, 1981).

Zizek, Slavoj, *The Sublime Object of Ideology* (London: Verso, 1989).

Zizek, Slavoj, *Looking Awry, An introduction to Jacques Lacan through popular culture* (Cambridge, MA: MIT Press, 1991).

Index

empty and full speech, 38, 54, 55, 86
enunciation, 153, 191
Ernst, Max, 19

father, 5, 92, 94, 96, 97, 99, 106, 107, 108, 109, 110, 111, 118, 120–3, 132, 137
feminine sexuality, 123–5, 137
feminine writing, 135, 142
feminism, 131, 139, 145
fetishism, 157, 158–60
foreclosure, 107, 109, 110, 187
'fort da' game, 53, 68, 85, 183, 184
four discourses, 41–3
Freud, Sigmund, 1–10, 12, 18, 19, 20, 27, 28, 36, 63, 68, 75, 76, 97, 99, 107, 120–1, 149, 153, 161, 162, 168, 171, 178, 183

gaze, 35, 137, 155, 158, 159, 160
Genet, Jean, 61, 181

Hamlet, 163–7, 194
hand, 52
Heath, Stephen, 92
Hegel, Georg W.F., 18, 31, 34, 35, 41, 67, 69
Heidegger, Martin, 37–8, 43, 54, 182
Holbein, Hans, 23, 188
hypnosis, 63

id, 2, 3, 39
ideal ego, 102–3
identification, 27, 103, 152
image, 45, 59, 66, 82, 149
Imaginary, 66, 84–5, 101–3, 109, 110, 111, 147, 160, 187
International Psychoanalytic Association, 70, 168
interpretation, 78
Irigaray, Luce, 117–18, 132, 135–9, 183, 190

Jakobson, Roman, 49, 50, 51, 191
Jameson, Fredric, 110, 163
Jones, Ernest, 15
jouissance, 99–100, 129, 155, 168
Joyce, James, 168

Kant, Immanuel, 78
Klein, Melanie, 65, 83, 111, 185
Kojève, Alexandre, 31, 66, 181
Koyre, Alexandre, 104
Kristeva, Julia, 139–44, 190

lack, 96, 98, 122, 123, 127, 139, 155, 156, 159–60
language, 12, 13, 14, 15, 20, 22, 26, 37, 38, 43, 44–58, 85, 87, 96, 108, 111, 117, 163
La Rochefoucauld, 40
Leclaire, Serge, 115
Lemaire, Anika, 12
Lévi-Strauss, Claude, 48, 49, 118, 119, 124, 176, 183
libido, 2, 4, 99
listening, 55
love, 36, 69, 70, 125–30
lying, 56
Lyotard, Jean-François, 191

Magritte, René, 22, 180
Marxism, 112
master–slave relation, 31–4
mathemes, 11, 114–16
Merchant of Venice, 69
metaphor, 49, 50, 51, 52, 91, 117, 149, 183, 191
metonymy, 49, 50, 51, 91, 149
Metz, Christian, 148, 150, 153, 191
Miller, Jacques-Alain, 11, 81, 115, 154
mimicry, 24–5
Minotaure, 14, 23, 61
mirror phase, 25, 36, 38, 53, 62–6, 72, 82–4, 102, 111, 140, 147
misrecognition, 40, 66
Mitchell, Juliet, 189
Möbius strips, 113, 188
mother, 5, 66, 67, 85, 94, 98–9, 106, 128, 132, 135–6, 137, 138, 140, 144, 157
mourning, 167
Mulvey, Laura, 158, 160, 192, 194
mysticism, 130, 137–8
myth, 20, 134, 176

narcissism, 40, 102, 125